This book focusses on the two plays of Shakespeare that have generally contended for the title of 'greatest' among his works. *Hamlet* remained a focal point of reference until about 1960, when it was displaced by *King Lear*, a play which at the same time ceased to be perceived as a play of redemption and became a play of despair. Foakes attempts to explain these shifts by analysing the reception of the plays since about 1800, an analysis which necessarily engages with the politics of the plays and the politics of criticism. Recent critical theorizing has destabilized the texts, has sought to abolish the frontiers of literature, and hence has undermined the notion of 'greatness' or any consideration of the plays as works of art. Foakes takes issue with such theories and reconsiders textual revisions, in order to argue for the integrity of the plays as reading texts, and to recover a flexible sense of their artistry in relation to meaning.

HAMLET versus LEAR

HAMLET versus LEAR

CULTURAL POLITICS AND
SHAKESPEARE'S ART

R. A. FOAKES

Professor of English, University of California, Los Angeles

 CAMBRIDGE
UNIVERSITY PRESS

PUBLISHED BY THE PRESS SYNDICATE OF THE UNIVERSITY OF CAMBRIDGE
The Pitt Building, Trumpington Street, Cambridge, United Kingdom

CAMBRIDGE UNIVERSITY PRESS
The Edinburgh Building, Cambridge CB2 2RU, UK
40 West 20th Street, New York NY 10011–4211, USA
477 Williamstown Road, Port Melbourne, VIC 3207, Australia
Ruiz de Alarcón 13, 28014 Madrid, Spain
Dock House, The Waterfront, Cape Town 8001, South Africa

http://www.cambridge.org

First published 1993
First paperback edition 2004

A catalogue record for this book is available from the British Library

Library of Congress cataloguing in publication data

Foakes, R. A. Hamlet versus Lear: cultural politics and Shakespeare's art/R. A. Foakes.
p.   cm.
ISBN 0 521 34292 9 (hardback)
1. Shakespeare, William, 1564–1616–Criticism and interpretation–History.
2. Shakespeare, William, 1564–1616–Criticism, Textual. 3. Shakespeare, William, 1564–1616.
King Lear. 4. Shakespeare, William, 1564–1616. Hamlet. 5. Politics and literature.
6. Transmission of texts. 7. Canon (Literature) 8. Tragedy. I. Title.
PR2965.F6 1993   822.3′3–dc20 92–7333 CIP

ISBN 0 521 34292 9 hardback
ISBN 0 521 60705 1 paperback

Transferred to digital printing 2004

Contents

Contents viii

Preface

It was only after this book was completed that Hugh Grady's *The Modernist Shakespeare* (Oxford University Press, 1991) became available to me. This general account of the shift from the new criticism to post-modernism in Shakespeare studies considers the impact of deconstruction, of the new historicism and cultural materialism, and of feminism in considerable detail. It includes a section on 'Postmodernist Aesthetics', pp. 204–11, which describes what he sees as the two major characteristics of 'contemporary Postmodernist aesthetics' as 'the abandonment of organic unity as an aesthetic value and the overthrow of a series of formerly privileged hierarchical oppositions through a Postmodernist anti-hierarchical impulse' (p. 207). His emphasis is thus on the relinquishment of outmoded aesthetic principles rather than on any replacement for them. He says that the 'end of the assumption of the art-work's organic unity' has been decisive in 'bringing about a basic change in how we read Shakespeare' (p. 210), sliding back from aesthetic questions to ways of reading or interpreting the plays. His book thus tends to confirm my sense that the effect of post-modernism (or more specifically, post-structuralist criticism, my main concern) on literary studies has been to turn away from aesthetic issues in what he calls with some reason 'an anti-aesthetic Postmodernist age' (p. 218).

I am indebted to many who have helped me in one way or another in the completion of a project that was begun some years ago, and had to be postponed during the long illness and subsequent death of my beloved wife Barbara. To each and every one

> I can no other answer make but thanks,
> And thanks.

Among those who have answered queries, listened with interest and prompted me to further thought, or brought to my notice points I had missed, I am especially grateful to Alan Brissenden, John Russell Brown, Maurice Charney, Howard Felperin, Eloise Hay, E. A. J. Honigmann, Grace Ioppolo, David Jopling, Patrick McCarthy, Derick Marsh, Barbara Packer, Richard Proudfoot, and Alan Roper. I have benefited greatly from the close reading of draft chapters by Victoria Hayne and Robert Watson. I owe many courtesies to the staff of the Huntington Library, San Marino, the library at the Shakespeare Birthplace Centre, Stratford-upon-Avon, and the British Library.

In the course of working on this book I have been assisted by grants from the research fund of the University of California, Los Angeles. The writing of it has been expedited by a Fellowship at the Humanities Research Centre, Australian National University, Canberra, which provided a peaceful working retreat from the hurly-burly of Los Angeles, livened by the presence of an interesting group of colleagues. I have also been aided by a President's Fellowship of the University of California, and a Fellowship awarded by the American Council of Learned Societies.

A number of essays I have already published contain trial runs for some of the sections or ideas in the book; material from them is included here by kind permission of the editors or publishers. I list these essays in chronological order: ' "Forms to his Conceit": Shakespeare and the Uses of Stage-Illusion', Annual Shakespeare Lecture at the British Academy, London, 1980, *Proceedings of the British Academy*, 66 (1982), 103–19; 'Textual Revision and the Fool in *King Lear*', Essays in Honour of Peter Davison, *Trivium*, 20 (1985), 33–47; '*King Lear* and the Displacement of *Hamlet*', *Huntington Library Quarterly*, 50 (1987), 263–78; 'Making and Breaking Dramatic Illusion', in *Aesthetic Illusion: Theoretical and Historical Approaches*, ed. Frederick Burwick and Walter Pape (Berlin and New York: Walter de Gruyter, 1990), pp. 217–28. Part of Chapter 2 is related to 'Hamlet and Hamletism', forthcoming in *Shakespeare Survey*, 45 (1993).

NOTE

Quotations from Shakespeare's works are modernized except where original spelling or punctuation affects the meaning of a citation from an early Quarto or the First Folio. Line references are to *The Riverside Shakespeare*, ed. G. Blakemore Evans (Boston: Houghton Mifflin, 1974).

CHAPTER I

Introduction: Hamlet *versus* King Lear

Let me begin with two lists, so as to provide an orientation for the first part of this book. One is a short anthology of comments praising either *Hamlet* or *King Lear* as the best, the greatest, or the chief masterpiece of Shakespeare. The claims for *Hamlet* pretty much died out by the 1950s, while those for *King Lear* become commonplace only from the 1950s onwards, though notably anticipated by Hazlitt and A. C. Bradley. The second list records some of the major international events in the period 1956–65, which is when the great shift in the status of *King Lear* took place. I do not claim that there is a direct connection, or that what was happening politically in the world at that time explains the way Shakespeare's plays were assessed, but only that critics consciously or unconsciously reflect the mood of their time; and the mood of that period was dominated by the expansion of nuclear arsenals and the fear of a war that might destroy the world. This mood was indicated in two of the films that made a huge impact, Stanley Kramer's *On the Beach* (1959), a film about the end of civilization in a world devasted by atomic waste, based on a 1957 novel by Nevil Shute; and Stanley Kubrick's *Dr Strangelove: or, How I learned to Stop Worrying and Love the Bomb* (1963), a satirical reflection of the nightmares of the age. Here, then are the lists:

1 The anthology: (a) *Hamlet*

'*Hamlet* – the noblest and greatest of all [Shakespeare's] tragedies' (John Keble, 1830).
'Other works of the human mind equal *Hamlet*; none surpasses it' (Victor Hugo, 1864).
'*Hamlet* is the greatest creation in literature that I know of' (Alfred, Lord Tennyson, as reported by Hallam Tennyson, 1883).

'*Hamlet* is the greatest of popular dramas' (J. Dover Wilson, 1935).

'The play [*Hamlet*] is almost universally considered to be the chief
masterpiece of one of the greatest minds the world has known'
(Ernest Jones, 1949).

'[*Hamlet* is] one of the few great masterpieces of the European
spirit' (Salvador de Madariaga, 1948).

(b) *King Lear*

'[*King Lear*] is the best of all Shakespeare's plays' (William Hazlitt,
1817).

'*King Lear* seems to me Shakespeare's great achievement, but it
seems to me *not* his best play' (A. C. Bradley, 1904).

'This greatest of plays [*King Lear*]' (D. G. James, 1951).

'In the twentieth century *Hamlet* has yielded to *King Lear* the
distinction of being the play in which the age most finds itself'
(L. C. Knights, 1960).

'For a number of critics it [*King Lear*] is self-evidently the greatest
of Shakespeare's tragedies' (Emrys Jones, 1971).

'The play that has come to be regarded as the definitive achievement of Shakespearean tragedy' (Howard Felperin, 1977).

'The tragedy of Lear, deservedly celebrated among the dramas of
Shakespeare, is commonly regarded as his greatest achievement' (Stephen Booth, 1983).

2 Some major events 1954–65

1954, March   Americans explode hydrogen bomb on Bikini
atoll; fallout affected Japanese fishing boats, and also islanders
more than a hundred miles away.

1956, October   Uprisings in Hungary and Poland crushed by the
Soviet Union.

1956, November   Outbreak of Suez war; Britain, France and
Israel invade Egypt, are defeated and humiliated.

1957, October   Sputnik, first Soviet space rocket, placed in orbit.

1958, February   Launching of the Campaign for Nuclear
Disarmament.

1959, January   Fidel Castro takes over in Cuba. First two
Americans killed in Vietnam.

1960   France explodes its first atomic device.

1960, March   Sharpeville massacre in South Africa.

1960, May   U2 spy plane shot down over Russia; after repeated denials that they were spying, the United States was forced to admit it when Gary Powers was produced alive.

1961, January   Inauguration of President John F. Kennedy.

1961–3   Build-up of American arms; Kennedy announced in 1963, 'In less than three years we have increased by 50 per cent the number of Polaris submarines – increased by 70 per cent the proportion of our strategic bombers on fifteen minute alert – increased by 100 per cent the total number of nuclear weapons in our strategic alert forces ... increased by 60 per cent the tactical nuclear forces displayed in Western Europe.'[1]

1961, April   Bay of Pigs; invasion of Cuba backed by the CIA fails disastrously.

1961, August   East Berlin closed off from the West by completion of the Berlin Wall.

1962, October   Cuban missile crisis.

1963, November   Assassination of President Kennedy.

1964, August   Tonkin Bay incident; two American destroyers said to be attacked by North Vietnamese gunboats.

1964, October   Krushchev ousted by Leonid Brezhnev.

1965, October   China explodes its first atomic bomb.

1965, February   First sustained bombing of North Vietnam by Americans; first marine battalions land in Vietnam; 200,000 combat troops there by December.

1965, August   Watts riots in Los Angeles

Hamlet and *King Lear*, archetypal tragedies of youth and age, have always challenged for regard as Shakespeare's greatest work. Although Hazlitt and Keats gave supremacy to *King Lear*, *Hamlet*, as the quotations above show, remained the central, and for many the greatest, work of Shakespeare until the 1950s. About 1960, however, an intriguing double shift took place. On the one hand, *King Lear* regained its ascendancy in critical esteem, and since that time most critics seem to have taken it for granted (see the quotations above from Emrys Jones, Howard Felperin and Stephen Booth) that they can refer to it as Shakespeare's greatest play. On the other hand, *King Lear* changed its nature almost overnight: the main tradition of criticism up to the 1950s had interpreted the play as concerned with Lear's pilgrimage to redemption, as he finds himself and is 'saved' at the end, but in the 1960s the play became Shakespeare's bleakest and most despairing vision of suffering, all hints of consolation undermined or denied. I was intrigued by such sudden changes in critical estimation and interpretation of the two plays, and set out to investigate how and why they occurred.[2] This investigation in turn raised other issues, and led to the present book.

There is no simple explanation for this shift in the 1960s, but it strikingly coincided with a period of political change, as indicated in the chronology above, that affected the mood of people in Britain and in the United States. The 1950s saw the development of the hydrogen bomb in 1952, an explosion of one being shown on television in 1954;[3] by the end of the decade, 'anxiety over fallout had become a powerful force around the world'[4], and had led to the founding of the Campaign for Nuclear Disarmament in Britain (1958), and the National Committee for a Sane Nuclear Policy in the United States. The orbiting of Sputnik, launched into space in 1957, seemed to bring home to millions the possibility of the destruction of life on the world, or its contamination by fallout, a possibility realized fictionally in the best-selling novel *On the Beach* by Nevil Shute. France exploded its first atomic device in 1960, and 'Everyone understood that more nations with bombs meant more chances for disaster from a faulty transistor, an insane authority, or (more realistically) an escalating local conflict.'[5] Polaris submarines using foreign bases, as in Scotland, further alarmed inhabitants of such countries. The Alain Resnais film, *Hiroshima mon Amour*, recalling the effect of the first atomic bomb on Japan, began to circulate in 1959. Fidel Castro took over in Cuba in 1959, and in the next few years a war between superpowers seemed imminent. The wretched Bay of Pigs affair, an attempted invasion of Cuba backed by the CIA, failed in 1961, the year in which the Berlin Wall closed off East Berlin from the West. When Soviet missiles were placed in Cuba, provoking the Secretary General of the United Nations to announce in October 1962, 'The very existence of mankind is in the balance', fear of nuclear destruction perhaps reached its peak.[6] If nuclear fear gradually diminished into a more cynical acceptance that the world was going to be permanently near the brink, at two minutes to the midnight of obliteration, there was no going back to a pre-nuclear world.

These are some of the events of the period around 1960 that deeply affected people in Britain and America, and which have a bearing on the way *Hamlet* and *King Lear* were interpreted. Criticism, as most now realize, is never an innocent activity; it always has a hidden agenda, even if the critic remains largely unconscious of it. For criticism always reflects the ideology of the critic and the conditions of the age in which he writes, however much it may claim to be independent and concerned only with the text. No critic can escape from the problems of his own time, or avoid reading literature in the context of these concerns. Without going so far as to assert that 'writing and reading are always socially determinate events', as if the author has no free play of mind, I would in general agree with the new historicist observation that 'the histories we reconstruct are the textual constructs of critics who are, like ourselves, historical subjects'.[7] My own reconstructions have, I am aware, the same limitation, and yet we can only begin to understand what critics are saying, and why they take the positions they assert, what ideological presuppositions are embedded in their writings, by attempting to gain a historical perspective and discover how and why critical response to *Hamlet* and *King Lear* has changed over the years. I realize that the shifts that happened about 1960 in the standing and interpretation of these two plays could only be assessed in relation to a much larger historical sense of the critical treatment of the plays. Hence in the first two chapters I offer an analysis of the main trends and ideological tendencies in the criticism of the two plays since about 1800. I use the term 'criticism' in the widest sense to include not only academic criticism, but references or reworkings in fiction, plays and poetry by other writers, productions and film versions, and what Ruby Cohn has called 'offshoots', like Edward Bond's play *Lear*.[8]

These chapters are not designed as a history or survey of criticism, for their aim is to historicize or provide a genealogy for the central preoccupations revealed in a range of critical responses. They present a selective account, and one that may often be partial in ignoring fine tuning, for I am not concerned with details so much as with the overall implications of a range of readings. Others might include critical readings I have ignored, and omit some I have emphasized, especially in the period since the 1950s, when the growing numbers of assistant professors needing to publish a book in order to gain tenure in America, and the inevitable professionalization of the academy in Britain and America as concerned more with research and publication than with teaching, have led to a massive proliferation of critical writings on Shakespeare; but I suspect that the characteristics I describe in Chapters 2, on *Hamlet* and 3, on *King Lear*, would emerge as prominent in any overview, even if they might be nuanced in different ways. Each play generates a complex and interesting story of critical response, two features of which especially affect the development of the argument of this book in the later chapters.

The first of these features relates to politics. Although Hamlet was, as a character, abstracted from the play and privatized as a representative of everyman by Romantic and later critics, he also became in the nineteenth century an important symbolic political figure, usually typifying the liberal intellectual paralysed in will and incapable of action. By contrast, *King Lear* was depoliticized, even by the radical Hazlitt, perhaps at that time because of a possible association with the mad old monarch, George III; and until the 1950s the play was, in the main, seen as a tragedy of personal relations between father and daughter, or as a grand metaphysical play about Lear's pilgrimage to discover his soul. All this changed after 1960, since when *King Lear* has come to seem richly significant in political terms, in a world in which old men have held on to and abused power, often in corrupt or arbitrary ways; in the same period *Hamlet* has lost much of its political relevance, as liberal intellectuals have steadily been marginalized in Britain and in the United States. In such a summary account I state the case forcefully to gain attention, and much too simply; and the first two chapters fill out the picture with much more detail and shading. The criticism of *Hamlet* and *King Lear* returns again and again to political issues, overtly or covertly, disconcerting as this may be to those who cling to an Arnoldian or new critical notion of criticism as the disinterested study of texts.

The second feature is to some extent indicated in the anthology of quotations from critics with which this introduction begins, and concerns aesthetic assessments of the plays. Each play has had its champions to assert vigorously that either *Hamlet* or *King Lear* is the 'greatest' of Shakespeare's plays, and, as the quotations show, *Hamlet* was in the ascendancy before the 1950s, while *King Lear* has achieved a pre-eminence since that period, to the extent that its status is now hardly questioned. Yet in all the vast mass of critical writing on these plays, there is hardly any consideration of the grounds for such judgements. Aesthetic questions are generally ignored, or the artistic value of the plays taken for granted. Indeed, criticism has increasingly been equated with interpretation, so that the post-structuralist claim that criticism is a discursive practice no different from other discursive practices such as those we call literature, and the further claim that 'only the critic *executes* the work'9 and constructs its meanings, appears from one point of view as the culmination of a long tradition in which interpretation has become the central activity of criticism, especially in the academy. The meanings critics find relate to their own values and their own world as well as to the play, and, broadly speaking, tend to reflect or overtly embody their own political or social ideology, whether conservative, quietist, liberal or revolutionary. In universities, criticism has displaced literature as the source of power in English studies, for the critical processing of literature can be taught more easily than literature itself, and through the creation of journals and schools of critisim provides professional enhancement and prestige.

In this professional sense, critical discourse generally has a political concern, but whereas deconstructive accounts of Renaissance literature tended to ignore history, the new historicists in the United States and cultural materialists in Britain have reinterpreted Shakespeare's plays in relation to the power structures of the age of Elizabeth and James I, or in relation to the politics of Conservative Britain in recent years. One effect of these critical moves has been to open up to scrutiny the motives and ideologies often concealed, or at any rate not consciously realized, under claims by earlier critics that they were engaged in an objective pursuit of truth. If most older criticism offered an interpretation of the meaning of *Hamlet* or *King Lear*, usually qualifying some earlier reading, and was not much concerned with the matter of Shakespeare's artistry, post-structuralist criticism has gone further, by abolishing the canon, tearing down the boundaries of literature, recognizing all texts as variants of the same kind of discursive practice, and so elevating critical interpretation to an importance equivalent to, if not greater than, that of the literary text the critic 'constructs' for us. Such criticism effectively also does away with aesthetic values. It is produced mainly in universities and colleges, where it forms the basis for a pedagogical technique, and is more useful than literature itself (in its traditional meaning), for literature demands not merely to be understood, but to be appreciated as an experience, and as art. In some ways these developments have been illuminating, for they have made us recognize that all readings of plays are relative, and that plays

change according to the interpreter, being scripts for performance as
well as reading texts or dramatic poems. But this very emphasis on
relativity has led to attacks on the concept of organic unity in
Shakespeare's plays proposed by Romantic critics like Coleridge,
and to the dismissal of any idea of permanent or transhistorical
artistic values. At the same time, it seems to me that something of
central importance is lost in the processing of Shakespeare, and that
we need to be concerned with appreciation as well as understanding,
and with the effect the plays have on us, not merely with what they
mean. In other words, we need a way of talking about Shakespeare's
artistry, and the later chapters of this book basically relate to this
theme. In particular, I am concerned in the last three chapters to
propose a concept of artistic value that is itself relative, not fixed, but
capable of changing with new generations of readers and viewers of
Shakespeare's plays, and with changes in the world around us. In
Chapter 5 especially I also consider the matter of the relation of
artistic value to meaning and to the problem of knowledge, while the
last two chapters present one method for the present time of bringing
these issues to bear on each of the plays.

Shakespeare studies have been jolted in recent years by the
rediscovery that in all likelihood the dramatist revised some, perhaps
many, of his plays. I say 'rediscovery' because the issue of revision in
Shakespeare's plays has a long history, after surfacing in the
eighteenth century.[10] In effectively silencing J. M. Robertson and
other 'disintegrators' of the plays early in the twentieth century,
bibliographers and textual critics established the conventional belief
that changes, omissions and substitutions in the texts of the plays
could be attributed to errors by printers and compositors, or to
interference in the playhouse. It was generally accepted that the task
of an editor was to present a composite text that would be as close as
possible to a putative lost original manuscript in Shakespeare's
hand, his 'foul papers'. Behind this conception in turn lay the
cultural authority of an idealized Shakespeare who, as a supreme
genius, never blotted or corrected a line. Conflated texts of plays like
Hamlet and *King Lear* including all lines from the Quartos and First
Folio that seemed to the editor authentically Shakespearian, were
accepted as the norm. When in 1931 Madeleine Doran issued a book
suggesting the possibility of revision in *King Lear*, little attention was
paid to it. An essay by Michael Warren published in 1977 arguing
that 'we have two plays of *King Lear*, sufficiently different to require

that all further work on the play be based on either Q or F, but not on the conflation of both',[11] seemed to some older critics shocking and unacceptable; but though debate continues,[12] the idea that Shakespeare reworked some texts has steadily gained more acceptance.

The one-volume Oxford Shakespeare (1986) indeed prints two texts of *King Lear*, from the Quarto and Folio as if these constitute separate plays, and relegates parts of *Hamlet* to an appendix as passages cut by Shakespeare in reworking the play. This edition undermines Shakespeare's authority further by reasserting some claims for disintegration, assigning parts of *Macbeth* and *Timon of Athens*, for instance, to Thomas Middleton. This destabilization of Shakespeare's plays can be seen as another manifestation of post-structuralist criticism, and would seem to problematize further the matter of Shakespeare's artistry, especially in relation to *King Lear*, if there really are two different plays with this title. I have no difficulty in accepting that Shakespeare revised plays, as many modern dramatists do; texts for performance may well be polished and modified in the theatre, where the process of staging can lead to cutting or alteration. However, the possible effect of such changes in the case of Shakespeare's plays has, I think, been exaggerated in the new enthusiasm for cutting Shakespeare down to size. So Jonathan Goldberg argues:[13]

That in the two Lears different characters may speak the same lines, that the same characters (characters with the same proper names) speak different lines, suggests the radical instability of character as a locus of meaning in the Shakespearean text. Nor can we assume that the text of a Shakespearean play will have a determinate structure; how could it when so much of the text was expendable? The Shakespearean text is a historical phenomenon, produced by ongoing restructurations, revisions, and collaboration; by interventions that are editorial, scribal, theatrical; by conditions that are material, occasional, accidental.

The play Shakespeare wrote vanishes into a morass of revision, collaboration and interventions by editors and actors, and cannot be thought of as a work of art if it has no shape, if it is conceived as a 'contemporary communal construct',[14] or if, in Stephen Orgel's words, the 'real play is the performance, not the text',[15] and the play should be thought of as an anthology of performances, each one different from the others.

Such attacks on the integrity of a play like *King Lear* relate to a wider post-structuralist onslaught on the cultural authority of Shakespeare, who has been toppled from his pedestal by those who now see in him 'the badge of cultural elitism and the instrument of pedagogical oppression'.[16] In the iconoclastic smashing of the idol there is both a sense of release from the dead weight of critical history, and a measure of solemn nonsense that has much to do with the concomitant elevation of the critic and of literary criticism as the new cultural authorities. Gary Taylor ends his long dismantling of Shakespeare's status by saying, 'Within our culture, Shakespeare is enormously powerful. Power corrupts and disfigures';[17] now I suspect that we should replace Shakespeare by 'critic' in this sentence, for the effect such attacks on Shakespeare seek to achieve is to substitute the critic for the author at the centre of power in the academy, and power corrupts the critic too.

A kind of corruption is seen in the excessive claims made in the effort to deconstruct and destabilize Shakespeare's plays. The evidence for revision has been used to question in an especially aggressive way the possibility of artistic coherence in *Hamlet* and *King Lear*, and I therefore devote Chapter 4 to a reconsideration of the significance of that evidence as it affects the shaping of the plays. Chapter 5, as indicated above, takes up in general terms the matter of artistic value in Shakespeare's plays, in relation to some recent considerations of artistry and of mimesis. The final chapters attempt to reconsider the plays in the light of an analysis of textual revisions, and seek to combine an awareness of the political implications of my own reading of the texts with a recovery of a sense of their artistry. Post-structuralist criticism – I use the term loosely to include deconstructionist, new historicist, cultural materialist, feminist, performance and revisionary textual criticism – has freed us from subservience to the text, and opened up a range of fresh perspectives on Shakespeare's plays. All these approaches have in common a rejection of the idea of a Shakespearean text as possessing a finite meaning or structure. We live in heady days for the critic, who asserts that he or she constructs the literary work, which has no ontological status, and which, like criticism itself, can be experienced only as a form of production. If post-structuralist criticism has usefully problematized Shakespeare's plays, and revealed new perspectives on them, the access of critical power and authority has produced various forms of critical arrogance and exaggeration, so that some seem to enjoy trashing Shakespeare, like schoolboys suddenly released from subservience to a formidable headmaster, and taking their revenge on him. They are also, of course, seeking to establish their own control over English studies in universities and colleges. In their processing of Shakespeare, the very possibility of a concept of artistry in the plays has almost vanished, and the aim of chapters 6 and 7 of this book is to attempt to restore that possibility.

CHAPTER 2

Hamlet and Hamletism

HAMLET PRIVATIZED AND POLITICIZED

The Romantic idealization of Shakespeare as a universal genius established him as a figure of enormous cultural authority, yet at the same time democratized him as a representative consciousness, available for each of us to interpret in his or her own way, untrammelled by scholarship, and regardless of social rank. If Shakespeare 'gave proof of a most profound, energetic & philosophical mind',[1] he was also, for Coleridge, 'a Nature humanized, a genial Understanding directing self-consciously a Power & a[n] ⟨implicit⟩ wisdom deeper than Consciousness';[2] Shakespeare was the wonder of mankind, who yet 'with all his wonderful powers' made us 'feel as if he were unconscious of himself & of his mighty abilities: disguising the half-god in the simplicity of a child or the affection of a dear companion'.[3] Since the 'mighty abilities' were displaced into Shakespeare's unconscious, everyone might find a 'dear companion' in him, a reflection of himself, or could reconstruct Shakespeare as a version of himself. And if Shakespeare had, as Edgar Allan Poe put it, a 'marvellous power of identification with humanity at large', that identification could be traced especially in Hamlet, for 'He wrote of Hamlet as if Hamlet he were.'[4]

The myriad-minded Shakespeare, to use Coleridge's term, had, of course, created a galaxy of characters, but in order for the reader to comprehend the philosopher-poet, the genius whose wisdom penetrated into the depths of human consciousness, he had to be translated into a persona the reader or critic could identify with; and Hamlet, reconstituted as a man with his own existence outside the play, was above all other characters identified with Shakespeare himself. 'The universality of Shakespeare's genius is in some sort reflected in Hamlet',[5] asserted an anonymous writer in the *Quarterly*

Review in 1847; and in pouring forth 'all that during the recent years had filled his heart and seethed in his brain', it 'cost Shakespeare no effort to transform himself into Hamlet', according to Georg Brandes, writing in 1911.[6] In France, Hippolyte Taine regarded Hamlet as having 'a delicate soul, an impassioned imagination, like that of Shakespeare', and went on to conclude, 'Hamlet is Shakespeare.'[7] If Hamlet thus became 'in a unique sense the mouthpiece of Shakespeare', this was a way not only of making Shakespeare accessible, but also a way of finding an image into which each reader could project himself or herself. If Hamlet embodied the philosophic depths and the profound imaginative greatness of Shakespeare, he also reflected everyman, since 'It is because Hamlet is eternally human that the play retains its lasting hold on our sympathies. We are all potential Hamlets.'[8]

Hamlet seemed so many-sided that he could take on the characteristics of the reader or play-goer: 'above all, we feel the universal validity, the typicalness, of Hamlet. As he thought and felt, or in some like manner, have we all at some time thought and felt and acted, or rather failed to act.'[9] It was possible to focus on his nobility, his generosity, his philosophizing, his lack of resolution, his exquisite sensibility, his impulsive energy, and so forth; in the glowing words of Anna Jameson (1840), anyone could

meditate on those things on which he meditates, accompany him even to the brink of eternity, fluctuate with him on the ghastly sea of despair, soar with him into the purest and serenest regions of human thought, feel with him the curse of beholding iniquity, and the troubled delight of thinking on innocence, and gentleness, and beauty ... In him, his character and situation, there is a concentration of all of the interests that belong to humanity. There is scarcely a trait of frailty or of grandeur which may have endeared to us our most beloved friends in real life, that is not to be found in Hamlet.[10]

The special feature of Hamlet was perhaps that he seemed to combine so many strong attributes with common weak ones, so that if in one aspect he appeared a hero, displaying 'conscious plenitude of intellect, united with exceeding fineness and fulness of sensibility and guided by a predominant sentiment of moral rectitude',[11] from another perspective he could appear 'the standing type and embodied emblem of irresolution, half-heartedness, and doubt'.[12]

Hamlet could thus always be reconstructed as a modern, a contemporary of the reader, since, in the words of Victor Hugo

(1864), 'His strange reality is our own reality, after all . . . Unhealthy as he is, Hamlet expresses a permanent condition of man.'[13] The world, said Henry Morley (1893), is full of Hamlets, 'with intellectual power for large usefulness, who wait, day by day and year by year, in the hope to do more perfectly what they live to do; die, therefore, and leave their lives unused', while lesser men get on with business as usual.[14] If Hamlet, with all his (or Shakespeare's) accomplishments of mind, was usually seen as weak, overwhelmed by events, or unable to act and achieve his goal of revenge, he could serve as both a paradigm of and excuse for ordinary people who in the normal way regard themselves as having potential, but fail to live up to their ideal of themselves, or fall short of the achievements they hope for.

Hamlet thus became a key figure in that shift towards an emphasis on subjectivity that began in the late eighteenth century and flowered with the Romantics. David Garrick had played the role 'with uncommon spirit',[15] and William Richardson in 1774, no doubt having in mind Dr Johnson's reservations[16] about a play in which for him the hero was 'rather an instrument than an agent' (1765), and also Voltaire's dismissal of it as a 'vulgar and barbarous drama' (1768), defended Hamlet as a character in whom a sense of virtue was the ruling principle, but who, in spite of 'the most active zeal in the exercise of every duty', is 'hated, persecuted, and destroyed' by his enemies.[17] But Hamlet soon began to be appropriated into a new image, shedding his heroic role to be recreated in the sentimental image of Wilhelm Meister in Goethe's novel (1778) as someone faced with an impossible task: 'A lovely, pure, noble and most moral nature, without the strength of nerve which forms a hero, sinks beneath a burden which it cannot bear and must not cast away.'[18] Incapable of heroism, Hamlet was conceived as a soul unfit for the performance of a great action. In England Henry Mackenzie (1780) perceived a 'delicacy of feeling, approaching to weakness' in Hamlet, a melancholy that is 'the effect of delicate sensibility, impressed with a sense of sorrow, or a feeling of its own weakness'.[19] His weakness in failing to carry out what he resolves to do was noted by Schlegel, and became for Coleridge the centre of Hamlet's character.

The effect was to generalize Hamlet into everyman confronting the problem of deciding how to act: 'he is a man living in meditation, called upon to act by every motive human & divine, but the great purpose of life defeated by continually resolving to do, yet doing nothing but resolve'.[20] Hamlet's specific 'purpose' of revenge for the murder of his father is transformed into 'the great purpose of life', everyone's life. Coleridge's famous remark, 'I have a smack of Hamlet myself',[21] further absorbs the character into the Romantic poet's own persona, abstracting him from the play, and giving him an independent existence outside the text. For Charles Lamb, the essential Hamlet was not the figure as played on the stage, 'dragged forth as a public schoolmaster, to give lectures to the crowd', for 'nine parts in ten of what Hamlet does are transactions between himself and his moral sense, they are the effusions of his solitary musings'.[22] He identified Hamlet with intellect, as embodied primarily in the soliloquies conceived as private meditations. Even the radical William Hazlitt found himself only able to echo Coleridge in his essay on the play, broadening the latter's identification of Hamlet as himself into 'It is we who are Hamlet. The play has a prophetic truth, which is above that of history.' Hazlitt thus permits anyone to say he has a smack of Hamlet, anyone, that is, who

has become thoughtful and melancholy through his own mishaps or those of others ... he who has felt his mind sink within him, and sadness cling to his heart like a malady, who has had his hopes blighted and his youth staggered by apparitions of strange things ... whose powers of action have been eaten up by thought.[23]

Abstracted from the play, Hamlet became a free-floating signifier, taking on the subjectivity of the critic, and typically reflecting his anxieties.

Hamlet was frequently reconstructed as a nineteenth-century intellectual, and critics projected on to him their own problems, their scepticism, lack of resolution, over-refinement of sensibility, or paralysis of will. This was indeed perceived by E. K. Chambers (1894), who saw Hamlet as a 'modern born out of due time', a 'high-strung dreamer':

A prolonged study of the character leaves one with the startling sense that out of the plenitude of his genius Shakespeare has here depicted a type of humanity which belongs essentially not to his age but to our own ... The key-note to Hamlet's nature is the over-cultivation of the mind. He is the academic man, the philosopher brought suddenly into the world of strenuous action.[24]

Hamlet is disabled by a fatal habit of speculation, which becomes in A. C. Bradley's famous formula (1904) a pathological condition that

is linked to 'Hamlet's failure'.[25] Hamlet was usually conceived as
having a duty enjoined upon him by the Ghost, a duty to carry out a
'great deed laid upon a soul unequal to the performance of it', as if
the issue of revenge were quite unproblematic; for A. W. Verity
(1904), who saw revenge as a 'great deed', Hamlet lacked the
qualities desirable in the modern world, that is to say, the world of
imperialist Britain:

> He does not see life steadily or see it whole; and not seeing, cannot deal with
> his fellows on equal terms. We see this tendency in Hamlet's sweeping
> generalisations, in his scorn of compromise with those opposed to him.
> Idealism has turned to antithesis – utter disgust with the world and
> humanity; and world-weariness is not an incentive to the performance of
> hard duty.[26]

The need for men of action with a resolute dedication to 'hard duty'
was presumably what he thought the age called for, and Verity
deplored the increase in his time in the number of men 'of the
Hamlet type',[27] echoing E. K. Chambers in regarding the habit of
speculation as fatal. The idea of Hamlet as diseased or mad suited
such readings, since no one who was 'healthily active' would give in
to self-indulgence like Hamlet and fail to do his duty.[28]

For other critics Hamlet, however unhealthy, represented a
'permanent condition of man', for 'we are all Hamlets in our time',
enduring his 'difficulties and doubts, his postponements and hesi-
tations, his weariness of life and shrinking from death . . .'[29] Hamlet
could indeed appear to be not the representative of those who fail in
a world called to do its duty, but rather

> the typical modern character, with its intense feeling of the strife between
> the ideal and the actual world, with its keen sense of the chasm between
> power and aspiration, and with that complexity of nature which shows itself
> in wit without mirth, cruelty combined with sensitiveness, frenzied im-
> patience at war with inveterate procrastination.[30]

Here Georg Brandes (1911) hints at a bafflement felt in the face of
the growing complexity of modern life, which seemed to Stopford
Brooke (1913) to throw up more and more people like Hamlet, so
that he claimed 'There are millions of Hamlets.'[31] For him they were
still a minority; the vast majority of practical, active men he thought
could not begin to comprehend the Hamlet type, who seemed to
them mad or diseased:

They draw attention to many acts and words of Hamlet as tainted with madness; and the most eager to prove this point, and their own acumen, are the specialists in insanity who, believing themselves to be an unanswerable authority on what is madness and what is not, are the very blindest and most foolish of guides in this matter – men, some of whom at least, if they had their way, would end by shutting up in asylums all the poets, artists, and prophets, all the men and women who do not care for money, who are bored by science, and who think that the real fools are those who care for the things of the world.[32]

Stopford Brooke's views were perhaps, like his religious opinions, 'dangerously broad', in the words of the *Dictionary of National Biography*. Nevertheless, his account shows that the irresolute Hamlet who failed to carry out the actions required of him could be seen in at least three ways through the nineteenth and early twentieth centuries, first, sympathetically, as a projection of the academic mind, the intellectual devoted to speculation but aware of his deficiencies; secondly, also sympathetically, as embodying a condition increasingly common in the modern world as men sought to cope with ever more complex social conditions; and thirdly, unsympathetically, as someone who failed to carry out his duty through a paralysis of will in a world that required men to be practical and active.

The political overtones of some of the passages cited above are probably self-evident, and the free-floating Hamlet, once cut loose from the play, was soon politicized and explicitly identified with the problems of the age, both in Europe and in America. So, for example, Emerson, in his essay 'The American Scholar' (1837), gave currency to an image of Hamlet as typifying the 1830s; he depicted his age as one of introversion; 'We, it seems, are critical. We are embarrassed with second thoughts. We cannot enjoy any thing for hankering to know whereof the pleasure consists.' He saw his age as 'infected with Hamlet's unhappiness – "Sicklied o'er with the pale cast of thought"',[33] and Hamlet becomes a type of the nineteenth-century intellectual trapped in inaction. Matthew Arnold also identified Hamlet with the problems of the age, the modern world, in which 'the calm, the cheerfulness, the disinterested objectivity' of the ancient Greeks have disappeared, and the 'dialogue of the mind with itself has commenced; modern problems have presented themselves; we hear already the doubts, we witness the discouragement, of Hamlet and of Faust [i.e., Goethe's Faust]'.[34] If here the political implications are veiled in a desire for change, for objectivity, for action, they emerge to some extent in Tennyson's *Maud* (1855), which the poet saw as depicting 'a little Hamlet, the history of a morbid, poetic soul, under the blighting influence of a recklessly speculative age'.[35] The link between Hamlet and Tennyson's hero is obscured at the end of the poem, because although this 'poetic soul' suffers a kind of madness after killing Maud's brother in a duel and losing her love, he ends by going off to fight for his country. Hamlet was more strongly politicized in Europe, where the sensitive, melancholy figure projected in Goethe's Wilhelm Meister, was reconfigured as typifying intellectuals who were unable to translate their revolutionary ideals into action. In his famous poem of 1844 beginning 'Germany is Hamlet' ('Deutschland ist Hamlet'), Ferdinand Freiligrath portrayed a Hamlet whose 'boldest act is only thinking', and ended by identifying himself with Hamlet as a 'poor old dreamer'. This poem strikingly sums up in its opening phrase the sense shared by others that Hamlet's 'strength and weakness' were 'the strength and weakness of the German people', seen as profoundly reflective and idealizing, but lacking the strength to achieve the 'greatness and grandeur of freedom'.[36]

Hamlet also was seen as embodying Slavic characteristics, both in Russia, where again he seemed to mirror the condition of intellectuals for whom debate became a substitute for action, and in Poland, where Mickiewicz 'wrote of Poland as a Hamlet'.[37] Censorship meant that literary commentary became important in Russia, where it could be used self-consciously as means of coding social and political criticism, as in the work of the distinguished critic V. G. Belinsky, who was very influential both in establishing a central position for Hamlet in Russian consciousness, and in relating Hamlet to the realities of the age, treating him as an 'idealist in conflict with a corrupt world'[38] who finally overcomes his paralysis of will to find strength in 'The readiness is all.' After Belinsky's death in 1848, Hamlet came increasingly to be associated with the cynicism, alienation and disengagement of sensitive intellectuals unable to change the system.[39] There were ideological links between the Russian recreation of Hamlet and that in Germany, where G. G. Gervinus saw Hamlet in 1849 as 'an idealist, unequal to the real world, who, repelled by it, not only laments in elegiac strains over its deficiencies and defects, but grows embittered and sickly about it, even to the injury of his naturally noble character'. In his 'bitterness of feeling', Hamlet appeared a 'type of our German race at the present day'.[40] So potent was this image that the Furness Variorum edition of the play in 1877, after the victories of the Franco-Prussian war, was dedicated to the 'GERMAN SHAKESPEARE SOCIETY OF WEIMAR REPRESENTATIVE OF A PEOPLE WHOSE RECENT HISTORY HAS PROVED ONCE FOR ALL THAT GERMANY IS NOT HAMLET'.[41]

In 1864 Victor Hugo had depicted Hamlet as combining melancholy and outrage, and as someone 'incapable of governing a people'.[42] A. A. Chernyshevsky, swayed by Hugo's reading, put a similar view in terms appropriate to his own country: 'Hamlet dies as he lived, cheerless, without belief in himself ... with the bitter awareness that the government needs Fortinbras and not him.'[43] The commentary by Edward Dowden on the play (1875) provides a further analogy. For him Shakespeare believed in a moral order 'which includes man's highest exercise of foresight, energy, and resolution'; so if it is doubtful whether Hamlet is delivered from his 'disease of the will', never mind; Fortinbras arrives to bring 'the restoration of a practical and positive feeling'.[44] Hamlet is blamed by Henry Morley for his unhealthy inaction and failure to use his powers, while the 'man of ready action', Fortinbras, with lesser powers, does what he can, and becomes king.[45] Like Morley, E. K. Chambers thought the government needed Fortinbras; in a play that showed 'the ruin of the great soul because it is not strong, practical', Fortinbras becomes 'the true saviour of society'.[46] The ideological position of these British critics was very different from that of the Russians, but in both countries men of action were needed rather than the over-sensitive, hesitating, irresolute intellectual typified by Hamlet.

HAMLET AND HAMLETISM

Hamlet, reconstructed as a reflection of a modern consciousness, was thus identified with the problems of the age, and politicized as mirroring those who from weakness of will endlessly vacillate. This Hamlet was further abstracted from the play into an embodiment of what came to be known as Hamletism (the verb, to Hamletize, came later). No other character's name in Shakespeare's plays, and few in other works of literature, have come to embody an attitude to life, a philosophy as we say, and been converted into a noun in this way. Those nouns developed from names of characters usually represent a fairly specific idea, such as the irresponsibility of wishful thinking in

Micawberism, or the striving with lofty or absurd enthusiasm for visionary ideals in Quixotism; Hamletism, however, took on a wider resonance, came to embody a 'philosophy' of life, and to represent a body of ideas, as developed out of a figure already abstracted and freed from the context of the play of *Hamlet*. Hamletism as a term had become established by the 1840s, and came to have a range of meanings, all interconnected, and developed from an image of Hamlet as well-intentioned but ineffectual, full of talk but unable to achieve anything, addicted to melancholy and sickened by the world around him, a Hamlet such as might be reconstituted from the first and third soliloquies, Hamlet contemplating self-slaughter, speaking of death as a kind of sleep, or Hamlet in the graveyard, with a skull in his hand confronting death.

Herman Melville apparently expected his readers to recognize his use of 'Hamletism' in *Pierre*, significantly subtitled *The Ambiguities* (1852), to express the idea of a 'nobly-striving but ever-shipwrecked character'.[47] As the term gained currency later in the century it gathered more varied and extensive connotations. In England it was especially associated with dithering, with men who ought to act but are inhibited from doing so by the 'pale cast of thought'. So the *Daily Chronicle* could advise its readers in 1905 to 'forget Hamletism and all its ills'.[48] Hamletism implied a negative, cynical or despairing attitude to life, as in D. H. Lawrence's novel *Women in Love* (1920), in which Birkin rejects love, weary, as he says, with 'the life that belongs to death – our kind of life', and categorizes his sense of the uselessness of words by saying to Ursula, 'One shouldn't talk when one is tired and wretched. – One Hamletises, and it seems a lie.'[49] To Hamletize is to substitute words for deeds, to postpone indefinitely taking a decision and instead give way to reflection and endless reconsideration. The culmination of Hamletism is perhaps to be seen in T. S. Eliot's Prufrock:

> No, I am not Prince Hamlet, nor was meant to be;
> Am an attendant lord, one that will do
> To swell a progress, start a scene or two,
> Advise the prince: no doubt, an easy tool,
> Deferential, glad to be of use,
> Politic, cautious and meticulous;
> Full of high sentence, but a bit obtuse;
> At times, indeed, almost ridiculous,
> Almost, at times, the Fool.[50]

Behind Prufrock we may glimpse Polonius, but as there is no prince in the world of the poem, but only, as the centre of attention and of self-consciousness, Prufrock, he in effect has the Hamlet role: in denying that he is Prince Hamlet, Prufrock in fact Hamletizes, and speaks for his age in his inability to conceive being Hamlet the Prince, the heroic figure portrayed on the eighteenth-century stage, 'The courtier's, soldier's, scholar's eye, tongue, sword', as Ophelia calls him, or the 'sweet prince' familiar to Horatio. Hamlet the Prince had been deflected into a Prufrock figure, ever failing to be decisive: 'There will be time to murder and create ... And time yet for a hundred indecisions'; in the end Prufrock will not dare to 'Disturb the universe' by action.[51] Prufrock is satirized, but treated affectionately too, and his consciousness, embodied in dramatic monologue, takes the reader with him ('Let us go then, you and I ...'), as if we all share his sense of inadequacy.

I do not know when the term was introduced into other languages, only that Jules Laforgue was said to have introduced it into French in 1886.[52] The idea, however, was current much earlier. In Russia Hamlet was identified by Chernyshevsky with the idea of the 'superfluous man', or 'a member of the tiny minority of educated and morally sensitive men, who, unable to find a place in his native land, and driven in upon himself, is liable to escape either into fantasies or illusions, or into cynicism or despair, ending, more often than not, in self-destruction or surrender'.[53] Turgenev elaborated the figure in his *Diary of a Superfluous Man* (1850), in which he imagined a man of thirty (the age of Hamlet in Act v), who keeps a diary in the last few weeks of a life that is meaningless, that, as he says, has almost driven him out of his mind with ennui.[54] He fails in his pursuit of love, and dies in the spring as everything else comes to life. He has derived pleasure only from the contemplation of his own unhappiness. In a short story of the previous year, 'Hamlet of Shshtchigry District', Turgenev listens to the life story of a strange man educated, like Hamlet, in Germany, who lives bored on his family estate, and sees himself, like Prufrock, as insignificant and useless; he refuses to name himself, only saying, 'call me the Hamlet of Shshtchigry county. There are lots of such Hamlets in every county.'[55] In his famous essay of 1860 contrasting Hamlet and Don Quixote, Turgenev depicted Hamlet as representative of persons who are thoughtful and discriminating, but 'useless in the practical

sense, in as much as their very gifts immobilize them' and turn them into sceptics.[56]

Hamlet indeed haunted the mental worlds of Russian writers and intellectuals through the nineteenth century. Hamlet, or rather 'the problem of contemporary Hamletism',[57] is not explicitly mentioned in Dostoevsky's *Notes from Underground* (1864), but lies behind the image of the central character, apparently a civil servant, who believes that to be too acutely conscious is the lot of intelligent men of his period, and that 'not only too much consciousness, but any sort of consciousness is a disease'; hence he finds the 'inevitable and the legitimate result of consciousness is to make all actions impossible'. Too much consciousness prevents action, and out of the resulting inertia comes boredom, and the feeling of being 'crushed by doing nothing'.[58] Later still, various aspects of Hamletism are embodied in works of Chekhov, who recreates the figure of a superfluous man in his story 'The Duel' (1891); the central figure is Layevsky, described by another character as 'a failure, a superfluous man, a neurotic, a victim of the age'.[59] In refusing to take responsibility for the life of lies he leads, Layevsky says, 'I'm as bad as Hamlet.' This story was in its way a response to Turgenev, who is blamed in the course of it for 'inventing failures',[60] and ends with Layevsky, the Hamlet-figure, living in poverty, but working off his debts, and so taking on responsibilities. Layevsky is thus to some extent redeemed; but the idea of Hamlet as a failure recurs in other works, notably in *Ivanov* (1887–9). The central figure in this play neglects his wife, talks endlessly and does nothing; he says, 'I do nothing and think of nothing, but I'm tired, body and soul . . . I'm bored here too', and he compares himself to Hamlet, who is thirty in the last act of the play, with the difference that for him at the age of 'thirty' he is 'tired and useless': he says, 'Wherever I go I carry misery, indifference, boredom, discontent, and disgust with life.'[61] Ivanov ends exhausted and ashamed, and shoots himself, committing the suicide contemplated at times by Hamlet. He differs from the figures in the works of Turgenev and Dostoevsky in that he blames himself more than society for what he is, and is not concerned, as Dostoevsky is, with the life after death; yet all these responses to the character of Hamlet carry the burden of Hamletism, the idea of someone consumed by ennui, nauseated by himself and the world, sensitive and over-conscious, refusing to accept responsibility, and unable to do anything about it.

In France Hamletism took somewhat different though related forms, especially after the visits to Paris by Kemble, Edmund Kean and William Macready to play the role between 1827 and 1844. Macready's performance was described by Théophile Gautier in his *History of Dramatic Art in France* (1859) with especial emphasis on the graveyard scene, in which, after he threw down the skull of Yorick, Macready drew out a fine cambric handkerchief and wiped his fingers with disgust.[62] This suggested an image of a refined, over-sensitive Hamlet, an image that was fixed in the French imagination by the series of lithographs made by Eugène Delacroix between 1834 and 1845 in the context of the visits by English players to France. Delacroix represents Hamlet in most of his drawings as a beardless youth, and in one early composition, that of Hamlet with the gravediggers, his model seems to have been a woman he knew. He depicts Hamlet as a delicate pallid figure, 'with white, feminine hands and tapering fingers, an exquisite nature, but without energy'.[63] Baudelaire identified himself with Hamlet, and hung Delacroix's lithographs on the walls of his apartment;[64] the defeatism and mood of ennui in his *Spleen*, and the paralysis of the artist trapped in words in his *Igitur*, both reflect aspects of Hamletism. Hamlet was mythologized well into the twentieth century in France as a dreamer who either, as Mallarmé saw him, opts for an ideal of pure being, and finds 'his vocation thwarted, his pure world violated, by the necessity to act',[65] or alternatively suffers from boredom, a *taedium vitae*, that prevents him from doing anything.

Hamletism had a special place in the fin de siècle world of French writers and artists, and Laforgue made a pilgrimage to Elsinore on New Year's day in 1886 so that he could stand by that sea 'whose monotonous waves assuredly inspired in Hamlet this epitaph on the history of humanity: "Words, words, words."'[66] Life and death seemed equally absurd, and Mallarmé's ideal of pure being merely an illusion, so that only self-mockery was left to counter the eternal boredom.[67] If the Macready/Delacroix handkerchief of disgust sym-bolized one aspect of Hamlet, the plume in Hamlet's cap, a standard part of his costume on the nineteenth-century stage, and also illustrated by Delacroix, symbolized another, especially in France, where 'plume' means both 'feather' and 'pen'. Hamlet was for Laforgue, as for Mallarmé, a decadent writer, reading in the book of himself, a book he has penned.[68] Max Jacob thought the First World War killed off this decadent Hamlet,[69] but if the Hamlet of

Mallarmé or Laforgue, or the Hamlet as acted by Mounet-Sully (Jean Sully Mounet), was no longer dominant,[70] Hamletism remained a mordant presence in the consciousness of French intellectuals. As late as 1950, in the wake of two world wars, Paul Valéry imagined the figure of Hamlet brooding over millions of ghosts in the graveyard of Europe:

Today, from an immense platform at Elsinore which stretches from Basel to Cologne, and which reaches the sands of Nieuport, the marshes of the Somme, the hilltops of Champagne and the granites of Alsace, our European Hamlet contemplates millions of specters. But he is an intellectual Hamlet; he reflects upon the life and death of human truths ... He is overwhelmed by the accumulation of discoveries and knowledge we have piled up; he is incapable of coping with this unlimited activity. He muses on the boredom of repeating the past; he muses on the folly of always wanting to be an innovator ...[71]

It is a vision of bleakness in which Hamlet himself becomes a giant spectre or ghost symbolizing the European intellectual brooding over desolation and not knowing what to do with all the skulls around him. Valéry's metaphor transforms the graveyard scene so that Europe itself becomes a vast cemetery in which Hamlet picks over the skulls of great artists and thinkers of the past, Leonardo, Leibniz, Kant and Hegel, whose work has led to nothing. This is the culmination of the French obsession with Hamlet holding the skull of Yorick in the graveyard scene, an obsession that goes back to Delacroix's painting of a 'delicate and wan' figure, 'with white and feminine hands, an exquisite but weak nature', and a 'somewhat irresolute air', as Baudelaire described the picture.[72]

Behind the Hamletism of Laforgue, decadent, despairing, capable only of mockery in defeatism, lies this image of Hamlet as exquisite, weak, feminine and delicate. The adjectives Baudelaire used suggest the ease with which Hamlet might be feminized, and indeed, from the time when Sarah Siddons played Hamlet in 1777 (only in the provinces of England, and later in Dublin, not in London), numerous actresses have essayed the role.[73] Some of the most notable male Hamlets accented the delicacy and sensibility of the character in their performances, as did, for example, Henry Irving in England, and Edwin Booth in the United States, who was regarded by one reviewer as ideal for the part because of 'feminine qualities in his style – subtlety, tunefulness, gentleness, mobility'.[74] One American admirer of Horace Howard Furness, whose Variorum edition of the

play had appeared in 1877, pursued the logic of the feminization of Hamlet in analysing what he saw as the development of 'the feminine element' in Hamlet's character in the revisions made between the first Quarto of 1603 and the final version in the 1623 Folio.[75] His ideological presuppositions embodied in an essentialist idea of manhood and womanhood were similar to those of Henry Morley and E. K. Chambers, in that for him Hamlet lacked 'the energy, the conscious strength, the readiness for action that inhere in the perfect manly character'.[76] Since Hamlet's nature is 'essentially feminine',[77] is it possible, Edward Vining asked, that Gertrude gave birth to a daughter, and passed her off as a son, Hamlet, who is 'in reality but a woman attempting to play a man's part'?[78]

Absurd as this may be, the great Danish actress Asta Nielsen in 1920 recorded in a silent film, much influenced by Vining's book, a much reworked version of *Hamlet* in which the hero is really a woman in love with Horatio.[79] If this was an extreme to which the feminization of Hamlet could go, it seems, paradoxically, that some of the actresses who took on the role were liberated by the fact that they were women from the need to portray Hamlet as possessing feminine characteristics. It is difficult to recover the impact of those powerful actresses who most impressed in the role, like Alice Marriott in London, Charlotte Cushman in the United States, or Sarah Bernhardt in France, England and the United States; and it is perhaps not possible to be sure how conscious audiences were throughout the performance that the slender figure of Bernhardt in black silk tights and a blonde wig of wavy, bobbed hair, who played Hamlet in Paris and London in 1899, was indeed a woman.[80] Max Beerbohm thought of her as 'Princess of Denmark',[81] and others saw in her vivacious, restless and excitable Hamlet qualities feminine enough but not appropriate to the part. Bernhardt used a prose translation, abandoned the handkerchief and plume, and played Hamlet as active and energetic, as one, according to a male reviewer, whose 'febrile agitation bears no resemblance to our ideal of the musing, melancholy Dane'.[82]

Bernhardt's representation of Hamlet provoked both admiration and hostility. A common response of male critics is summed up by William Winter in his account of Shakespeare on the American stage, in which he assumes that Hamlet is a 'born victim of melancholia',[83] and that 'semi-masculine women' playing the role destroy its spiritual truth, especially when, like Bernhardt, they

make Hamlet manly and resolute. If Bernhardt in particular seemed
for some to open up new perspectives on the part, the overwhelm-
ingly male critical response could finally dismiss as all wrong a
transvestite Hamlet. Female Hamlets could thus be disturbing in
challenging the dominant male tradition of associating Hamlet with
traits regarded by men as feminine, a tradition that leads eventually
to a psychological reading of Hamlet as unable to find his identity in
a patriarchal world that stifles his search for the woman in himself;
Ophelia's suicide then becomes 'a little microcosm of the male
world's banishment of the female'.[84] Such a reading recovers the
play and Hamlet's role as a 'study in frustration and failure',[85] but
with a new emphasis. Hamlet's frustration parallels that of the male
artist who, as a man, was expected to do something practical in the
world; and Hamlet's inability to achieve could be related to the
woman in himself, so that he could appear feminine as in Delacroix's
painting, just as the artist, in his ineffectuality, occupied with words
or paint on a canvas, might seem effeminate or androgynous. Tonio
Kröger in Thomas Mann's story, who identifies himself with Hamlet, comments on himself as artist: 'a properly constituted, healthy,
decent man never writes, acts, or composes ... Is an artist a male
anyhow? Ask the females! It seems to me we artists are all of us
something like those unsexed papal singers ...'[86] The association of
sensitivity with femininity finds its culmination in 1981 in a critical
appropriation of Hamlet as 'sensitive, intellectual; and feminine'.[87]

The dominant image of Hamlet in the later nineteenth century,
'shrinking from his appointed task', as Bradley saw him, the
embodiment of irresolution or paralysis of the will, a representative
of the 'ineffectiveness of the speculative intellect in a world of action'
according to E. K. Chambers, was fascinating to the prevailing
ideology of masculine power in the period, because everyone was a
potential Hamlet. Anyone, however noble or fine, might fail by
yielding to weaker impulses. Hamlet's 'constitutional defect of
character'[88] provided a dramatic example of inaction in a world that
summoned men to duty and resolute action; but Hamlet indeed also
embodied something fine and noble, a mixture of strength and
weakness such as all men share. Bradley gave a powerful formulation
to this combination of opposites in his image of Hamlet as ill and
suffering from a pathological condition, yet possessing speculative
genius. In an imperialist age it was ideologically important for
Britain to be seen as having a mission to bring civilization to

benighted peoples, often through 'the power of that great civilizer, the Sword',[89] and Western superiority required men of decision and resolution to exercise that power, whether of the sword or the district officer. Hamlet was a disturbing figure in relation to such an ideology, and the repeated treatment of him by critics as a failure was perhaps an inevitable consequence.

Although Hamlet's failings could be seen as an evil or sickness, he could also serve as a counterpart and projection of the artist or intellectual who felt out of place in a world of philistinism, and who might lament the deficiencies of Hamletism, but at the same time celebrated the disenchanted dreamer spinning words in pursuit of an elusive ideal, or persuaded of the uselessness of action. The poets who identified themselves with Hamlet in France could be perceived as decadent aesthetes, but were also reacting to a time that was for them out of joint, and rejecting the world of getting and spending, with its prevailing ideology. Hamlet embodied the sense of aliena-tion felt by the artist, and became a model in life for writers such as Laforgue, and in art for such figures as Thomas Mann's fictional writer, Tonio Kröger, who, like Laforgue, journeys to Elsinore, to stand on the terrace where Hamlet saw the Ghost. The feminization of Hamlet may be seen as both exemplifying further his failure to meet masculine demands of action and resulution, and also as a way of displacing on to women, and so devaluing, his sensitivity, his habit of introspection, his strength of feeling. In opening the way for women to play the role on stage, however, this process boomer-anged, for women showed they could undermine stage tradition by presenting a resolute Hamlet, and so prove 'unpleasingly mannish'[90] in raising male anxieties about their unfulfilled potential.

HAMLET IN THE MODERN WORLD

By the late nineteenth century Shakespeare's cultural status was changing. Through much of the century his plays had been part of a popular theatrical tradition, performed in the context of all kinds of entertainments, farces and afterpieces, on stages of varying kinds of sophistication in Britain and America. When Mr Wopsle in *Great Expectations* (1861) faced a running commentary from the audience while playing Hamlet with three other actors representing the whole of the Danish nobility, he was a 'provincial amateur' attempting to make his mark in one of the many London theatres. By the end of the

century Shakespeare's plays had been absorbed into legitimate
theatre and high culture and the plays were being performed on
their own in the increasingly centralized and professionalized
theatres of the West End of London and the larger cities, which
catered for more refined middle-class audiences, and were distinguished from those catering for popular entertainment. The
Shakespeare Memorial Theatre was established in Stratford-upon-
Avon as a shrine for an annual celebration devoted to the bard. Mr
Wopsle's Hamlet had been treated as available for friendly banter
by the audience, and 'on the question whether 'twas nobler in the
mind to suffer, some roared yes, and some no, and some inclining to
both opinions said "toss up for it"'.[91] Dickens was, of course,
presenting a satirical picture of such performances, but the gulf
between Shakespeare as popular entertainment and Shakespeare as
cultural idol can be seen in Bernard Shaw's reaction in 1897 to
Forbes-Robertson's essentially classical performance of the role,
presenting a 'dramatic hero as a man whose passions are those which
have produced the philosophy, the poetry, the art and the statecraft
of the world'.[92] This was the Shakespeare who merited the 'Book of
Homage' produced in 1916 on the tercentary of his death, Shakespeare for highbrows.

In America even more strikingly Shakespeare was reabsorbed
during the early part of the century into popular culture, and
'presented as part of the same milieu inhabited by magicians,
dancers, singers, acrobats, minstrels, and comics. He appeared on
the same playbills and was advertised in the same spirit.'[93] For long,
indeed, as Lawrence Levine has shown, the plays were seen as
expressing a populist American ideology, buttressing American
values: as late as 1906 Martha Baker Dunn, looking back over a long
association with Shakespeare's plays, could say:

Shakespeare's message is the message of a robust manhood and womanhood: Brace up, pay for what you have, do good if you wish to get good;
good or bad, shoulder the burden of your moral responsibility, and never
forget that cowardice is the most fatal and most futile crime in the calendar
of crimes.[94]

Even Hamlet fitted the picture in so far as he was seen to be
responsible for his fate, and his role was acted in a vigorous,
melodramatic style by actors like Edwin Forrest long after such a
style had ceased to be dominant in England. In the later part of the
century the more refined, even effeminate, style of playing Hamlet

practised by Edwin Booth held sway. Eventually a cultural shift parallel to that in England took place, as local stock companies were replaced by 'combination companies' organized from the east coast cities, and eventually the 'actor-managers who had dominated the nineteenth-century theater were replaced in the twentieth century by the producer-booking agents centered in New York City'.[95]

Both in Britain and in America the elevation of Shakespeare coincided with and was related to the establishment of the study of English literature as a discipline in its own right in schools, colleges and universities. As long ago as 1882 the far-sighted A. A. Lipscomb pronounced in *Harper's Magazine* that because of Shakespeare's rise 'in the firmament of intellect', special training was necessary to comprehend his works, and he predicted that Shakespeare was destined to become 'the Shakespeare of the college and university, and even more the Shakespeare of private and select culture'.[96] Shakespeare's cultural status was validated by his profundity and great genius, and his concern as the 'supreme teacher' with 'the higher intellectual and moral life'.[97] The reverence for Shakespeare demanded by Coleridge was revived in the academy, where his special status and central position in a literary syllabus were taken for granted, as is shown in the growing industry in providing scholarly editions and critical interpretations of his works. Shakespeare was also institutionalized in other ways, in, for example, the commencement in the 1870s of the New Variorum Edition, promoted by Horace Howard Furness, whose work and whose library are associated with the University of Pennsylvania; and in the founding in Washington, DC of the Folger Shakespeare Library.[98] In England a Shakespeare archive was built up in Stratford-upon-Avon, and an important Shakespeare collection in the Birmingham Public Library. The Deutsche Shakespeare Gesellschaft in Germany began to publish its *Shakespeare-Jahrbuch* in 1865, and the twentieth century has seen the establishment of several other scholarly periodicals devoted wholly to Shakespeare.

This process has been well summed up, with reference to the academic institutionalization of Shakespeare, if perhaps with some exaggeration, by Lawrence Levine: 'By the turn of the century Shakespeare had been converted from a popular playwright whose dramas were the property of those who flocked to see them, into a sacred author who had to be protected from ignorant audiences and

overbearing actors threatening the integrity of his creations.'[99] As
Hamlet was taken over in this way by high culture and the academy,
so the play and the character were revalued, with an increasing
elaboration of their complexity and the difficulty of comprehending
them. Hamlet the character was put back into the play as the texts
(Q1, Q2 and the Folio), as well as the sources, came in for greater
scrutiny, though he retained a remarkable ability to escape and turn
again into a free-floating signifier. A number of scholars and critics
rejected the idea of Hamlet symbolized in the figure of the ineffectual
dreamer, or idealist paralysed by the demands of a world of action,
and sought to reinstate Hamlet as active hero. This was not an easy
task in a democratic age when the traditional idea of the hero had
lost most of its force, and princes were increasingly becoming
decorative rather than functional, targets for gossip or scandal
rather than agents of power. One way was to discover in Hamlet a
'heroism of moral vacillation',[100] as a character who, baffled in his
desire for justice, ends in self-contempt, yet 'can be nice and
courteous, kindly and amiable, wittily fastidious and greatly indig-
nant, urbanely ironical and serenely disillusioned, even when [he]
privately despises and detests the very nature of [his] own existence'.[101] This list of characteristics has little to do with heroism, and
hardly succeeds in turning into virtue what had usually been
considered Hamlet's central weakness. A more subtle approach
would stress rather Hamlet's healthy sensibility, and see him as a
'champion of sensibility in a world that has descended to the level of
beasts'.[102]

Here lay a more persuasive strategy for rehabilitating Hamlet, by
relocating him in the context of the play's action, and perceiving
him, to put it in the simplest and crudest terms, as a 'knight-errant,
the champion of right in a corrupt society'.[103] This was to shift the
emphasis from the 'malady' of Hamlet, his morbid condition or
melancholy, to the sickness of the society in which he is placed. This
idea was developed in a more sophisticated way in the wake of
Laurence Olivier's film version by Peter Alexander in his *Hamlet
Father and Son* (1955). Olivier's film (1947) was in some measure an
offshoot of his energetic triumph as Henry V (1944), and he
appeared in *Hamlet* as the image of a golden-haired warrior, bearing
across the chest and shoulder of his doublet braid suggestive of a
military officer. It seemed to Harry Levin that Olivier's Hamlet
coalesced with the swashbuckling image of Douglas Fairbanks;[104]

but this image was contradicted by much else in the film, notably by the voiceover at the beginning saying, 'This is the story of a man who could not make up his mind.' Alexander rejects the dithering, ineffectual image of Hamlet and presents him instead, with reference to Shakespeare's sources in Saxo and Belleforest, as 'the ideal prince, tough and resourceful'.[105] Hamlet seemed to him to unite the 'heroic passions of antiquity with the meditative wisdom of later ages', but the best image he could find for a modern equivalent was Raymond Chandler's fictional detective Philip Marlowe, and he cited Chandler's well-known comment on him: 'down these mean streets a man must go who is not himself mean, who is neither tarnished nor afraid. The detective in this kind of story must be such a man. He is the hero, he is everything.'[106] The image of the hero in the modern world is radically diminished if it settles into that of a tough but humane private eye, a figure who operates on the fringes of society, marginalized politically, and powerless.

Alexander's effort to shift attention from the faults of Hamlet to his virtues was applauded by Levin, who included a review of Alexander's book in his *The Question of Hamlet* (1959). Hamlet as a secular modern hero could perhaps only be reinstated in terms of a shrunken concept of heroism, that of an individual who 'keeps facing up to and (however desperate) maintaining some control over the flux of action that he stirs around him', a heroism depending less on 'acting or even knowing than upon *being*'.[107] Stressing the place of reason and conscience in the play could amplify such a concept of Hamlet as heroic in spite of his inactivity, as 'an innocent caught in the machinery of a situation engineered solely by Claudius',[108] one whose virtue has to be taken away from him in the killing of Polonius to enable him to 'serve as God's scourge, destined for death himself, and minister, agent of the good'.[109] Here the secular hero turns into God's agent; and Hamlet as a Christian hero in a providential play, concerned not for his life, but for his soul, and refusing to act because he fears damnation, until in the end he becomes 'the hand of Providence destroying evil', is a more plausible reconstruction than the shadow of an ancient Homeric or Germanic hero which Reuben Brower would identify in him.[110] Christian readings tend to assume as justified Hamlet's conviction that he is God's 'scourge and minister', and excuse his sending Rosencrantz and Guildenstern to their deaths on a variety of grounds, such as that his indifference to their deaths is of the same nature as his indifference to his own. In such ways what have traditionally been seen as Hamlet's faults have been absorbed into a providential pattern.

It is perhaps not surprising to find a psychological critic also applauding Hamlet as wholly exonerated: 'the hero is not at fault. Whatever is wrong is wrong with Hamlet's entire world, a world which recreates every adolescent's fantasies about growing up.'[111] This is to excuse Hamlet's 'faults' not on Christian or metaphysical grounds that the play is really a spiritual tragedy,[112] but rather by using the play's uneasiness about the boundaries between fantasy and reality to explain Hamlet in terms of every teenager's fantasies, and so sidestepping the question of Hamlet's weaknesses or failings. One other attempt to rehabilitate Hamlet has been made in the claim that when the play was originally performed, the Renaissance attitudes of the audience would have secured 'their acceptance of him as morally heroic'; but this argument simply assumes that Hamlet always evinces a 'noble mind', even when, in the best tradition of schoolboy heroes, he gives such a 'thorough thrashing' in Ophelia's grave to Laertes that the latter is 'unable to speak again in the scene'.[113] All these efforts to restore to Hamlet an heroic image may be interpreted as meeting a felt need to validate the character as a model and the play as worthy of study, and as establishing an opposition to the pervasive Hamletism of the late nineteenth and early twentieth centuries. But they only work in terms of an impoverished concept of heroism, or by simplifying the play to fit a religious dispensation.

The prevailing view of Hamlet was quite different: forms of Hamletism lie behind the 'verbal invalids',[114] troubled introspectives and tainted protagonists who are to be found in works by a whole range of early twentieth-century writers, such as Henry James, Thomas Mann, Italo Svevo or T. S. Eliot, as well as such figures as James Joyce's Stephen Dedalus and Joseph Conrad's Lord Jim. The various attempts to restore an heroic Hamlet indeed seem not very effective in relation to the continuing pervasive presence of Hamlet as a projection of dissatisfaction or disgust with oneself or with the world, of high aspiration and the inability to achieve anything significant, and above all of a death-wish, or a failure to act against a corrupt society. The word 'failure' haunts Hamlet in this century, even as Hamlet haunts the consciousness of writers and intellectuals. For Joyce's Stephen Dedalus he becomes (as Hamlet/Shakespeare, assimilated into the author), a 'deathsman of the soul', responsible for the 'bloodboltered shambles' in Act v, that seem to Stephen a 'forecast of the concentration camp';[115] Hamlet's weakness thus seems to load him with anticipatory responsibility for the horrors of the twentieth century. In Sartre's *La Nausée* (1938), Hamlet lies behind the existential despair of Antoine Roquentin, whose disgust with existence is focussed in his sense of being superfluous,[116] recalling Turgenev's *Diary of a Superfluous Man* and Chekhov's Layevsky. Boris Pasternak translated the play and scripted Kozintsev's film version, and in comments associated Hamlet with Christ as an heroic figure: '*Hamlet* is not a drama of weakness, but of duty and self-denial';[117] yet his own fictional hero, Dr Zhivago, turns out to be a failure, weak and indecisive, unfaithful to his wife, and far from being a model of duty and self-denial. The novel is, of course, about his initial enthusiasm for the revolution giving way to disillusion and disgust, as he comes to feel he is, like Hamlet in the first of the poems attributed to Dr Zhivago and printed at the end of the novel, trapped in a false role in a world he sees as hypocritical.[118] In Saul Bellow's novel *Herzog* (1964), the central character asks himself, 'Do I want to exist, or want to die?', rephrasing Hamlet's 'To be or not to be'; he is nauseated by the burden of selfhood, and all too conscious of himself as a failure.[119]

The image of Hamlet that informs these and other such works remained powerful because it could serve to focus various forms of disenchantment with the self or society, in relation to the malaise of intellectuals who felt disaffected with the power-structures and ideologies of their capitalist or communist worlds, and also in terms of a reactionary critique of those who show a sense of alienation from their bourgeois society. For Herzog, 'the modern character is inconsistent, divided, vacillating'.[120] Roquentin aspires to oblivion,[121] Herzog feels himself to be 'next door to the Void',[122] and both characters might be thought of in relation to Freud's *Civilization and its Discontents* (1930). Here, in a sweeping view of the evolution of civilization as a struggle between 'Eros and Death, the instinct of life and the instinct of destruction', the price of advance in civilization is seen as a 'loss of happiness through heightening the sense of guilt', and this is manifested as anxiety or malaise. Although Freud does not comment specifically on the play, Hamlet was in his mind, for he cites in this connection the line, 'Thus conscience does make cowards of us all.'[123]

Long before he explained the malaise of Hamletism in such

olympian and transhistorical terms, Freud had written briefly on the
psychology of Hamlet, and influenced Ernest Jones, who in 1923
argued that Hamlet was the victim of a powerful unconscious
conflict as a result of his Oedipus complex, so that in him 'the Will to
Death is fundamentally stronger than the Will to Life'.[124] Such a
view was deflected into quasi-religious terms by G. Wilson Knight
(1930), who saw Hamlet as the 'ambassador of death walking amid
life', affecting others 'like a blighting disease'.[125] In this influential
essay, Wilson Knight betrayed his political interest in strong government by seeing Hamlet as undermining by his sickness 'the health of
the state' in a world of positive assertion, and growing 'more and
more dangerous'.[126] Knight was exceptional in associating Claudius
with a healthy state, but a politically hostile attitude to Hamlet can
be found in other influential treatments of Hamlet in this period,
such as that by George Santayana (1936), who saw 'a sort of
passionate weakness and indirection' in Hamlet's will, that left him
floating without direction in a world he cannot escape or understand,[127] or that by L. C. Knights (1946), who castigated Hamlet for
self-indulgence and a 'desire to escape from the complexities of adult
living'.[128] For Knights, Hamlet provided 'an indulgence for some of
our most cherished weaknesses', and was a bad example, 'incapable
of leading us far towards maturity and self-knowledge'.[129]

The most widely read study of Hamlet at this time was probably
John Dover Wilson's *What Happens in Hamlet* (1935, and frequently
reprinted), which, as Terence Hawkes has wittily shown, restored
order and a conservative understanding of the play in a long-
pondered response to W. W. Greg's subversive account of the
Ghost's story as 'not a revelation, but a mere figment of Hamlet's
brain'. If the tale of the murder of old Hamlet is an hallucination on
Hamlet's part, then Claudius is innocent, which is why he can watch
unmoved while his supposed crime is represented on stage in the
dumb-show preceding 'The Mousetrap'; and when he rises and
leaves the stage, it is because he has become convinced that Hamlet
'is a dangerous madman'.[130] Dover Wilson's concern was to restore
what he thought of as a correct view of the play, by showing how
Hamlet, 'a genius suffering from a fatal weakness', copes with his
'task'; thus he would solve 'dramatic problems, which have arisen
through forgetfulness of Shakespeare's purposes' and restore a sense
of Shakespeare as a great dramatist who knew his business.[131] Even
so, he could only explain Claudius's unconcern in relation to the

dumb-show by arguing that he simply was not looking, because he was deep in conversation with Polonius and the Queen. The 'correct' interpretation restores a Hamlet with noble qualities, but fatally flawed: 'From the very beginning Shakespeare has been playing variations upon the Hamlet theme . . . suggesting that sense of frustration, futility and human inadequacy which is the burden of the whole symphony.'[132] Shakespeare, he wrote, 'never lets us forget that he [Hamlet] is a failure, or that he has failed through weakness of character'.[133]

A somewhat later essay that was very influential, especially in America, was Maynard Mack's 'The World of *Hamlet*' (1951–2), in which the play is presented as concerned with Man, 'Man in his aspect of bafflement', envisaged as 'moving in darkness on a rampart between two worlds'.[134] Mack's tactic, one often emulated but rarely used so well, was to transform Hamlet into an embodiment of 'Man' in general rather than modern man, and so, from an apparently independent and lofty standpoint, to present a sort of transcendent, metaphysical reading in which the mystery of the play is emphasized, and Hamlet's problem is an image of our own in that he exemplifies the human predicament in being tainted with sin and descended from a fallen Adam. Hamlet, naturally 'sensitive and idealistic', has to learn not simply 'to endure a rotten world, he must also act in it', and does so finally by putting himself in the hands of Providence with 'There's a divinity that shapes our ends.' But in all this, Hamlet confronts a condition not of his own making, and cannot do anything about it; he shares in 'the play's emphasis on human weakness, the instability of human purpose, the subjection of humanity to fortune – all that we might call the aspect of failure in man'.[135] Mack subtly relates Hamlet's inactivity to the overlapping meanings of recurrent words in the play like 'act', 'play' and 'show', and in a world of seeming, Hamlet raises questions about the nature of reality when to act is to play or to pretend. Mack put Hamlet back into his world; but still, for all the metaphysical dimension to his argument, Mack sees the play as conveying a 'powerful sense of mortality' by its emphasis on 'failure in man'. In this way we are enabled to accept Hamlet's failings and failure as representative of our own, as the play becomes 'a paradigm of the life of man'.[136]

Here 'failure', the term that recurs so often in accounts of Hamlet, takes on its loftiest meaning, as it relates Hamlet's failure to a much larger metaphysical idea of failure in Man as a necessary aspect of his

mortality, his failure ultimately to grasp the mystery of the meaning
of life and death. At the same time, the very word 'failure' implies an
element of condemnation measured against its implied opposite,
success, and a sense that one could do better. Mack's essay, by
stressing this term, aligns itself with other critical accounts of Hamlet
that depict him, whatever noble qualities he may have, as 'a failure,
an utter failure' in terms of action, and as 'the type of "modern" or
post-Renaissance man: a man essentially divided within and against
himself' in his scepticism.[137] It is an idea of failure that readily passes
into failure in social or political terms. If Hamlet typifies the
emergence of the bourgeois subject with his self-consciousness and
claim to interiority, to a privacy of inner life ('I have that within
which passeth show'),[138] then as the archetype of modern man, he is
'simply a failure, the most formidable and the most fascinating
failure that literature has known'.[139] At a more basic level, Hamlet
may be presented, as in the most recent Arden edition (1982), as 'a
man with a deed to do who for the most part conspicuously fails to
do it', as if Hamlet neglects his 'vocation' or duty of revenge, which
the editor takes as a *donnée* in the play.[140]

If Hamlet is a failure in his 'evasion of the task imposed on him',[141]
what would make him a success? Failure for Mack becomes an
inescapable condition of Man, but if it is an aspect of a new
bourgeois construction of the subject, it can be interpreted in a
variety of ways, all of which may be seen as variants of Hamletism.
The image of Hamlet as artist or player that possessed writers like
Laforgue and Mann persists in critical accounts of Hamlet as a role-
player who fails in his task when, with the King at his mercy in the
prayer scene, he 'becomes corrupted in that moment of hubris by the
taint of a fatal aestheticism'.[142] Another version of Hamlet highlights
nausea, in the wake of Nietzsche and Sartre, either as a condition of
existential despair in the face of an inexplicable and corrosive world,
or as a pervasive sex-nausea, a misogyny that is a mode of anger
Hamlet directs 'towards the Other for destroying his old self-
centered world'.[143] Yet another reading would link Hamlet with
Conrad's Lord Jim and other modern figures as 'opaque not only to
others but to himself or herself', raising a possibility that 'At the
centre of Hamlet, in the interior of his mystery, there is, in short,
nothing', an essence beyond his grasp or the text's power of
signification.[144]

HAMLET OUR CONTEMPORARY

A major shift has taken place since Goethe, Schlegel, Coleridge and Hazlitt deconstructed the Prince and turned Hamlet into a subject without a social role, a private reflection of each of us as common man, or, in Hazlitt's words, 'as little of the hero as a man can well be'.[145] The privatized Hamlet, abstracted from the play and turned into a projection of each of us as individuals ('I have a smack of Hamlet myself'; 'It is we who are Hamlet'), democratized criticism by opening up the possibility of any number of subjective interpretations, and the range of responses to this most famous of literary creations has indeed been very wide. Once set free from the play, Hamlet was not easily put back into it. Yet the privatized Hamlet, though still withdrawn from the play as an autonomous figure, was gradually restored to the public arena. The shift that brought Hamlet back from the private to the public world has taken several forms. One was overtly political, and the others, however much presented in metaphysical or aesthetic or psychological terms, tend also to have significant political undertones.

The political adaptation begins early, as in Freiligrath's identification of Hamlet with young German intellectuals dreaming about the revolution they were unable to bring about, and is especially evident in Germany and Russia in the nineteenth century. In England Hamlet came to exemplify for many nineteenth-century critics the unhealthy condition of those modern men who rejected the prevailing imperialist ideology, and failed to achieve anything or to do their duty. From a conservative point of view, Hamlet seemed to embody the failure of a 'great nature confronted with a low environment',[146] or, in a harsher aspect, he represented a 'spirit of disintegration' as a man 'isolated, self-nauseated, labouring in a sense of physical corruption'.[147] In the twentieth century Hamlet came to represent for W. B. Yeats 'this filthy modern tide' overwhelming all he valued,[148] and D. H. Lawrence deplored what he saw in Hamlet as 'the reaction from the great aristocratic principle to the great democratic principle'.[149] In Russia after the revolution Hamlet was a problem, for it was difficult to accommodate him to the 'active and heroic ideals' of socialist realism,[150] but after the death of Stalin, Grigori Kozintsev directed the play and made his notable film version in 1964, in which, he claimed, 'Before our eyes, faith in the greatness of man conquers the forces of reaction.'[151] In the West, Hamlet was momentarily rescued for a left-wing perspective in the Second World War by Max Plowman, who identified him in 1942 as 'self-conscious man encompassed by a world of violence . . . our world, in fact, is the world of Hamlet; a world that has suffered injury and cries out for justice'.[152] But since then Hamlet is more likely to be seen from the left or the right as a failure in action, or, in Charles Marowitz's words, as 'the supreme prototype of the conscience-stricken but paralysed liberal, one of the most lethal and obnoxious characters in modern times'.[153]

By the 1960s, in any case, a larger sense of disillusion had set in, as seen in Jan Kott's influential absurdist account of the plays in his *Shakespeare our Contemporary* (English version 1964), which gave a new slant to the idea of Hamlet as a representative modern man. For it was a work written by someone who, as Peter Brook said in his foreword, 'assumes without question that every one of his readers will at some point or other have been woken by the police in the middle of the night'.[154] *Hamlet* was inevitably politicized in the context of the Cold War. The young Peter Hall directed a notable production of the play at the Royal Shakespeare Theatre in 1965, when people, mostly young themselves, stood in line for hours to get tickets. Hamlet was played by the tall, adolescent David Warner, dressed in the student fashion of the day, and wearing the ankle-length scarf then popular. He was gauche, gangling, anti-romantic, there was nothing to suggest a prince, and, as the conservative *Financial Times* reported, Hamlet appeared 'a beatnik, not only in his dress and appearance, but in his behaviour as well'.[155] The term 'beatnik' was introduced, in echo of 'sputnik', in 1958, and members of the 'beat generation' were identified in *Encounter* in 1959 as the new barbarians in America rebelling against bourgeois values.[156] Hamlet the beatnik caught the imagination of audiences then, and Peter Hall's address to the cast of his consciously political production shows why it met with conservative disapproval. Hall was a Cambridge graduate, and had read the critics; after referring to Granville-Barker, Brecht and Jan Kott, he said:

Shakespeare himself was entering a dark valley – a place of cynicism, tragedy, and disgust . . . For our decade, in my view, the play will be about the problems of commitment in life and in politics, and also about the disillusionment that produces an apathy of the will . . . There is a sense of what-the-hell-anyway, over us looms the mushroom cloud. And politics are a game and a lie, whether in our own country or in the East–West dialogue, which goes on interminably, without anything very real being said ... [at the end] you are left with Fortinbras, the perfect military ruler ... I would not particularly like to live in a Denmark ruled by Fortinbras.[157]

In the world of the H-bomb cynicism seemed the only stance; what possibility was there of commitment? The disillusionment Hall speaks of was perhaps a factor in the play's apparent loss of contemporary relevance after 1970, in England at any rate. It was not produced by the Royal Shakespeare Theatre between 1970 and 1980 except in the tiny studio theatre, the Other Place, in 1975, where it was staged in modern dress, with Claudius looking more like a company director than a king. The London productions by Peter Hall at the end of 1975, with Albert Finney as Hamlet, and by Toby Robertson in 1977, with Derek Jacobi in the leading role, seemed to be searching for contemporary relevance, the first by emphasizing chance in a dramatic world where all action seemed rather meaningless, the second by emphasizing spying and intrigue. *Hamlet* seemed no longer to have much to say to the age, and when it was revived in Stratford in 1980 in a production devised in metadramatic terms, played on a stage within a stage, receding into a rehearsal and props room, Sheridan Morley, reviewing it in *Punch*, could see little point in the production, or 'in doing this Hamlet here and now'.[158]

Hamlet has usually been seen in political terms in one of two ways. The first regards him as a 'great nature' rendered ineffectual or nauseated by a society in which action seems useless, an image related to the Coleridgean and Bradleyan view of him as required to act but failing to do so. The second would see him as a conscience-stricken intellectual who recoils from violence and is thus unable to take action, an image related to the late nineteenth-century aesthetic identification of Hamlet with the artist alienated from a world that does not value him, or thwarted in his pursuit of the ideal by unavoidable involvement in the world of action. These are familiar variant faces of Hamletism. Much academic criticism evades a directly political reference by transposing discussion on to a philosophic or metaphysical plane, and treating Hamlet as an embodiment of a generalized weakness in Man; but in the widespread fascination of such criticism with Hamlet as a failure, it would seem that a political version of the character as typifying ineffectuality, failure in social or political commitment, underlies even the most abstract and apparently detached accounts of the play.

In fashionably deconstructive and linguistic terms, for instance, the play can be read as 'extraordinarily given to the *via negativa*. Here, perhaps more than anywhere else in his work, Shakespeare specializes in nonbeing and inaction, in forms of verbal suicide, in interruptive modes, in junctures and caesurae, in unnamings and unspeakings.'[159] But such a reading, like all negative readings, implies a positive, which in this case the critic identifies with the killing of the King: 'out of the negative, the positive; out of not-being, being; and out of inaction, action'.[160] To act in the world, to do, to achieve, is, within the terms of the play, to destroy, to kill; and translated into the social and political world of modern Western man, it is to accept the dominant ideology, the profit-motive and forms of successful achievement of our society. The critics who revive again and again the sense of failure in Hamlet the character or the play rarely consider what success involves, but its meaning is implied in the opposites of weakness and indecision, the *via negativa*, the death-wish. Strength, self-assertion, decisiveness, a positive attitude to life, relate well to a conservative political agenda.

Hamlet is representative of the first modern men to the extent that as a subject he feels cut adrift from his social role, in this case prince and heir to the throne of Denmark, by which the identity of men and women was established in a feudal society. As has often been observed, Shakespeare's was an age of transition bringing the emergence of the as yet unintegrated bourgeois subject, and the 'unified subject of liberal humanism' may indeed be 'a product of the second half of the seventeeth century'.[161] Hamlet does finally mend the division between himself as subject and the role he perceives as required of him by committing himself to the values of the ruling ideology, those of Claudius. In academic terms, the central problem in *Hamlet* has frequently been identified as Hamlet's delay, which is a way of talking about a failure to act; and the notion of delay has thus often been formulated in terms of Hamlet's failure to carry out his 'task' or 'duty'. In a more general modern sense, the problem becomes what Peter Hall called 'commitment to life', and there is, of course, a valid sense in which the idea of commitment can be narrowed down to focus on issues like revenge. Some recent critics have understood Hamlet's delay more as a dramatic device that allows the dramatist to 'examine the nature of this act of violence [i.e., revenge]',[162] and so interrogate 'commitment'; and such enduring relevances help to account for the continuing interest in the play, marked by three major editions in the last decade or so.[163]

If it is in some ways a long transition from Coleridge and Hazlitt ('We are all Hamlet') to Prufrock ('I am not Prince Hamlet'), in losing the Prince, we have gained something too. As Hamlet has become increasingly identified with modern man, not as prince but as subject, so his problem has in effect been redefined as questioning the nature, usefulness, and indeed the possibility of action in a world we cannot comprehend – our democratic world, in which the structures of power have become ever more remote, inscrutable and unaccountable to ordinary people, as, for instance, the Irangate affair and the trial of Colonel North in America show. The best-known literary response to Hamlet in recent times, Tom Stoppard's *Rosencrantz and Guildenstern are Dead* (1967), illustrates this well. We lose sight of Hamlet through much of this play, and instead of seeing with Hamlet as observer, we see all through the eyes of Rosencrantz and Guildenstern, who do not understand what is going on. 'We are little men,' they say, 'we don't understand the ins and outs of the matter.'[164] The company of players who visit the court become central, and for them all actions are, of course, fictions, mere show. In offering to perform for Rosencrantz and Guildenstern, they specialize in death, or rather in a range of deaths: 'It's what the actors do best. They have to exploit whatever talent is given to them, and their talent is dying. They can die heroically, comically, ironically, slowly, suddenly, disgustingly, charmingly, or from a great height.'[165] Later in the play, in its one moment of violent action, Guildenstern loses his temper, and stabs the Player with his own dagger. The stage direction reads: 'The Player stands with huge terrible eyes, clutches at the wound as the blade withdraws; he makes small weeping sounds and falls to his knees, and then right down.'[166] It might be a stage direction for the death of Claudius; and indeed, when the Player lies still, Guildenstern talks, in tragic fashion, of silence and destiny; but his fellow-tragedians all applaud the Player, who rises to remark disarmingly, 'O come, come, gentlemen – no flattery – it was merely competent'.[167]

Guildenstern is taken aback to find it was a stage dagger he stabbed with, and this ostentatious comic reminder of the nature of stage deaths might seem to undermine all the deaths in the play, not only those of Rosencrantz and Guildenstern, but those of all who end as corpses in the last scene of Shakespeare's play, which the

tragedians stage as a finale. The end of *Hamlet* is presented in this
play merely as bathos, or a *coup de théâtre*, and, emptied of its
emotional force, is emptied too of any tragic weight. But there is
more to it than this, for Stoppard was responding to something
deeper in Shakespeare's play, the questioning of action itself that can
be construed as constituting its philosophical undercurrent. From
the point of view of Rosencrantz and Guildenstern, Hamlet is all
action, this is all they see, uncomprehendingly; they are caught up in
it from time to time in a marginal way. But there is one moment
when they have an opportunity to intervene, when they are with
Hamlet on the boat travelling to England. They open Claudius's
letter to find it contains orders for the immediate execution of
Hamlet on his arrival there. After debating what to do about the
letter, Guildenstern concludes, 'All in all I think we'd be well
advised to leave well alone.' They are the talkers who do nothing; as
Rosencrantz says, 'We don't question, we don't doubt. We
perform.'[168]

If 'interiority, this consciousness which is also being, defines the
humanist subject, the author and origin of meaning and choice',[169]
then Rosencrantz and Guildenstern renounce meaning and choice,
and treat life as a game of chance. They perform the roles assigned to
them by authority, and when faced with a genuine moral and
political problem, they leave well alone; they Hamletize. But action
is a serious matter for Hamlet himself, who overhears their conversation about the letter, and sends them to their deaths instead. In
Rosencrantz and Guildenstern are Dead, Shakespeare's play is glimpsed
from time to time in flashes of incomprehensible brief action, and
later Stoppard boiled *Hamlet* down to a fifteen-minute version,
reducing it to a rapid chain of events, and so revealing it as farce.[170]
For speeding up the play in this way (as Charles Marowitz and
Joseph Papp have also done) empties significance from the plot as
such, as if to show that the play's power lies not in the events, but in
its investigation of the problem of doing anything significant in a
society whose moral and political order is remote and corrupt.
Stoppard was no doubt impressed by Samuel Beckett's Ham in
Endgame, who is a kind of Hamlet, his consciousness tormented, in
the story about himself he repeatedly tries to finish, by his failure to
act. But in *Rosencrantz and Guildenstern are Dead*, Stoppard's reworking
of *Hamlet* is conservative in transferring emphasis (as in T. S. Eliot's
Prufrock) from Hamlet to two characters whose consciousness re-

mains uninvolved, and who seem to represent for him the 'little men' of the modern world, for ever talking, ironic, detached, uncommitted.

In the preface to his 'unraveling and reweaving' of *Hamlet* (1969), Joseph Papp said '*Hamlet* is a crisis-ridden play, and if ever humanity was in a crisis, it is now'; he strove to relate the play to the Second World War and the war in Vietnam, and turned Claudius into a military dictator.[171] This radical and overtly political approach was very different from Stoppard's, and more in tune with the productions Jan Kott describes as taking place in Poland. In one of these, in Cracow in 1959, the play was presented as a 'drama of political crime', with Hamlet as a rebel, passionate and brutal, and the text was, in Kott's words, 'deprived of the great soliloquies'.[172] In other words, the emphasis was on action, violence and political intrigue. The director omitted the major soliloquies, which for many academic commentators are central; many critics indeed are disconcerted or refuse to believe the evidence when faced with the probability that Shakespeare revised the play and cancelled the whole of the last big soliloquy, 'How all occasions do inform against me . . .' The Polish treatment of the play is at the opposite extreme from that of Stoppard. Effectively, Stoppard expanded material from the soliloquies into the endless word-games of Rosencrantz and Guildenstern, and telescoped the action so as to reduce it to nonsense, inscrutability or mere histrionics. What Stoppard did parallels what many academic critics do in appearing to treat the play in purely philosophical, moral, psychological or metaphysical terms, as though any of these can stand alone, and the play can be read through the character of Hamlet as exploring the grounds for any kind of meaningful action. The play is such an exploration, indeed, but it is more than this; for in order to challenge the power of Claudius, Hamlet is forced to adopt his methods, and involve himself in the world of policy, that is to say, in deception, concealment, diplomacy, and accept that there is no scope for what Sir Philip Sidney thought of as the end of all earthly knowledge, 'virtuous action'.[173] The play is inescapably political, as novelists, poets, essayists, dramatists and critics, consciously or inadvertently, have shown over the last two centuries.

The idea of Hamletism as an attitude to life, a 'philosophy', as we casually put it, developed after the Romantics freed Hamlet the character from the play into an independent existence as a figure

embodying nobility, or at least good intentions, but disabled from
action by a sense of inadequacy, or a diseased consciousness capable
only of seeing the world as possessed by things rank and gross in
nature, and hence a failure. Hamletism gained currency as a term to
describe not only individuals, but the failings of intellectuals,
political parties or nations, and so *Hamlet* was restored to the public
arena to characterize the condition of Germany, or Europe, or the
world, or the decline of aristocracy in the face of democracy. As the
idea of Hamletism prospered, so it came to affect the way the play
was seen, and the most widely accepted critical readings of it have
for a long time presented us with a version of Shakespeare's play
reinfected, so to speak, with the virus of Hamletism, and seen in its
totality as a vision of failure in modern men or even in Man himself.
Since about 1800 Hamlet has become representative of modern
anxieties, and has been democratized into a figure symbolizing the
dismay of ordinary people in the lonely crowd at their inability to
change what they see as wrong in their environment. Whether the
attitude is cynical, a throwing up of the hands, as in Stoppard's play;
or authoritarian, as in the criticism of those who rap Hamlet over the
knuckles for not carrying out his task; or radical, as in the work of
those, like Peter Hall, who have been concerned with commitment
in life and in politics, Hamlet can be made to fit. But the dominant
image that recurs again and again is well summed up in the fine
delineation by Seamus Heaney in his 'Viking Dublin' (1975),
written by a Northern Irish poet brooding on the past and present,
in the context of the political problems of Northern Ireland:

> I am Hamlet the Dane,
> skull-handler, parablist,
> smeller of rot
>
> in the state, infused
> with its poisons,
> pinioned by ghosts
> and affections,
>
> murders and pieties,
> coming to consciousness
> byjumping in graves,
> dithering, blathering.[174]

CHAPTER 3

The reception of King Lear

KING LEAR AND REDEMPTION

If the story of the reception of *Hamlet* keeps returning to Hamletism and politics, the reception of *King Lear* has to do for the most part with an evasion of political issues. I start with the Romantics, who first claimed for the play the special status it now has. They saw themselves as recuperating *King Lear* as a reading text from the approval by Dr Johnson of the happy ending devised by Nahum Tate, on the grounds that the death of Cordelia was 'contrary to the natural ideas of justice, to the hope of the reader, and, what is yet more strange, to the faith of chronicles'.[1] Tate's was, of course, the version played on the stage during this period, with its happy ending – restoring Lear to a power he promptly hands over to Cordelia and Edgar, who are to marry – and from 1810 till the death of George III in 1820, the play was not staged at all in London because of the analogy that might be drawn between Lear and the mad old king on the throne. Tate's version, made in 1681, is conservatively political in making the action move towards a restoration of the monarchy, and 'an endorsement of obedience and civil order';[2] and the reasons for banning of the play in 1810 were also political. But in the final years of the reign of George III it was perhaps inevitable that the Romantic critics should avoid political issues and concentrate on the personal relations of Cordelia and Lear. Schlegel pointed the way in 1811 by defending Cordelia's death as necessary, since the old King can only die; he put it as a rhetorical question: 'what more truly tragic end for him than to die from grief for the death of Cordelia?'[3]

Charles Lamb went further in internalizing Lear: 'while we read it, we see not Lear, but we are Lear, – we are in his mind, we are sustained by a grandeur which baffles the malice of daughters and storms'.[4] Thus we can enter into the 'sublime identification' of the old King with the heavens, and recognize that after his experience, after the terrible 'explosions' of his passion, there is nothing left but for him to die.[5] The rest of the play tends to fade behind this intense identification of the critic with Lear himself. Hazlitt is notable as the first radical critic of Shakespeare, one who stressed the political implications of plays like *Coriolanus*, and saw the complexities of *Henry V*; yet he too treated *King Lear* in personal terms, cited Lamb as his authority for dismissing Dr Johnson's approval of Tate's ending, and, like Lamb, stressed the 'force of individual passion' in Lear as the old man encounters the 'petrifying indifference' of his daughters.[6] In his general reflections on the play, even Hazlitt does not notice the subversive potential of Shakespeare's text as contrasted with Tate's, but particularly emphasizes that 'the greatest strength of genius is shewn in describing the strongest passions', and this would seem to explain what he meant by saying that *King Lear* is 'the best of all Shakespeare's plays, for it is the one in which he was most in earnest'.[7]

Coleridge was fascinated by Edmund, and offered a masterly analysis of his character in terms of the power of intellect and will that compels admiration 'without reference to any moral end'. His comparison of Edmund to Napoleon, and his noticing the 'inveterate habits of Sovereignty' in Lear, show a consciousness of some of the political issues in the play that is surprisingly absent from Hazlitt's account.[8] In his essay on *Coriolanus*, Hazlitt recognized the sympathy of the imagination for the heroic, the powerful: 'The principle of poetry is a very anti-levelling principle';[9] and he went on to treat this play entirely in political terms, noting, 'We had rather be the oppressor than the oppressed. The love of power in ourselves and the admiration of it in others are both natural to man: the one makes him a tyrant, the other a slave.'[10] Yet Hazlitt treats Lear as a father, and the play *King Lear* chiefly in terms of 'the ebb and flow of the feeling'.[11] It is as if the grandeur of the play defeated him, or at least deactivated his radical principles; he stood in awe of it, saying, 'We wish that we could pass this play over, and say nothing about it. All that we can say must fall far short of the subject.'[12]

'The excellence of every art is its intensity', Keats wrote in a letter of January 1818, his example being *King Lear*, that 'fierce dispute, / Betwixt Hell torment & impassion'd Clay'.[13] This is a more idealized and metaphysical version of Hazlitt's reading, and the effect of Romantic commentary on the play was at once to elevate it to a position of supremacy as an awesome work, as 'the most perfect specimen of the dramatic art existing in the world', in Shelley's words,[14] and at the same time to internalize the play, as centrally concerned with what Hazlitt called the 'force of passion'.[15] The Romantics located the tragedy within the mind of Lear, and tended to reduce the external action to a domestic drama centred on the old King's quarrel with his daughters. Although both Hazlitt and Coleridge, who observed 'some little faulty admixture of pride and sullenness in Cordelia's – Nothing',[16] had reservations about Cordelia's behaviour in the opening scene, the general emphasis of the Romantic critics tended to foster the idealization of Cordelia. Hazlitt brought his essay on the play to a climax by citing the reconciliation of Lear with Cordelia (IV.7.43–69), and describing the 'awful beauty' of their mutual consolation as prisoners (V.3.3–21).[17] It was a short step from such a perspective to the conversion of Cordelia into 'a saint ready prepared for heaven', an almost sacred embodiment of love, as in Mrs Jameson's account of her influence as 'like that of a celestial visitant'.[18]

During the nineteenth century other aspects of the play came under scrutiny, but still its primary interest was seen to reside in the relations of parent and child. Hence the matter of Cordelia's death, whether it has any meaning or can in any way be justified, became a central issue, giving rise to a series of readings which emphasized the redemptive power of Cordelia's love at the end. Hermann Ulrici may have been the first critic to note in 1839 the larger political implications of a play that 'sets before us the public fortunes of a great nation'; but he went on to distance the politics of the play from his own time, for such 'wide-spread corruption of morals', he said, could not occur in a modern Christian society.[19] Distancing the play into a remote and primitive age helped to provide analogies for the idea of its grandeur or sublimity, and at the same time made its political concerns seem irrelevant to the age of the critic, so that the effect was to reinforce a critical emphasis on personal relationships in *King Lear*. Nahum Tate's version had ruled the London stage since 1681, and when William Macready revived the play at Covent Garden in 1834 in the first production to restore Shakespeare's text (if heavily cut), the settings suggested an ancient world of prehistoric monoliths, and 'druid circles' rose 'in spectral loneliness out of the heath'.[20] The visualization of the play in terms of a prehistoric Britain of ancient druids and Stonehenge-like

monoliths was to remain a recurrent feature of the staging of
King Lear.[21]

Alternatively the play was seen as analogous to ancient epics, such
as 'the Trojan legend and the "Nibelungen Lied", which similarly
celebrate the downfall of barbarous races, whose place is occupied
by descendants of a more advanced civilisation'.[22] For Gervinus,
writing these words about 1850, Cordelia was the precursor 'of a
better generation'.[23] A further comparison, suggested by Shelley,
was taken up by Swinburne (1880) and Edward Dowden (1881),
who linked *King Lear* with the drama of Aeschylus. Swinburne was
exceptional in his century in finding a dark and hard fatalism in the
play, but, like Dowden, he used the analogy with Aeschylus to
distance the play as 'elemental and primaeval'.[24] Dowden passed
rapidly from a comparison of *King Lear* with the *Agamemnon* to a
rhetorical flight on its grandeur as akin to that of a great Gothic
cathedral.[25] He saw the characters as 'ideal', so that Cordelia
became 'a pure redeeming ardour', and the play as a whole
possessed 'some vast impersonal significance', a mystery too grand
for critical analysis.[26] Echoing Hazlitt, he threw up his hands: 'Of the
tragedy of *King Lear* a critic wishes to say as little as may be', since
words are inadequate to respond to such sublimity.[27]

In alluding to the *Agamemnon*, Dowden did not mention the
political concerns of that play or of *King Lear*, and the first critic to
concern himself with the contemporary political implications of
Shakespeare's play was Denton Snider, who argued in 1887 that it
'reaches to the very heart of the age of the Tudors and Stuarts, and
reveals to us the disease of absolute authority, showing how such an
authority wrecks society on the one hand, and, on the other, wrecks
the monarch who exercises it'.[28] Rather than distancing *King Lear*
into a primitive age, or into Classical myth or Classical tragedy,
Snider saw the play as topical in the largest sense in showing the
break-up 'by an inner disease' and subsequent restoration of what he
called the 'Institutional World', which he thought was healed and
purified at the end.[29] His reading was therefore in alignment with
redemptive interpretations, but transferred the emphasis to the
political: 'A history of society in small is shown in the drama; we see
how a period gets corrupt and perverted, then how it is purified.'[30]
As Swinburne's was a rare voice in recording a sense of bleakness in
the play, so Snider seems to have been alone in reading the play in
relation to the politics of Shakespeare's own world; and his account

was forgotten in the overwhelming impact of A. C. Bradley's masterly synthesis in 1904 of the main lines of nineteenth-century criticism of *King Lear*.

Bradley's main points derive in part from his response to earlier critics. Like Lamb, he found the play too sublime for the stage, imperfectly dramatic, and demanding a 'purely imaginative realisation'; hence it is not, as Hazlitt claimed, Shakespeare's best play, but rather his greatest, as generating a sense of vastness, 'the feeling not of a scene or particular place, but of a world'.[31] Bradley thus once more dehistoricized the play, grouping it with 'works like the *Prometheus Vinctus* and the *Divine Comedy*, and even with the greatest symphonies of Beethoven and the statues in the Medici Chapel'.[32] Thus *King Lear* was made to transcend period and genre as a work of poetic imagination that tends to the symbolic or allegorical. The analogy with the *Divine Comedy* was pursued by Bradley to reinforce a redemptive reading that rejected Swinburne's pessimistic interpretation; he found 'a consciousness of greatness in pain, and of solemnity in the mystery we cannot fathom'.[33] Although Bradley stopped short of a Christian justification of suffering as redemptive, his sense of ecstasy at the end, his insistence that an actor should show Lear dying in 'unbearable *joy*',[34] paved the way for a series of readings of the play in Christian redemptive terms during the first half of the twentieth century.

Bradley's impact was enormous, but it did not overwhelm all opposition to a redemptionist reading of *King Lear*, an opposition that is represented, for example, in the emphasis by E. K. Chambers (1906) on the pagan environment of the play and the ruthlessness of the last act,[35] in G. Wilson Knight's perception (1930) of the play as the 'most fearless artistic facing of the ultimate cruelty of things',[36] and in D. G. James's sense (1951) of its 'bleak and merely exploratory vision' as offering 'no crumb of Christian comfort'.[37] However, redemptive interpretations were much more common, and more influential. Even Wilson Knight, who anticipated absurdist readings of the play, shared Bradley's vision of mankind being ennobled by a purgatorial suffering, as Cordelia brings an 'awakening of Lear from the Wheel of Fire to a new consciousness of Love'.[38] Harley Granville-Barker (1927) also quarrelled with Bradley in arguing for the effectiveness of the play on the stage, but shared Bradley's sense that the play shows, as he put it, Lear's 'agony, his spiritual death and resurrection'.[39] R. B. Heilman's influential study of the play's

imagery (1948) also emphasized Lear's 'religious feeling'; for him the
play presented a conflict between the 'rationalistic obtuseness' of
characters like Edmund, and the 'illumination' that comes to the old
King in something like a 'Christian transvaluation of the values of
Lear's pagan world'.[40]

By this time (1939) R. W. Chambers had promoted a more
specifically Christian reading of the play as a remodelling of its
sources into 'the final victory of good'; Edgar in this view becomes
a 'Christian gentleman' (a phrase borrowed from Granville-
Barker), and Cordelia a martyr.[41] Others took up this theme,
representing the play as a 'sublime morality play' showing 'The
Salvation of Lear', and even finding in it an assertion of 'the
perfection of God's harmonious order'.[42] Many of those who quarrelled with such readings, which at their most extravagant could
discover 'the teaching of the Cross'[43] in *King Lear*, continued
nevertheless to find redemption or something very like it in the
play, if not expressed in specifically Christian terms. A secular
version might offer renewal or restoration; and Robert Ornstein,
comparing Lear once again to Job, as R. W. Chambers and others
had done, sees Lear as born again through patience and humility.[44]
Perhaps the most widely known interpretation of this kind was
offered by Kenneth Muir in his introduction to the important
New Arden edition of *King Lear* in 1952; in this he stressed the
joy of reconciliation as the 'goal of Lear's pilgrimage'.[45] The term
'pilgrimage' has, of course, religious connotations, and Muir,
acknowledging his debt to Bradley, again aligns Lear with Job, as
suffering in order to shed the old man and be born again: 'He loses
the world and gains his soul.'[46]

Most of such accounts of the play treat it as one of cosmic scope,
concerned with universals, with Man abstracted from the petty
concerns of ordinary life – as if the play could only be understood by
analogies with Christian or Greek myths, which were brought
together in Geoffrey Bickersteth's image of Lear as a Promethean
figure embracing Cordelia, who is associated with the Christian
myth as a symbol of divine love.[47] The concern of the play with
power and rule was not always ignored, but was subordinated to the
personal 'pilgrimage' of Lear, a quest often generalized into the
suffering of Man on a journey to find redemption. There was a
counter-movement by critics who related the play more closely to
the thought of Shakespeare's own age, and the most influential of

these, Theodore Spencer in *Shakespeare and the Nature of Man* (1942), saw the play as showing how the 'evil in man's nature' brings chaos 'in a kingdom and a soul'.[48] He stressed especially in *King Lear* the violations of 'natural law' as defined by Hooker and other Elizabethan thinkers, while considering the play in terms of 'the relations of children to their parents . . . of man to the state, and . . . of the gods to man';[49] and he noted that though Shakespeare gives little attention to 'political chaos', this is as 'obvious as the chaos in man and in the universe'.[50] Spencer's brilliant account may have influenced Edwin Muir's argument (1946) that Lear and his allies represent 'an order of society so obviously springing from the nature and needs of man that it can also be called natural',[51] while Edmund and his allies embody a realpolitik that links them on the one hand with Machiavelli and on the other with fascism in Italy and communism in Russia, as representing 'political action which ignores all moral considerations'.[52] Edwin Muir indeed claims that a 'sacred tradition of human society' lies behind *King Lear*, one which has been 'smashed' by individualism.[53] Both Spencer and Muir were writing in the context of the disruptions of the Second World War, and shared a conservative nostalgia for 'True universality in the form of an ordered pattern of relationships', which is what they found in Shakespeare.[54]

The insights of critics like Spencer and Edwin Muir were skilfully assimilated into the redemptive tradition by John F. Danby in *Shakespeare's Doctrine of Nature* (1949), a book that remained influential through the 1950s, when it was twice reprinted. Danby again saw the play as centrally concerned with Renaissance conceptions of nature, perceived as benignant (in the tradition of writers like Hooker), or as malignant (in the tradition of writers like Hobbes). Edmund in particular he regarded as exemplifying a new rationality, 'the impulse to acquire, to provide for one's security, to extend one's prestige'.[55] Edmund thus symbolized the 'New Man' in an age of competition, and belonged to the new society Danby saw and deplored as developing in the sixteenth century and after, 'the new age of scientific inquiry, of industrial development, of bureaucratic organisation and social regimentation'.[56] In this view, Edmund becomes the antithesis to 'the benevolent thesis Shakespeare's age inherited from the Middle Ages'.[57] That 'thesis' was embodied in Cordelia as representative of benignant nature; Cordelia thus was idealized as 'the perfection of truth, justice, charity'[58] by Danby, and

her invasion of England at the head of a French army 'is simply
right'.[59]

Edgar and Lear also belong in this 'theology of nature'. Lear's
'neurosis . . . of old age and absolute power combined' in the opening
scene is cured for him to develop into a 'full humanity'.[60] Lear,
indeed, seems for Danby to embody many of Edmund's qualities
until he is humbled, but then his cry in III.4, 'Take physic pomp . . .',
becomes 'the logical outcome of Shakespeare's own achieved insights, the wisdom the tragic period establishes'.[61] Danby's moral
idealization of Cordelia and Edgar is rooted in a political schema in
which they represent the values of an older and better kind of
society, into which Lear too is assimilated, while Edmund, Goneril
and Regan embody the competitive self-assertion and greed of a new
society described in terms more relevant to twentieth-century capitalist countries than to the seventeenth century. Danby thus effected
a significant modification of the Bradleyan tradition, to which he
owed a good deal. Bradley notoriously offered to give *King Lear* a
new title:

There is nothing more noble and beautiful in literature than Shakespeare's
exposition of the effect of suffering in reviving the greatness and eliciting the
sweetness of Lear's nature . . . but Lear owes the whole of this to those
sufferings which made us doubt whether life were not simply evil, and men
like the flies which wanton boys torture for their sport. Should we not be at
least as near the truth if we called this poem *The Redemption of King Lear*, and
declared that the business of 'the gods' with him was neither to torment
him, nor to teach him a 'noble anger', but to lead him to attain through
apparently hopeless failure the very end and aim of life?[62]

Bradley ended his chapters on *King Lear* by pointing to *The Tempest*,
as if Prospero takes over from Lear in preaching to us 'from end to
end, "Thou must be patient." "Bear free and patient thoughts."'[63]
For Bradley the play thus displayed a conflict of good and evil,
detached from specific social or political concerns, which were
generalized into Lear's process of learning to 'disarm the falseness of
flattery and the brutality of authority' in a world convulsed by evil,
but in which good is 'the principle of life'. Thus Bradley's appeal to
the 'sweetness of Lear's nature' elided his terrible tyranny, sanc-
tioned him as a figure representative of good, and implicitly lent
approval to the kind of hierarchical society he stands for.[64]

This approval is marked in Bradley's view of Edmund, whom he
reduced to the status of a common criminal: 'Practically, his attitude

is that of a professional criminal. "You tell me I do not belong to you", he seems to say to society: "Very well: I will make my way into your treasure-house if I can. And if I have to take life in doing so, that is your affair." '[65] If Edmund does not conform, that is his fault, and he should not blame the 'society' which Bradley assumed we approve. Bradley helped to reinforce what remained for so long the dominant critical view of *King Lear*, as, in Keats's words, a 'vale of soul-making', a play in which suffering is justified as necessary to school the heart. Danby shared Bradley's somewhat sentimental reading of *King Lear* as a preparation for *The Tempest*, ending his book with the claim that in the last plays 'Lear and Cordelia find each other again and live happily ever after.'[66] But in amplifying his conception of Edmund, Goneril and Regan as typical of a ruthless, self-seeking capitalism, Danby at once pulled *King Lear* into the twentieth century, and used the play as a way of rejecting 'the impulse to acquire, to provide for one's security, to extend one's prestige' in favour of a vision of a better world in which Cordelia became part of 'the utopian dream of the artist and of the good man'.[67]

Danby's reshaping of Edmund from Bradley's common criminal into a capitalist reflects a shift from an unthinking acceptance of the order of society as it was in his time (1904), shown in Bradley's essays, to a general rejection of what Danby saw as a competitive and corrupt society in his own age (1949). But in sentimentalizing Lear, knocking away all the rough edges, and distancing him and Cordelia into the 'utopian dream' of a 'perfect community', Danby effectively continues a conservative tradition of associating Lear with all that is good, and playing down the tyranny of the old King. The play was reconstructed in terms of the personal sufferings of a good old man, and the kind of reading Danby offered was given wide currency in Kenneth Muir's introduction to his edition (1952). The persistence of redemptionist readings of the play in the years following the end of the Second World War may be related, as G. R. Hibbard has suggested,[68] to the emphasis during that period on reconstruction and social justice, especially in Britain, where a serious effort was being made to ensure, in Gloucester's words, that

> distribution should undo excess,
> And each man have enough. (IV.1.70–1)

But if such readings mark a willingness, with Lear, to 'forget, and

forgive' (IV.7.83) the enmities of the Second World War, they still at
a deeper level maintain a long tradition of interpretations of *King
Lear* that implicitly endorse the structure of society the play takes for
granted. For redemptionist readings tend to associate Edmund,
Goneril and Regan with the worst features of destructive competiti-
veness in the modern world, even with 'the rise of fascism'; and they
sanction as an alternative a concept of order which may be described
in terms of piety, or a lost 'communal tradition', but which is not
distinguished from the hierarchical order taken for granted in the
play.[69] The social order the play assumes is in fact an absolute
monarchy, with its rigid structure of ranks and values. There is a
deep contradiction built into Danby's vision of a benevolent medieval order of society; for if, as he claimed, Shakespeare always
'affirmed the primacy of the private sphere to the political', it is not
at all clear how the political, the idea of a society, relates to the
personal, to the idea of a 'full humanity'.[70]

KING LEAR AND DESPAIR

At one point Danby somewhat oddly observes that Lear's speech to
Cordelia when they are taken prisoners ('Come, let's away to prison
. . .') 'points to the continuing possibility of [the] concentration
camp',[71] and his nostalgia for a golden age located in a pre-capitalist
society no doubt has some connection with his revulsion against the
atrocities of the Second World War. Some critics, unaffected by or
rejecting such considerations, continued to represent *King Lear* in
metaphysical terms as a play that shows us pain overcome in Lear's
'unbearably joyful knowledge of a reality and truth that triumph
over death and fate and time',[72] Lear himself being 'born again', as
he puts on 'the new man',[73] or as he is finally redeemed at the end of
his 'spiritual pilgrimage' towards self-discovery.[74] But by 1960 a
marked shift in the interpretation of the play was taking place, and
such critical voices seemed increasingly out of touch, even if a
Bradleyan approach was not without its defenders; and some subtle
variations could be played on a metaphysical approach to the play,
as by Stephen Greenblatt (1982), who saw it as a 'secular version of
the ritual of exorcism', transcending 'all ideology'.[75]

In his anxiety to challenge those, like Swinburne and E. K.
Chambers, who found the play pessimistic, 'no more than a deeply
moving contemplation of man's helplessness', L. C. Knights (1960)

argued that 'For what takes place in *King Lear* we can find no other word than renewal'; the philosophy of egotism embraced by Edmund, Goneril and Regan is revealed as a 'self-bred delusion', while 'What Lear touches in Cordelia . . . is, we are made to feel, the reality, and the values revealed so surely there are established in the face of the worst that can be known of man or Nature.'[76] 'Renewal' is a more cautious word than 'redemption', and Knights was careful to avoid religious connotations in writing of 'reality' and 'values', as he sought to close in some measure the gap between affirmative and bleak interpretations of the play. Danby had sharpened this polarity in relating it to an opposition between a good medieval order and a corrupt modern form of society. Some critics sought to transcend these polarities by treating the play primarily as concerned with personal relationships 'treated as an end and not as a means' between characters 'imagined not only as members of each other but also as members of a Nature which is active both within themselves and throughout the circumambient universe'.[77] The appeal to 'Nature' appeared to resolve, and certainly marginalized, the opposition between Christian and secular versions, negative and positive interpretations; and the matter of the social order, so central on one level to Danby, was also realigned as 'the condition, as it is the resultant, of sweet and affirmative being, without which man relapses into a beastly and self-destructive individualism'.[78] Such an approach made it possible to rescue some moments that offer 'promise of grace and benediction'[79] without asserting a beneficent final dispensation in *King Lear*; and other critics, like Richard Sewall (1959) and John Holloway (1961), developed similar readings. Both linked Lear with Job, and settled for a limited affirmation 'in the face of the most appalling contradictions'.[80] For Holloway, the division of the kingdom was a facet of 'that universal disruption of Nature, that Descent into Chaos, which for millennia had been a standing dread of mankind'; but he thought the play recovers from this apocalyptic vision to close with a modest affirmation, and a sense of 'a human sacrifice'.[81]

The most subtle and comprehensive attempt to reconcile what he saw as two sentimental readings of the conclusion to *King Lear* was presented by Maynard Mack (1965). He rejected interpretations of the end as either total victory or total defeat; rather, for him, 'the victory and the defeat are simultaneous and inseparable'.[82] We recoil from suffering, he argued, but 'it is a greater thing to suffer than to lack the feelings and virtues that make it possible to suffer'.[83] The play concerns 'Man's tragic fate', and this 'comes into being with his entry into relatedness, which is his entry into humanity'.[84] The 'bent of the play is mythic',[85] he said, and, recalling R. W. Chambers quoting Keats, he again thought of the action as 'a vale of soul-making'.[86] By emphasizing on the one hand personal relationships, and on the other hand the mythic aspect of the play, Mack was able to rescue a sense of 'whatever grandeur we achieve', of nobility, and of the survival of 'our moral and religious systems' from the deaths of Lear and Cordelia.[87] He even invoked, in a self-indulgence that might be accused of sentimentality, 'the image of Mary bending over another broken child',[88] as if Lear with the dead Cordelia showed us something more nearly like a religious than what Helen Gardner called a 'secular Pietà'.[89]

Mack began his book with a chapter on the stage history of the play, in which he was especially harsh in describing what he called 'efforts to rationalize *King Lear*' by performing a 'subtext' instead of what Shakespeare intended.[90] He focussed particularly on the productions by Herbert Blau (1961) and Peter Brook (1962). In his second chapter he categorized the play as a union 'of high-flown parable and vision with a homely verisimilitude',[91] but went on to stress the archetypal elements, links with the morality play and with romance, and 'possibly archetypal folk motifs'.[92] He concluded that its 'form of organisation' was 'as much homiletic as it is dramatic, and sometimes more the former than the latter'.[93] In this way, and in spite of his sense of Lear as a 'rancorous father',[94] or of the need to establish in the opening scene 'a deep sense of Renaissance England',[95] the essence of the play lay for him in his conception of its vision, which he aligned with the morality play:

This is what the Morality play was, a vision acted upon a platform whereby the invisible became visible and man's terrestrial pilgrimage was glimpsed whole in its entire arc of pride and innocence, temptation and fall, regeneration and salvation or ruin and damnation. This is also, essentially, what *Lear* is, save that in the case of *Lear* we must add to the arc of pilgrimage Shakespeare's more tragic vision of the creature whose fate it is to learn to love only to lose (soon or late) the loved one, and to reach a ripeness through suffering and struggle, only to die.[96]

In this way Mack recuperated a sense of Lear's progress as pilgrimage, and revitalized a metaphysical emphasis in his reading of the text, bringing into play a wide range of the terms that in effect locate it within a traditional Christian framework; and even if 'the heavenly destination is no longer clear, the sense of journey to some form of consummation remains'.[97]

I have dwelt at some length on this book because it is the most incisive and skilful attempt to preserve the best features of a long tradition of reading the play both in terms of personal relationships and at the same time in metaphysical terms, while acknowledging, and to some extent pillorying, those who, by the 1960s, were, as Mack put it, indulging 'the mid-twentieth-century *frisson du néant* at its most sentimental'.[98] It was a clever tactic to turn the accusation of sentimentality back on those who had been establishing what, by 1965, threatened to become the dominant line of interpretation of *King Lear*. Until about 1960 or so redemptive readings, or at least readings emphasizing the positive more than the negative aspects of the ending, had predominated, but thereafter there came a marked swing to bleak and pessimistic accounts of the play. In 1960 two essays helped to establish the idea of 'The New *King Lear*', to cite the title of one, in which Barbara Everett rejected a Christian interpretation, and the treatment of the work as a morality play.[99] In another essay, J. Stampfer pulled back Lear's 'purgation' and 'spiritual regeneration' into the middle of the play, finding catharsis there, while seeing at the end only a release of the worst of our fears, 'the fear, in other words, that we inhabit an imbecile universe'.[100]

The shift in response to *King Lear* was prompted by an increasing sense of the play's relevance to the age; as Mack remarked, 'After two world wars and Auschwitz, our sensibility is significantly more in touch than our grandparents' was with the play's jagged violence, its sadism, madness, and processional of deaths . . .'[101] Others found a reference to concentration camps, and especially Auschwitz, useful in assessing the bleakness of the play in relation to the possibility of a Christian interpretation.[102] The two important productions pilloried by Mack perhaps did most to change perception of *King Lear*. One was Herbert Blau's San Francisco Workshop production, mockingly dismissed by Mack, who commented, 'intoxicating stuff – but what resemblance does it bear to the play Shakespeare wrote?'[103] The problems with the idea of 'the play Shakespeare wrote' will be considered later; suffice it here to say that like other plays, *King Lear* is continually redefined by each new generation, and, as this chapter implicitly argues, resists being reduced and sanitized into a universal allegory about the pilgrimage of Man. (Perhaps no other work has induced in a succession of critics such an addiction to capital letters, used as a means of claiming a metaphysical grandeur and removing the play from ordinary social and political considerations.) In his account of directing the play, Blau consciously located his production in relation to the theatre of the absurd, especially the drama of Genet and Samuel Beckett's *Endgame*, to the atom bomb, and to the war in Korea. He aimed in his presentation at a 'provisional summing up of the disturbed questing of our entire theater in a period infected by the demoralizations of the Cold War'.[104] Blau published this account in 1964, at a time when the development of hydrogen bombs, begun in the 1950s, the proliferation of missiles provoked by the Cuban crisis of 1961–2 and the erection of the Berlin Wall were especially disturbing. Blau wrote, 'the presence of the Bomb . . . shattered all belief', and again asked, in the wake of Hiroshima and Belsen, 'what could you believe in?'[105] The half-forgotten horrors of the atom bomb had been brought to life vividly in Alain Resnais's film *Hiroshima mon amour*, which began to circulate in 1959, and Blau reinterpreted *King Lear* with reference to this film as rediscovering and nourishing love 'by proceeding from horror to more horror'.[106]

The emphasis on 'nothing' in Blau's production was still more marked in Peter Brook's more influential version of 1962, made into a film in 1967. The beginning of the text was cut, so that the film could open with Lear's great cry, 'Know that we have divided / In three our kingdom . . .'; the long-drawn-out 'Know' brought out the pun on 'No', and negation became the theme. Further cutting removed most of the play's moralizing and words of comfort or consolation, and reduced the roles of Edgar and Albany especially. The film, set in a barbaric Jutland landscape where life is at best crude and primitive, emphasized desolation, loss, brutality. Lear's knights lay waste to Goneril's palace, and Oswald squeals like a pig when savagely killed by Edgar. Special highlighting was given to Gloucester's words.

> As flies to wanton boys, are we to th'gods,
> They kill us for their sport.   (IV.1.36–7)

These lines had been usually cut in productions of the play until the 1930s, as representing an unacceptable nihilism;[107] by contrast, Brook kept them in and cut the remaining forty lines of dialogue between Edgar as Poor Tom and his father in this scene, as part of a deliberate attempt to remove any 'reassuring catharsis' in relation to either Lear or Gloucester.[108]

Brook could shape his interpretation by visual emphasis, omissions, reassignment of speeches, and the invention of elements not in the text, such as the burning of the French fleet towards the end of his film version. The critics who gave powerful currency to a bleak reading of the play after 1960 were, of course, dealing with the full text, i.e., in editions that invariably offered an eclectic text combining the Quarto and Folio versions (see below, pp. 82–3). Nevertheless, they tended to emphasize those aspects of the play that supported a reading denying any affirmation, and insisting on the 'supreme tragic horror'[109] of the ending, or on the nihilism of an action that it was claimed represented 'the decay and fall of the world'.[110] Perhaps the best analysis of this kind, by N. S. Brooke (1963), sought to show that 'the process of the play seems . . . calculated to repudiate every source of consolation with which we might greet the final disaster'.[111] 'Who is it can say we are at the worst?' indeed. The play was seen as a descent into chaos, as 'we are left with the spectacle of how suffering can renew itself unremittingly until the very moment of death'.[112] Jan Kott, who greatly influenced Brook, read *King Lear* through Beckett's *Waiting for Godot* and *Endgame* as the fall and disintegration of 'the modern world' as well as the Renaissance world, saying 'All that remains at the end of this gigantic pantomime, is the earth – empty and bleeding.'[113] William Elton (1966) painstakingly analysed the background of Renaissance religious thought in order to argue that the play is a pagan tragedy showing the 'annihilation of faith in poetic justice . . . within the confines of a grim pagan universe'.[114] Thus both contemporary analogies and Renaissance beliefs were invoked to confirm a sombre reading of the play.

A subtle and influential reading of this period is to be found in Stanley Cavell's essay 'The Avoidance of Love'. This first appeared in 1969, and in its latest presentation, in 1987, the author still notes in his preface that the essay 'bears the scars of our [i.e., the American] period in Vietnam'. These scars show in the negative emphases in an account of the play that presents Edgar and Lear as motivated by shame or guilt in avoiding recognition by Gloucester or Cordelia, whose love for Lear is 'incompatible with the idea of having any (other) lover'. If Lear is reborn, it is only 'into his old self', so that tragedy itself becomes ineffective in the play: 'it is one thing, and tragic, that we can learn only through suffering. It is something else that we have nothing to learn from it.' This is a version of the play that was appropriate to the desolations of the war in Vietnam, and retains its relevance for those who feel 'we are surrounded by inexplicable pain and death; and no death is more mysterious or portentous than others'.[115]

KING LEAR DESTABILIZED

If by 1966 the stimulus of the Brook/Kott account of *King Lear* made it seem that this play was 'above all others the Shakespearean play of our time',[116] a dissatisfaction with Brook's negative approach, his idea that 'as characters acquire sight it enables them to see only into a void',[117] led to a recovery of more positive interpretations of the ending. However, in some ways later commentary on the play has remained deeply affected by the insights of the 1960s, as if a critical innocence – the innocence of, for example, Danby's reading – was for ever lost. As noted earlier, even Maynard Mack, who dismissed Brook's version as having little to do with 'the play Shakespeare wrote', nevertheless acknowledged that the experience of Auschwitz and two world wars had altered our perception of the play. Brook made more specific political connections when his production toured in Hungary: there Lear became 'the figure of old Europe, tired, and feeling, as almost every country in Europe does, that after the events of the last 50 years people have borne enough'.[118] In interviews Brook also specifically linked Lear to contemporary old men who wielded political power in a rather dictatorial way, de Gaulle and Adenauer,[119] and said, 'One could easily see in Lear the incarnation of the process that takes place within a certain form of Stalinism.'[120] After such knowledge, what forgiveness? It would seem that the recapturing of a sense of something positive at the play's end would have to take a new form, not a glowing sense of redemption, miracle or nobility so much as the more modest claim that 'It is *because* our situation is so bleak and terrible that we must love one another.'[121]

A muted affirmation was strikingly suggested at the end of Grigori Kozintsev's Russian film version (1970). Kozintsev commented at length on his ideas about the film; he wanted 'the living traits of a despotic ruler' to show through the 'legendary figure' of King Lear, and no doubt had Stalin in mind.[122] But in contrast to Brook, Kozintsev also attempted to restore the sense of Lear as representa-

tive of a feudal order clashing with Edmund as a Renaissance
careerist, a 'true hero of the era of primary accumulation'.[123] But
where Danby, for example, had seen the old order as good and the
new as evil, Kozintsev felt that 'Shakespeare saw both the evil of the
old order and the savagery of the new.'[124] He found therefore a
measure of optimism in the paradox of the ending, when we feel the
victory of the 'worthy over the unworthy, even though their moral
victory be a factual defeat at the same time'.[125] In his film version
there is something less than optimism. The country is ravaged, as
soldiers carry the dead bodies of Lear and Cordelia through ruins;
indeed, Kozintsev linked his film visually with the pictures in the
museum at Hiroshima.[126] A trickle of water symbolizes continuity,
and perhaps the possibility of hope and renewed fertility. The Fool
remains alive, consoling himself by playing on his pipe; he was
modelled on a musician in an orchestra of prisoners in a Nazi
concentration camp, who were beaten to make them play better.[127]
At the very end there is a close-up of Edgar staring out of the frame
as if he has become one of the people he may now lead. In his
account of this ending, Kozintsev said nothing of Edgar; he stressed
rather the image of

Rags, and the soft sound of the pipe – the still voice of suffering. Then,
during the battle scenes, a requiem breaks out, then falls silent. And once
again the pipe can be heard. Life – a none too easy one – goes on. Its voice
in *King Lear* is a very quiet one, but its sad, human quality sounds distinctly
in Shakespeare's work.[128]

This emphasis was anticipated in Frank Kermode's *The Sense of an
Ending* (1967), in which he observes that in *King Lear*, 'tragedy
assumes the figurations of apocalypse', but then 'the world goes
forward in the hands of exhausted survivors'.[129] If Kozintsev
softened the harshness of both the 'real world of tyranny' he
depicted, and 'the turbid chaos of primitive existence',[130] a new
sense of that tyranny and the exhaustion of survivors marked
Edward Bond's chilling reworking in his play *Lear* (1970). Bond
escalated the violence in his play, in an action in which all personal
relationships break down and offer no hope for the future. Cordelia
survives being raped by rampaging soldiers only to rebuild at the
end a state as horribly cruel and repressive as the one her father
ruled at the beginning; thus the final effort of the old, blind Lear,
who has at last learned the meaning of pity, seems merely futile. He
is shot as he hacks at the great wall he built to protect his

possessions, and she has now reinforced, in a symbolic act apparently intended by Bond to suggest it can be demolished; but the effect on stage is rather to confirm that things go on as before. The group of workers present is marched off, and the stage direction requires that 'One of them looks back',[131] in a gesture that may be meant to suggest that Lear's effort is not entirely wasted, but it is so indefinite as to be lost on an audience, if noticed at all. Rather we come away with the sense, as Lear says towards the end, that 'nothing's changed'.[132]

To judge from his own preface to the published text, Bond wanted to show the inadequacy of personal reconciliation to bring about change, and sought to demonstrate that the only way to transform an authoritarian society is to challenge the state:

Our own culture is based on the idea that people are naturally violent. It is used to justify the violence and authoritarianism that saturate our state, although in fact it is the state that provokes violence and authoritarianism ... But the social moral of Shakespeare's *Lear* is this: endure till in time the world will be made right. That's a dangerous moral for us. We have less time than Shakespeare.[133]

Bond's thinking seems muddled, and his play might be taken as showing that people are naturally violent. But he assumed that Shakespeare as a conservative simply accepted the ideology of an age that urged the maintenance of a strong, single authority to prevent the breakdown of society; Bond asserts an opposite view, that the state is the source of repression, that, as Lear says late in his play, after he has acquired some insight, 'Your law always does more harm than crime, and your morality is a form of violence.'[134] Bond's *Lear* thus is not so much a reworking as a counter to Shakespeare's play in pushing to an extreme the emphasis on tyrannical violence and repression, and diminishing the possibility of a positive humanity into Lear's appeal, 'Our lives are awkward and fragile and we have only one thing to keep us sane: pity, and the man without pity is mad.'[135] An unfocussed notion of pity does little to modify the sense of a country brutalized by a never-ending cycle of civil war;[136] and here the contrast with *King Lear* becomes especially significant, for it is through love in this play that a potentiality for change is conveyed, and at the end it seems that nothing will ever be the same again. Bond's *Lear*, by contrast, may be taken to imply that successive regimes will continue to refurbish the wall Lear built, a wall that no doubt refers to the Berlin Wall, and symbolizes the barriers that nations and individuals set up around themselves.

Bond wished to change society, but represented human nature as fixed, so that his reworking of *King Lear*, as displaying the dialectic of violence in a competitive society bound up in inevitable conflict and destruction,[137] appears closer to Brook's interpretation than I imagine he intended. Although reviewers of Brook's film[138] and literary critics like Maynard Mack and Helen Gardner complained about the reductiveness of treating *King Lear* as *Endgame* ('It was the most grievously reductive production of a great masterpiece I have ever seen'[139]), they were being reductive themselves in failing to respond to the dimensions of the play which Brook's vision of a barbaric world opened up during a period when a new barbarism seemed to be setting in with the Cold War and the building of the Berlin Wall. A number of critics continued to find a bleak reading of the play persuasive, as a work that 'advances us deeper and deeper into nothing'[140] and shows in its plot movement a 'cruel progression towards unrelieved despair'.[141] It became no longer possible to settle for a simple Christian or redemptive reading; if the play ends with an image recalling a pieta, this is cruelly ironic, for Shakespeare 'dramatizes the final possibility: there is no God';[142] and if Lear may be seen as a sort of Job-figure, one who gains in self-knowledge, it is a 'miracle' that brings us an 'ironic image of the indifference to remote, frail, and petty life of the heavenly powers to whom Lear had thundered his demand for care, concern, and justice'.[143]

Rather than seeing the play finally in negative terms, others found in *King Lear* 'a deep distrust of all attempts at closure',[144] and treated it as an open-ended work. In one of the cleverer of such deconstructive moves, Howard Felperin argued that the subplot involving Gloucester enacts a traditional conventional tragedy in which Gloucester's salvation is stage-managed by Edgar, who, with Albany, simply reaffirms a 'Christian vision' in the face of experience that denies it.[145] Lear, by contrast, moves towards a new sense of existential indeterminacy, and 'enacts in advance our own dilemma as interpreters, alternating between antithetical visions of experience, only to abandon both in favor of a pure and simple pointing to the thing itself' in a kind of aporia, a 'negation of the possibility of unity, coherence, and resolution'.[146] The perception of indeterminacy, open-endedness or incoherence was reinforced by the increasing awareness during the last twenty years of the instability of

Shakespeare's text. The recognition that the difference between the Quarto (1608) and Folio (1623) texts might be due to revision by the author,[147] and hence that there is no single, authoritative version of *King Lear*, also involved acknowledging that each editor had been in the habit of presenting his own eclectic text made from a collage of Quarto and Folio; and this knowledge reinforced the claims of the more advanced critics of recent years that 'the script is *essentially unstable*'.[148]

Such a view takes us beyond the notion of ambivalence or absence of closure as perceived by Frank Kermode and reasserted by such critics as James Siemon, who argued that all the commonplaces of the text and tableaux of the action of *King Lear* represent 'attempts to contain the action in manageable form' that 'are inadequate to their task'.[149] A more subtle reading that took its cue from Kermode was Stephen Booth's essay on indefinition in *King Lear* (1983). He claimed that with the deaths of Edmund, Goneril and Regan, the play 'has formally concluded while its substance is still in urgent progress', and that the 'culminating event of the *story* (the entry of Lear with Cordelia in his arms)' comes after the '*play* is over'.[150] His italics separate what he sees as pattern or form that asserts 'the presence of an encompassing order in the *work* (as opposed to the world it describes)' from the inconclusiveness of the ending that marks a 'failure of form'.[151] Claiming that the play undermines our confidence in any fixities, he goes on:

I have argued that *King Lear* both is and is not an identity – that our sense that it inhabits only its own mental space is countered by a sense that it and those of its elements that I have discussed are unstable, turn into or fuse into other things. The identities of the characters and our evaluations of them belong in the catalogue of elements that duplicate the simultaneously fixed and unfixed quality of the whole of *King Lear*.[152]

If then, as he says later on, 'our evaluations of the play are unfixed',[153] this is due to a radical instability in the play itself.

This instability has been related by Harry Berger Jr. to the difference between the experience of reading the play and seeing it performed. In performance we respond to 'the stories the characters tell', but the text as read reveals something different: 'these are stories they prefer to hear about themselves rather than others which strike closer to home and which they would find harder to bear'.[154] So in reading about the play Berger 'learned most' from accounts of Edgar that discovered cruelty in him, or saw him as 'the most lethal

character' in the play.[155] The act of interpretation becomes a
struggle in which 'we define the character's personhood . . . in such a
way as to preclude our closing the book on the character'.[156]
Traditionalist critics have continued to resist the idea of such post-
structuralist indeterminacy, but have themselves been revisionist in
finding no adequate single response. So Bernard McElroy used a
term given currency by Norman Rabkin, 'complementarity', to
argue that the play presents two attitudes, a 'transcendent dream of
human redemption' on the one hand and a 'pessimistic indictment of
the absurd human condition' on the other, which exist side by side
'in perfect artistic unity and harmony in the play'.[157] He did not,
however, substantiate his claim for perfect artistic unity in relation
to two readings that, as he says, are logically incompatible.

McElroy took as his starting point Danby's view of the play as
showing an older hierarchical order giving way to a new ruthless
individualism. Michael Long stood this view on its head by claiming
that the play enacts a rejuvenation of a culture that has been frozen
by old law; but the 'emergent spring' he sees, in contrast to the
nihilism of the Brook/Kott interpretation, is not for him the controlling effect finally replacing 'winter'; indeed, he observes what he
calls an 'interdependence of . . . contraries' at the end.[158] Emrys
Jones found the second half of the play less painful than the first,
and, harking back to Bradley, related it to Shakespeare's late
romances, notably *Cymbeline*; yet he saw no clear pattern in an
episodic work, but rather a sense of 'increasing randomness and
inertia' as part of Shakespeare's governing artistic idea in *King
Lear*.[159] Returning to a Christian perspective, Joseph Wittreich
associated it with biblical myths of apocalypse, but though he starts
by asserting that the play culminates in a 'king's redemption', he
ends by arguing that it is not Christian, and that no simple reading
will do; *King Lear* indeed 'quarrels with all perspectives', suggesting
that 'even if the world is not meaningless its mysteries are beyond
man's comprehension'.[171] It would seem that after the 1960s there
could be no return to a straightforward redemptionist interpretation
of *King Lear*, or to an uncomplicated bleak reading.

Attending to the play's historicity in relation to Shakespeare's
own age offered an approach that might possibly restore a coherent
meaning to the play. J. W. Lever pointed the way in his *The Tragedy
of State* (1971), arguing that the dramatists of the Elizabethan period
'were aware of a wider transformation of society taking place

throughout Europe and undermining all traditional human relationships'.[161] Then Rosalie Colie, leaning on Lawrence Stone's *Crisis
of the Aristocracy 1558–1641*, specifically identified *King Lear* as a play
with its major theme 'tied to the problems of an aristocracy caught
between an old ethos of unreckoned generosity, magnificence, and
carelessness, and new values stressing greater providence, frugality,
and even calculation'.[162] In some ways her sense of the play as
morally approving 'the advocates of old values'[163] is reminiscent of
Danby, but her emphasis is quite different, and she ends by arguing
that *King Lear* sanctions neither the old nor the new values. Stone's
book also prompted Alvin Kernan to see the play as an enormous
historical pageant 'in which the Middle Ages move on into the
modern world' with a kind of faint optimism in the 'saddened
knowledge of full reality'.[164]

There is a sense of uncertainty about these efforts to place *King
Lear* in an historical or political context. They revive the idea of the
play as reflecting the transition from an old to a new order or set of
values, the old identified as medieval in terms of aristocratic
generosity, or in terms of natural law, with Shakespeare usually
presented as approving the older values, even if the play remains
open-ended. In the 1980s this transition has been redefined in
several ways. For example, James Kavanagh sees it as showing a
clash between an aristocratic and an emergent bourgeois ideology;
Shakespeare's fearlessness in representing opposed ideologies 'de-
stabilizes the reconciliation effect that the text seeks to achieve within
a given cultural ideology';[165] at the same time, a modern audience is
swayed 'by those elements that support a culturally familiar reductive humanism'.[166] John Turner, on the other hand, claims that 'the
true subject of *King Lear* . . . is not an old order succumbing to a new
but an old order succumbing to its own internal contradictions'.[167]
Metaphysical consolations at the end of the play are ineffective
'without the primary reciprocities of social justice', which have
vanished.[168] This account again restores the image of an heroic past
in *King Lear* giving way to a present of 'abiding injustice'.[169] More
subtly, Stephen Greenblatt focusses on Shakespeare's use of Samuel
Harsnett's *A Declaration of Egregious Popish Impostures* in creating Poor
Tom; he claims that Harsnett's rejection of the practice of exorcism
as merely theatrical, and the dismissal by the Protestant Church of
demonic possession as fraud, are related to a view of *King Lear* as a
play 'haunted by a sense of rituals and beliefs that are no longer

efficacious'.[170] So the ending of the play, he claims, can be seen in a new way: 'Lear's sorrows are not redeemed; nothing can turn them into joy, but the forlorn hope of an impossible redemption persists, drained of its institutional and doctrinal significance, empty and vain, cut off even from a theatrical realization, but like the dream of exorcism, ineradicable.'[171] This is well expressed, but such a conclusion is not really dependent on Shakespeare's minor use of Harsnett: the interplay between beliefs and rituals commonly held or practised, and the sense of their inefficacy, is perhaps even more marked in *Hamlet*, notably in the alternative conceptions of death as providential and as mere oblivion presented in the play (see below, pp. 173–4).

In the 1980s the critical developments associated with new historicism in the United States and the related cultural materialism in Britain have provided theoretical grounds for understanding contradictions in *King Lear* by seeing the play as 'the. locus of a distinct, politically dynamic sequence of intersecting discursive practices, replete with competing ideologies'.[172] This phrase could equally well be applied to the interpretations of *King Lear* which these movements have produced. So, for example, Leonard Tennenhouse sees the play as a spectacle of power in which Shakespeare 'interrogates the very notion of the Crown as a corporate essence in perpetuity';[173] Lear violates the principles of primogeniture in dividing the kingdom between his daughters, but the power of patriarchy is restored through Edgar and Albany, and Cordelia has to die in order that the system of power through patrilineage can be maintained.[174] Annabel Patterson, on the other hand, finds a 'radical analysis' of the 'economic structure of his own society'[175] in Shakespeare's play, and sees the King's challenge, 'Expose thyself to feel what wretches feel', as centrally subversive, a speech of 'social inversion': 'If men can change places on the social hierarchy, then those places have no absolute value, and complete inversion becomes, to the seeing ear of madness, utterly thinkable',[176] as in Lear's speeches in IV.7. The end of the play, on this reading, retreats from 'structural analysis' into 'the domestic and familial, as a shelter from sociopolitical awareness'.[177] Kathleen McLuskie, bringing a feminist perspective to bear on the play, argues that a 'dispassionate analysis of the mystification of real socio-sexual relations in *King Lear* is the antithesis of our response in the theatre where the tragic power of the play endorses its ideological position at every stage'.[178] That ideological position relates to a misogyny 'constructed out of an ascetic tradition which presents women as the source of the primal sin of lust', so that the only alternative offered to 'the patriarchal family' is chaos.[179] Such analyses have in common a recognition of political and social tensions in Shakespeare's work, and share a view of *King Lear* as the site of conflicting ideologies, though they come to differing conclusions. Edgar's disguise as Poor Tom is turned into an act of socio-political transgression, insanity becomes a vehicle for political subversion, and the central issue of the play is reformulated as the subversion or maintenance of patriarchy. Shakespeare the transcendent genius concerned with universals is replaced by a dramatist very much the product of his age, and embroiled in social and political issues rather than concerned with abstract questions of justice or Providence.[180] The new readings of *King Lear* produced by this shift are markedly different from those that emerge from the more traditional placing of Shakespeare in the context of ideas in his age, as can be seen in the analysis of natural law that leads Robin Headlam Wells to the conclusion that 'Declaring by means of images of barbarism and insanity the terrible consequences which must inevitably follow the violation of natural law, plays like *Hamlet* and *King Lear* reveal, at the same time, a world in which providence, if it exists, is inscrutable and human reason pitifully ineffectual.'[181]

KING LEAR HISTORICIZED

If we consider all these accounts of *King Lear* in a more general perspective, certain trends emerge as significant. When the Romantics began to enthuse over the play as they read it in opposition to the reworked stage version by Nahum Tate, they privatized it in a different way from *Hamlet*. Where Hamlet the character could be absorbed into the critic ('We are all Hamlet') as an intellectual with problems, a projection of himself, Lear seemed awesome, and afforded no basis for comparison in ordinary life, so that the critic was absorbed into him ('while we read it, we see not Lear, but we are Lear, we are in his mind, we are sustained by a grandeur which baffles the malice of daughters and storms'). Coleridge offered no analogy in life for Lear, and after lecturing on the play in 1819, he said that 'the Lear of Shakespeare is not a good subject for a whole lecture, in my style',[182] by which he meant, it seems, that the play was too grand, for in a letter written the day before the lecture was given, he called it 'La Terribilita of Shakespeare's tragic Might';[183] while Hazlitt would have preferred to say nothing about a play that seemed, as Lamb said, 'essentially impossible to be represented on a stage'.[184] The pathos of a figure so old that he stands on the very verge of nature's confine, and the sense of sublimity induced by the reconciliation with Cordelia, disabled further criticism, and set the tone for later reactions to the play.

In the theatre Macready's restoration in 1838 of much of Shakespeare's text in fact enhanced the sense of remoteness because the play was set, as noted above (pp. 47–8), in an ancient world, with round-arched stone walls for a backdrop in the first act; but visible too was a stone circle, reminiscent of Stonehenge, from which the smoke of sacrifice rose.[185] This established a fashion, and megaliths and stone circles have featured in the settings of numerous productions, persisting down to the Granada television version of 1983, which set the play in Britain in the year 800, opening with the actors moving about 'in a mist-enshrouded replica of a stone circle, incongruously in use as a throne room'.[186] At the same time, critics found points of comparison in ancient legends, or in the earliest Greek tragedies, those of Aeschylus, or alternatively in the Book of Job. The effect in every case was to reinforce the sense of a play far distanced in time from the period of the actor or critic, and so monumental or grand in scope as to transcend any immediate topical or political inquiry, and to defeat criticism. Lear seemed representative of Man, capitalized and abstracted from ordinary men, enduring, like Job or Prometheus, suffering and tribulations beyond the capacity of the reader or audience, but learning patience and humility at the end of Life's pilgrimage. If the play thus acquired a sort of metaphysical grandeur, at the same time the reconciliation between Lear and Cordelia especially could be seen as humanizing the old King into man with a small 'm', in the 'ebb and flow of the feeling' celebrated, for example, by Hazlitt.[187] The power struggles involving Goneril, Regan, Edmund, Lear and Edgar in the first part of the play were usually left out of consideration in critical accounts, or touched on in passing.

The distancing of the play into a primitive and barbaric world, so common on the stage, and its distancing into ancient myths by critics, led to the curious effect that early attempts to view the play not merely in idealist terms, but in relation to social or political change, found hints of a transition in it from barbarity to a more

advanced civilization. Alternatively, the dominant readings of the
play in terms of the redemption or salvation of Lear were associated
with a sense too of a social order being broken up or corrupted and
restored or purified at the end; but this was a social order in the
abstract, so to speak, and not related to the critic's own world. The
theatrical and critical distancing of the play helped to give authority
to a long tradition of seeing *King Lear* both in transcendent terms as
the pilgrimage of Man enduring the worst that his enemies, fortune
and the gods can throw at him, but on the path to a final victory of
Love or Good over Evil, and also in terms of feeling, notably centred
on the reconciliation of father and daughter, and this tradition in
turn removed the play from the political arena. It is notable that
reworkings of the story of the play by later writers tend to domesti-
cate it as about the break-up of a family, and the effect on his
children and on himself of a father's tyranny over his daughters, or
the daughters' tyranny over their father; this can be seen, for
example, in Honoré de Balzac's *Père Goriot* (1835), in which the
father-figure is a growingly senile old man who sweated all his life in
a flour-mill to save money for his daughters; and in Turgenev's *A
King Lear of the Steppes* (1870), in which an illiterate peasant cedes his
property to his daughters, provoking him to attempt a revenge in
which he only manages to kill himself. An exception is Randolph
Stow's remarkable Australian novel *To the Islands* (1958), in which
the Lear-figure, an ageing white man who has devoted his life to
running a mission station for aborigines, realizes he has achieved
nothing but disappointment and hatred, and believing he has killed
a native, goes on a walkabout that brings him to face death at the
sea's edge. He has no daughters, and the effect of the novel is to
transpose elements of the Lear story into a primitive and mythic
world.

Only after the outbreak of the Second World War was serious
attention given to the 'political chaos' shown in the play, and
Edmund, Goneril and Regan began to be seen as precursors of the
machiavellian 'realpolitik' associated with fascism and Nazism.
The mythological distancing of Lear as embodying 'Man's tragic
fate' or pilgrimage towards redemption insulated him from any
direct link with modern tyrannies, and his world was identified with
an old order (a benevolent medieval one in John Danby's view)
which was under attack by new forces representing a ruthless,
competitive capitalism. It was not until about 1960 and after that

the play began to be considered in direct relation to a new political consciousness engendered by the Cold War, the rediscovery of the Holocaust, the renewed interest in Hiroshima, and the development of the hydrogen bomb, and then the building of the Berlin Wall. In this context the tyranny and obsession with power of Lear himself became more noticeable, and the similarity between his behaviour and that of Goneril and Regan, emphasized by Peter Brook in his 1962 production, turned the play, as noted earlier (p. 58), into a bleak vision of negation. During the 1960s critics found confirmation of bleakness in their readings of the text in the various editions of the full play, usually a composite version amalgamating Quarto and Folio texts. Their emphasis tended to be less political than Brook's (he saw a Stalinist figure in Lear), and more concerned with the indifference of the gods and the frailty of human life. In other words, the new political emphasis fostered by Kott and Brook was transmuted into metaphysical terms, with Lear progressing towards despair rather than towards redemption.

Since the culmination of nihilistic readings of *King Lear* in Edward Bond's reworking of the play (1970) as celebrating violence in a contemporary world perceived as dedicated to violence, there has been a retreat from such essentially pessimistic interpretations. Deconstructive critics have found a radical instability in the play that permits no confidence in any particular reading, and the sense of instability has been reinforced by the revival of interest by textual scholars in the differences between the Quarto and Folio texts, and the evidence that Shakespeare or someone else revised the play, effectively creating two different but perhaps equally valid versions. Deconstructive criticism denies external authority, and is not interested in history, so privileging the reader or critic over the literary text; the critic then no longer stands, like Hazlitt, in awe of the sublimity of *King Lear*, or sees the play as embodying determinate meanings or metaphysical truths, but creates the work by his reading of it, which remains necessarily incomplete. In effect, revisionist textual critics also privilege the reader over the text, since the reader makes up the text he prefers from the choices available to him. It is significant that the interest in textual revision that developed in the 1970s has grown to become a minor scholarly industry: although the two texts of *King Lear* were analysed acutely by Madeleine Doran as long ago as 1931, and E. A. J. Honigmann drew attention to problems of revision in variant texts in his *The Stability of Shakespeare's*

Text in 1965,[188] it is effectively since 1978 that the issue of revision in Shakespeare's works has become a vital one, to the extent that the recent Oxford Shakespeare prints both Quarto and Folio versions of the play.

Deconstruction and textual revisionism both reject external authority, and both achieved prominence during a period when *détente* prevailed, and a government perceived as corrupt in the United States confronted a supposedly 'evil empire' in the Soviet Union; when old men imposed their will on the major countries of the world seemingly with little concern for ordinary people. It would be hard to establish a direct connection, and I can only be impressionistic, but the timing of the rise of these particular approaches to Shakespeare may have significance in relation to world events, and especially the mood of the United States and Britain. Both approaches effectively dismantle the cultural status traditionally assigned to Shakespeare and to his plays, and emerge in a period when political authority in the West came to seem tainted and to be distrusted by intellectuals. The effect of the new historicism in the United States and of cultural materialism in Britain has been similar, although the critical methods grouped under these labels differ among themselves, and are in some ways a counter to deconstruction, in so far as they reintroduce historicism. But they do so by way of marginalizing the text as a construct of the social and political order of the Elizabethan and Jacobean ages. Plays themselves become documents of history, so that *King Lear* can be seen as concerned with power relations and the concept of the crown, with reference to the patriarchal ideology of King James I, and even as close to a 'fictional portrait of the king himself'.[189]

Again the effort is to demystify (an overworked term) the cultural authority of a text as having an absolute or independent value, and to insist that the critic produces the meaning of a text, which therefore has no objective status. Although it is not difficult to show, as Richard Levin has done,[190] that critics of this persuasion tend to slip into writing of the play as it really is, and accord a text the objective status their proclaimed critical relativism would seem to deny, their powerful attack on the canonical standing of texts like *King Lear* links with the efforts of deconstructionists and textual revisionists not only to destabilize the text, but to demote the play from its critical placing as a supreme work of art, the 'greatest' of Shakespeare's tragedies, into a battleground of conflicting discourses and ideological contradictions, subverting even as it contains and sanctions the idea of a patriarchal society. Viewed in this way, *King Lear* has no more claim to attention than any other text, and the new historicists acknowledge this by their anecdotal method, in which some minor event or curious happening is described at length in order to reveal some tangential relationship, often a slight or marginal one, to a play by Shakespeare. But in their continued attention to Shakespeare, they tend in fact to reinforce the cultural authority they would deny him.

Another group who have contributed to the dismantling of the authority of the text are feminists, who see *King Lear* in terms of a masculine identity crisis, or in terms of misogyny and the 'mystification of real socio-sexual relations'. During the 1980s all four approaches, political/nihilistic, deconstructive, revisionary and feminist, whatever their differences, have contributed to a redefining of the nature and status of *King Lear*, in what they see as a process of liberating us from an allegiance to such static notions as the truth or autonomy or coherence of the play, into a recognition of contradictions in it, of ranges of possible meanings, indefiniteness, and the clash of ideological stances. In their rejection of traditional assumptions, all these approaches have brought a new sense of excitement to the study of Shakespeare's age, and all would seem to reflect the larger condition of their own period, of America and Britain in the 1980s. In this decade both countries have been dominated by aggressively authoritarian figures, who ignored the majority in dismantling democratic institutions, cutting welfare and social benefits, and maintaining an imperialist attitude towards the rest of the world, as in the Falklands, Grenada, Nicaragua and Iraq. It is not surprising that the literary critics of this decade should have a distrust of authority.

But if the reaction of critics from the 1960s to the 1980s can be seen, however indirectly, as affected by the political situation of those decades, what can be said of the earlier criticism of *King Lear*? How could criticism remain so apparently unconcerned with political issues for so long, roughly from 1800 to the 1950s? Perhaps that is the wrong question to ask, though it is implicit in the assumption of some cultural materialists that earlier critics used texts like *King Lear* to perpetuate an imperialist ideology: 'Shakespeare, as a central component of British culture, has inevitably been incorporated into the dominant ideology and made an instrument of hegemony.'[191] A more sophisticated view is presented by Jonathan Dollimore, who argues that both traditional Christian redemptionist readings of *King Lear*, and liberal humanist interpretations that emphasize instead Lear's growth in stature through heroic endurance of suffering, are two sides of the same coin, and both need to be contested by a materialist account that stresses the play's concern with 'power, property and inheritance'.[192] In this reading Edmund becomes prominent for his 'revolutionary scepticism', as not simply evil, but as embodying a process whereby a 'revolutionary (emergent) insight is folded back into a dominant ideology'.[193] For Edmund's pursuit of wealth and power merely extends the 'obsession with power, property and inheritance' of a society based on patriarchal authority but resting its ideological claims on metaphysical notions of values like nobility and justice.[194]

Such an approach is offered as a new insight in the 1980s, but it seems as if in some respects the wheel has come full circle. For in 1819 Coleridge had analysed Edmund's character in ways not unlike Dollimore, even if his conclusions about the play are very different; and Coleridge's account helps to explain why for so long critics more or less ignored the politics of *King Lear*. From late in 1799 when Coleridge began to write regularly for the *Morning Post*, he was concerned in his journalism with events in France, and found he was constantly needing to revise his estimate of Napoleon Buonaparte. At first Napoleon had for Coleridge 'the splendour of a hero in romance',[195] combining military genius with a beneficial impact on France in introducing a new tone of morality after the bloodbath of the Terror and the period of revolutionary chaos. But as Napoleon swept through Europe, and turned himself into an emperor, Coleridge's view changed. Napoleon himself established a link with ancient Rome when he was proclaimed First Consul in 1802. Coleridge now saw more resemblance to the Caesars, to the period 'when Rome ceased to be a Republic and the Government was organized into a masked and military despotism'.[196] Napoleon combined the good and bad qualities of Julius Caesar, Augustus and Tiberius, and like the Roman emperors, he encouraged 'great public works' while destroying political freedom.[197] Later on Napoleon came to seem the enemy of the human race, as a man dedicated to the total conquest of Europe.

Napoleon was, indeed, a wholly new phenomenon, for whom there was no basis of comparison in recent history. In order to assess him Coleridge cast about for analogies, linking him with Charle-

magne, with Tamburlaine, and later still, in 1814, with Genghis
Khan. Napoleon was a radically disturbing figure, for, in countering
those who saw him simply as a hero, Coleridge felt it necessary to
acknowledge his genius, his prowess as a conqueror like Alexander
the Great, his enormous abilities, and yet to insist on something
more, in the degree to which he showed tremendous courage in
'daring to be a villain'.[198] For want of analogies from life, other than
conquerors from the remote past, Coleridge was led to see Napoleon
as a tragic figure, misusing 'that energy, persistency in resolve,
wicked or wise, and that activity of restless passion in a restless Body'
that made him such an extraordinary man.[199] At the worst, Coleridge saw Napoleon as corrupted by power, and transformed from a
benevolent dictator into a monstrous tyrant. In seeking a yardstick
by which to measure him, Coleridge was drawn to literature,
relating the political stage on which Napoleon performed his role to
dramatic stages, finding analogies for him in Satan in Milton's
Paradise Lost, and in *Macbeth*. Coleridge's subtler characterizations of
the French Emperor are informed by his critical analysis of counter-
parts in Milton and Shakespeare, and as time passed, after the fall of
Napoleon, Coleridge developed perhaps his most complex assessment in a reading of him through Edmund, or rather in a reading of
Edmund through Napoleon. Edmund too appears early on in the
play like a hero in romance, 'in the united strength and beauty of
earliest Manhood',[200] endowed with a powerful intellect and a strong
will. But the levity of his father wounds his pride and infects him
with the 'corrosive Virus' of envy, hatred, and 'a lust of that Power
which in its blaze of radiance would hide the dark spots on his
disk'.[201] At the same time, Coleridge noted how Shakespeare prevents the evil or guilt of Edmund from 'passing into utter monstro-
sity', as it would do if it originated in mere 'fiendishness of nature',
by providing circumstances – his bastardy, his being cut off from
domestic influences by being sent away from home and educated
abroad – that could not but affect him. Hence the possibility of
admiring Edmund: 'He [Shakespeare] had read Nature too heed-
fully not to know, that Courage, Intellect and strength of Character
were the most impressive Forms of Power; and that to Power in itself,
without reference to any moral end, an inevitable Admiration &
Complacency appertains, whether it be displayed in the conquests of
a Napoleon or a Tamurlane, or in the foam and thunder of a
Cataract.'[202] The image of the cataract turns these figures, and

Edmund by implication, into natural forces, abstracted from moral or political motives or intentions.

So in Coleridge's late assessment of Napoleon, the parallel with Satan fades behind the analogies with Macbeth and above all Edmund. It was through Shakespeare's great tragic characterization of figures with commanding genius or will to power, and at the same time possessing a potential for good, that Coleridge was able to find his richest way of interpreting Napoleon; and it was through Napoleon that Coleridge was able to develop a conception of Edmund as a revolutionary figure, corrupted in the end like Napoleon by his lust for power. Coleridge did not perceive Lear himself in terms of a patriarchal ideology of power, though he noted his 'incapability of resigning the Sovereign power in the very moment of disposing of it';[203] so if Napoleon provided a political and moral standard against which to measure Edmund, what of Lear himself? Interestingly, Coleridge offers no basis of comparison for Lear with any human being. He treats Lear as the centre of suffering in the play, and distances him on the heath in III.5 into a 'picture . . . more terrific than any a Michelangelo inspired by a Dante could have conceived'.[204] Lear was simply awe-inspiring, to be thought of as 'La Terribilita'. The living tyrant, Napoleon, emerging youthfully into eminence as a commanding genius, Coleridge linked with Edmund; he had no living analogy for Lear.

Later critics, from Hazlitt onwards, continued on the whole to regard Lear as above politics, as a remote or sublime figure, and paradoxically therefore to treat him in personal or moral terms. There were no obvious parallels to be drawn with living rulers, or it was too dangerous to make such connections, as in the case of George III. Lear was perceived primarily in terms of his sufferings, as the frequent linking of him with figures such as Job and Prometheus indicates. It seems that only after the Second World War, in the period of the Cold War, and in relation to a world increasingly dominated by countries ruled by old men obsessed with power, could Lear begin to be appreciated fully in political terms. As noted above (p. 60), in 1973 Peter Brook recognized what he called the 'politics of sclerosis' in linking Lear with Stalin and other ageing rulers like Adenauer and de Gaulle; the old men who maintain their hegemony in China, or Ronald Reagan, might offer further analogies. Perhaps the most striking connection made in recent years is that with the exercise of authoritarian power in South Africa, where the rigidities of apartheid disenfranchize most of the population and the Land Act allots only ten per cent of the land to black people. Lear seeks to maintain his power after giving away the source of it, his land; nothing can be made out of nothing, and 'so much the rent of his land comes to' (1.4.134), as the Fool tells him. Once Goneril and Regan have the land, they can seize all power, just as Edmund determines to 'have lands by wit' (1.2.183) to achieve the power his bastardy denies him. Although the play moves towards a Christian reconciliation in Martin Orkin's view, the circumstances and language of *King Lear* 'confirm the powerlessness of such values or responses really to inform let alone alter the dominant social order'.[205]

According to Orkin, *King Lear* is depoliticized in schools and colleges in South Africa, and is treated as dealing in moral truths about human nature, and the recovery of order or insight. Influenced by Dollimore, he observes how in the play, as in South Africa, the state denies responsibility for the misery it creates, while punishing those who object to it. *King Lear* becomes very much a political commentary on a modern tyranny. New historicist readings of the play have avoided such direct reference to a specific political situation, but their emphasis on power and patriarchy is the culmination of a shift in understanding that began in the 1960s. Their rejection of idealist readings, and the general emphasis of the last thirty years on the bleakness of the play, reflect an anxiety, implicit in the criticism of the new historicists and cultural materialists, about the prevailing ideology of their own society, and the powerful old men and women who run things. The new historicists tend to treat power relations in the play in terms of the Renaissance, and specifically the world of James I, depicted as a completely authoritarian ruler; but such readings bear on the present too, for if the play initiates its audiences into the 'injustice, confusion and violence of the past', these become in performance 'the injustice, confusion and violence of the present'.[206]

CHAPTER 4

Plays and texts

PROCESSING SHAKESPEARE

An analysis of the reception of the play *Hamlet* over the past 200 years shows that Hamlet himself has been the main focus of attention; that he has often been extrapolated from the play as if he had an independent existence, and has usually been seen as a failure, an embodiment of Hamletism. By the early nineteenth century Hamlet was privatized, turned into a projection of each of us, and opened up to a democratized range of interpretations; but in the mainstream of writing and criticism in that century he became a mirror in which the bourgeois subject saw himself or herself reflected as intellectual, aesthete or artist and as ineffectual or politically marginalized. Hamlet was, in effect, appropriated to fit the image of such figures, and his problems were translated into those of the critics of the age. Hamlet became modern man, and efforts to return him to a Renaissance context have met with little success. By contrast, the reception of *King Lear* until about 1960 shows a predominant emphasis on personal relationships, centred on the reconciliation of Lear and Cordelia as the key moment in the play, and treating Lear as an awesome figure, to be associated with remote and primitive times, and as quite removed from any immediate political or social relevance to the critic's own time.

Hamlet has been accommodated to the political agendas of the right and the left, on the one hand as a failure in terms of doing his duty, and displaying a weakness of character in not facing up to his task; and on the other hand as a victim of oppression, struggling against a powerful dictatorship. The latter reading has been especially effective in Eastern bloc countries before the changes in the 1980s; indeed, some think the reworking of *Hamlet* in a production by Alexandru Tocilescu in Bucharest in 1985, in which Claudius and Gertrude were presented as mirroring the Ceaucescus, helped to bring down their government.[1] *King Lear* was for long treated as above politics, though in fact powerful redemptionist readings in the twentieth century aligned Lear and Cordelia with a lost beneficent order nostalgically associated with all that is good, in contrast to the machiavellian or fascist ideology perceived as represented in Edmund and Goneril. In the 1960s *King Lear* was absorbed into the nihilism of absurdist drama, and then gradually brought back into relation with the tyranny of aged rulers like Stalin in the modern world. Criticism has always adapted the plays to the general political conditions of the contemporary world of the critic, and the variety of ways in which this adaptation has been made would support the view that criticism has always been 'involved necessarily in the making of cultural meanings which are, finally, political meanings'. This and similar claims asserted often rather stridently by cultural materialists and new historicists are new in their self-consciousness, in seeing texts as 'inseparable from their conditions of production and reception in history',[2] and in putting literary criticism to the service of their own political agenda of transforming society, but not in the general practice described. In the case of *Hamlet* especially it is noticeable that a strong correlation can be found in any one period between the political and social implications of various kinds of readings, such as (a) the numerous uses of the character and play in other fictions, and reworkings in poetry and drama; (b) the commentaries by essayists and gifted amateurs; (c) stage and film productions; and (d) conventional academic criticism.

All critical accounts and stage productions are ways of processing or adapting plays to the present world of the critic or director, even if they claim to be recovering the authentic play of Shakespeare. The story of the reception of *Hamlet* and *King Lear* shows that it is a gross oversimplification to attribute this processing to a conspiracy, or to blame it on 'a system of education which seeks, often under the aegis of the subject called "English", to process the text on behalf of specific political positions and ambitions'.[3] The 'system' may take for granted the status of Shakespeare as a cultural idol, but the teacher or critic brings his own prejudices and beliefs to bear on the play. What the reception of both plays shows is that critical readings cannot be finally understood except in the context of the politics of the critic's own era. It is not a matter of control by a system, or of a group of critics at any time sharing a particular political view, but rather a consequence of the inevitable exposure of the critic to the general political mood and context of his age. The critical fortunes of *Hamlet* and *King Lear* are bound up with this larger context, as is shown by the reassessment of *King Lear* about 1960 as a bleak and despairing play.

The post-structuralist displacement of the concept of organic unity in favour of a dynamic reading of texts as sites of competing discourses has given special prominence to strategies of subversion and containment in Shakespeare's plays. It has also fostered the dismantling of the concept of individual authorship, as if plays should be seen as 'the locus of a distinct, politically dynamic sequence of intersecting discursive practices, replete with competing ideologies'.[4] So Shakespeare's plays, it is argued, did not originate in a 'pure act of untrammeled creation', but as 'a subtle, elusive set of exchanges, a network of trades and trade-offs, a jostling of competing representations, a negotiation between joint-stock companies',[5] and so are to be interpreted in terms of 'the circulation of social energy'. The plays can thus be demoted from their ranking as masterworks, and Shakespeare's cultural authority undermined, since all texts become equivalent, including presumably those produced by the critics, and interesting only as negotiations between intersecting discourses, or, in Stephen Greenblatt's revealing phrase, between 'joint-stock companies'. The question that troubled Coleridge had to do with the aesthetic nature and quality of the plays, and in reaction to eighteenth-century judgments on Shakespeare which represented him as a *lusus naturae*, untutored, knowing no rules or art, Coleridge sought to establish an idea of artistic unity, at first as a process in the mind, a 'pleasurable sense of the Many . . . reduced to unity', and later, under the influence of Schlegel, he located organic unity in the plays themselves. What was a central issue for Coleridge now emerges only in the contempt poured on the very idea of artistic values as immanent in a work, or alternatively with reference to the form of a play as a 'primary expression of Renaissance power' that 'helps to contain the radical doubts it continually provokes'.[6] Coleridge's first concept of artistic form, as a process in the mind, is very relevant to the concerns of this book (see below, pp. 136–7), but the second one, locating unity in the work, is the target of much current Shakespeare criticism; for now the form is conceived only as a vehicle of meaning.

It is something of a paradox that the critics who demote Shake-speare at the same time reinforce his cultural authority, by their concentration on him to the exclusion of other authors in one of the richest periods of literature in English history. It is also something of a paradox that critics who are so concerned to reduce Shakespeare to an anonymous group of collaborators, a joint-stock company, and who claim 'there is no theoretically compelling reason to posit an identity between an author-function and any historically contingent individual',[7] insistently assert their own individuality as authors on title-pages, in acknowledgements, and in a mode of writing which claims for the critic an 'authority' in opening up for readers truths he or she has discovered and researched. The contradictory impulses of those who would abolish the 'author-god of traditional humanism'[8] are exposed by their own evident sense of authorship, and of themselves as exceptional subjects. This is seen, for instance, in Greenblatt's centring of his book *Shakespearean Negotiations* on his own desire for knowledge ('I wanted to know'), and his own personal voice ('if I wanted to hear the voice of the other, I had to hear my own voice');[9] but it is also present in the dogmatic assurance of tone in, for example, Michael Bristol's *Shakespeare's America, America's Shakespeare*.

Shakespeare may have become an American and a British institu-tion, a tutelary deity, a cult-object,[10] but to say such things is to comment on one direction the history of bardolatry and the mytho-logizing of Shakespeare have taken, and not say anything about the plays he wrote. And if the project of new historicism and cultural materialism is to 'dissolve the modern privileged notion of "litera-ture" altogether', this is to identify a particular socio-political agenda which will aim 'to merge literary texts back into the historical milieu from which academic studies such as "English" have irresponsibly prised them'.[11] The issue here is not one of responsibility as against irresponsibility, but one of a covert as against an overt politicizing of literature, or of a privileging of literature as aesthetic experience as against a deconstruction of literature as merely one factor in the negotiations through which cultural practices and structures of power are sustained and interrogated.[12]

There is an important difference between new historicism and cultural materialism in this connection, in that new historicism presents itself as politically neutral. This is to say that it proclaims its deep concern with the concept of power and its relation to subversion, and also with literature as part of a social and political process, but does so in relation to Shakespeare not in order to effect change, or with any clearly acknowledged political agenda, but simply as registering a political sensibility. If methodologically, in deprivileging literature and equating it with other forms of discourse, it seems daringly modern, in its apparent neutrality it appears resolutely old-fashioned. Cultural materialism, by contrast, lays claim to a political agenda, and is committed to changing the social and political order in Britain; so it applies its analysis of works of the past to the present world, and takes an axiomatic the principle that all interpretation has in the end to do with political commitment. Cultural materialists would see themselves as political agents, not merely as expressing a political sensibility. Both these isms may be seen as expressions of disaffection with the reactionary policies of the United States and Britain in the 1980s especially; but one, in the United States, seems born out of despair, and may be regarded as a further variant of Hamletism, while the other, in Britain, has grown out of a strong tradition of protest within the academy, and trust that change can be brought about.[13]

What both have in common with other post-structuralist moves is not only a rejection of the concept of the author as a 'pathetic and overwrought metaphysical category',[14] but a rejection of the very idea of the text of a play. Just as the author becomes a collaborator in a group activity that was affected by improvisation and continual revision, so the text is dissolved into an anthology of performances.[15] The question of revision in Shakespeare's plays, though an old topic of debate, has now become a fiercely contested one for textual critics in the context of this more general post-structuralist destabilizing of texts. Textual critics may carry on their analyses without paying conscious attention to what critical theorists are arguing; indeed, while the apologists of revision adopt post-structuralist approaches to printed versions, 'what they seem actually to hanker for is a return to an original and originating historicity'.[16] Editors and textual critics used to be concerned to determine 'what Shakespeare wrote', or what he 'evidently preferred',[17] and their primary aim in the case of *Hamlet* and *King Lear* has been to separate out those versions represented in the second Quarto (Q2, the 'good' Quarto) and the First Folio (F) in the case of Hamlet, the Quarto of 1608 (Q) and F in the case of *King Lear*, versions which in all standard editions until the 1980s were conflated in order to include for the reader all authentic Shakespearian lines. Instead of explaining differences between these texts as resulting from corruption in the printing-house or playhouse, editors now wrestle with the possibility that the plays were subject to deliberate alteration or revision. Thus, while having implications for the practice of authorship, the work of textual critics has tended to preserve the authority of Shakespeare in seeking to differentiate between texts and establish 'Shakespeare's final version'.[18]

But it is surely not mere coincidence that the question of revision in Shakespeare's plays, though an old topic of debate, has now become a fiercely contested one for textual critics in the context of a more general post-structuralist destabilizing of texts. Indeed, while general theoretical arguments designed to undermine the authority of authors and to deconstruct the privileged status of literature may be debated in general terms, the detailed study of plays like *Hamlet* and *King Lear*, for which more than one text survives, has raised the image of a dramatist engaged in a process of continuous reworking, and so has provided the most specific and substantial evidence to support the deconstruction of Shakespeare. At least one textual critic has recognized that bibliography has taken on the nature of a sociology of texts, and notes that 'since any single version will have its own historical identity, not only for its author but for the particular market of readers who bought and read it, we cannot invoke the idea of one unified intention which the editor must serve'.[19] The very idea of an authorial 'final version' is undermined if plays like *Hamlet* and *King Lear* can be shown to have gone through a process of reworking that has in effect given us more than one version of each play, and opened up the possibility that this process was continual, whenever the play was revived on the stage, so that there may have been no final version for Shakespeare. So textual criticism, in abandoning the attempt to establish the most authentic text of *King Lear*, and in asserting that we may have in effect two different plays entitled *King Lear*, contributes to the larger destabil-ization of the authority of Shakespeare, even though individual scholars may be hostile to or ignorant of post-structuralist theorizing in general. Michael Bristol has perceptively noted the connection, in support of his own polemical position: 'Critics with a post-structura-list orientation may well be able to make common cause with the new textual scholarship, because these are two groups who wish to make a united front against a common enemy, namely the advocates of a humanist ethos of the exceptional subject and of curatorial preservation of priceless artistic values.'[20] This polemical expression of a desire for victory would seem, in branding humanists as the 'enemy' – an enemy that is seen as having for many years autocratically controlled research – to reach a note of anxious shrillness. But the over-emphasis of such statements brings out sharply what is at stake, both in relation to the concept of the author or text on the one hand, and in relation to the concept of artistic value on the other. These issues need to be addressed, but I shall first take up the matter of the text and textual revision, and devote a chapter to these matters in relation to *Hamlet* and *King Lear*. In the case of these two plays, revisionist theories have made specific claims about textual changes that need to be taken into account in any consideration of Shakespeare's artistry. The question of authorship is ancillary to this, and will also enter into consideration.

SCRIPTS, PLAY-TEXTS, LITERATURE

In the effort to dismantle the authority of Shakespeare and of his texts, it has proved a convenient strategy for new historicism to abandon the traditional critical emphasis on a reading version of the plays, and to point instead to the acting text or script. Then it can be argued that the play 'is actualized in a specific social event, namely a theatrical performance of the play-text, and that this kind of social realization is always and inherently collaborative'.[21] So a play like *Hamlet* is said to be only realized through the joint activity of a group of artists working as equals in the theatre. The author dwindles into anonymity, and the text dissolves, in its 'scandalously indeterminate status',[22] into an endless series of reworkings and adaptations in ephemeral stage performances. The editors of the First Folio then come to seem almost wicked in canonizing and preserving Shakespeare's works, as if establishing written texts is 'an expression of a profound anti-theatricalism';[23] and a pursuit of textual accuracy, it is claimed, has more to do with asserting property rights to Shakespeare's works than with an effort to make available Shakespeare's plays, in the words of Heminge and Condell, 'absolute in their numbers, as he conceived them'.

Later editors and textual scholars come under attack for seeking to establish a text that would as nearly as possible represent authorial fair copy, as if their concern were to police theatrical performances in order to ensure textual purity.[24] As against such a concept of textual authority, stress is laid on the variations and improvisation that marked each performance of, say, *Hamlet*; and much weight is placed on evidence for improvisation in the surviving texts. Here critics and editors who have worked in the tradition of textual scholarship fostered by scholars like W. W. Greg and Fredson Bowers are vulnerable to the charge that in seeking to establish the text as Shakespeare conceived it, they have maintained too lofty an ideal of the author, forgetting that he was an actor himself, and have treated contemptuously as contamination any traces of theatrical interpolation. Thus Terence Hawkes can point to the removal by editors from their editions of *Hamlet* of the last sound Hamlet makes in F as he dies, 'O,o,o,o', which is not in Q2, and may be a playhouse addition, a dying groan. For Hawkes these O's have a 'musical power beyond ordinary words', and work to 'subvert order, to disrupt sequence, to impede the linear flow of meaning' by introducing another mode of communication.[25] If this is to burden a groan with more power than it can possibly exert, Hawkes has a point; the latest editions of Hamlet either relegate these O's to a collation note, or substitute for them the stage direction, 'He gives a long sigh and dies.'[26]

It is true, as this example illustrates, that editors have generally sought to present what they regarded as closest to an authentic text, based on the earliest printed texts, and the postulate of a lost authorial manuscript behind those. But their object has been basically to provide a reading version, with such information as would enable the user to understand editorial and staging problems. For the majority of the users of such editions Shakespeare's plays are experienced as texts to be read in the classroom or at home. New historicism and its allies would claim that Shakespeare's plays have 'shrunk to be sacred written texts',[27] shrunk, that is to say, from some fuller function in an oral tradition of performance, The 'acting text', which 'always was different from the written text', is thus privileged over a reading version, which lacks what actors and directors add, 'elements like tone, stage action, interpretation'.[28] But since each performance is a collaborative project that differs from other performances, there would seem to be no possibility of recovering from a multitude of stagings a single 'acting text'.

Typically post-structuralist criticism rejects the notion of a 'total artist and a totalizing society', and the idea of the work of literature as an artistic whole. Its special concern is with the fragmentary, the local, the liminal, the detail (see below, pp. 221–2). In privileging performance over text, new historicism highlights the marginal, actors' interpolations, improvisation, and context, and displaces to the margin what has customarily been treated as central, the written text. In so doing, it on the one hand treats drama as a special case in literature, as if 'dramatic literature has no existence except in historically concrete social practice';[29] and on the other hand takes no notice of the varying lengths of Shakespeare's plays, and the near-certainty that plays like *Hamlet* and *King Lear* were always heavily cut in performance. In relation to the first of these points, plays are indeed different from poems and novels in being designed in most cases for staging; however, a performance script is not the same thing as a play-text, but is a modified, often cut, restructured, reworked or topicalized version designed for use on a particular stage at a particular time. The play-text, by contrast, of a very long work like *Hamlet* or *King Lear* has rarely been performed except to satisfy a sort of antiquarian curiosity; when Hamlet was first staged in its entirety, it took six hours to play.[30]

A popular play like *Hamlet* has, in other words, since the Renaissance commonly existed in the form of a reading text as well as numerous acting versions. The difference between the title-pages of the first and second Quartos of *Hamlet* neatly illustrates the concern of Shakespeare, or his fellows, to establish a text of the play as a 'finished literary production'.[31] The title-page of Q1 (1603) offers the reader the play as acted by the Lord Chamberlain's Men in London, Oxford, Cambridge and elsewhere, and apparently represents an abridged reconstruction for staging derived from a manuscript behind the text that was eventually printed, with some theatrical markings, in the Folio.[32] The text in Q1 includes two comic additions, one in Hamlet's advice to the players and a second in mockery of Osric's use of perfume, that are not in Q2 or F, and presumably these were inserted for or by players. Q2 (1604–5), by contrast, announces a text 'Newly imprinted and enlarged to almost as much again as it was, according to the true and perfect Coppie' (and even if this is advertiser's blurb, it shows a faith in the idea of a stable text). It is a text for reading, even if it contains many printer's errors, derived from a manuscript that was, according to scholarly agreement, in Shakespeare's hand, probably his 'foul papers', or final draft before the text was prepared and modified for staging purposes. In relation to the second point above, it seems absurd to think of Shakespeare's plays as 'dwindling' into high art or shrinking into literary texts, when common stage practice has always been to alter, rearrange and above all cut plays for performance. The bad Quarto of *Hamlet* (Q1) has about 2220 lines, the good Quarto (Q2) 4056. In 1870 Edwin Booth brought back into performance several passages that had traditionally been curtailed or omitted in productions of *Hamlet*, among them the prayer-sequence in III.3, and Hamlet's narration to Horatio of his adventures at sea in v.2; but the resultant 2750-line version proved too long for his audiences, and he dropped Hamlet's speech, 'Now might I do it pat ...', and the narration in v.2 from later productions.[33] Playhouse interpolations, in the form of improvised jokes, dying O's or whatever, deserve more consideration than to be simply dismissed as corruptions, but they constitute a very minor element in such Shakespearian play-scripts as we have, and are much less important than, for example, stage directions which may likewise be Shakespearian or 'playhouse interpolation'. In any case, almost always it is the acting version that shrinks and dwindles, and that in the nature of things we cannot recover, and in the case of *Hamlet*, the reading text of Q2 is almost twice as long as versions commonly acted then and ever since.

It is therefore misleading to deconstruct Shakespeare as though his plays 'are produced by a multitude of determinations', and to claim that 'Every text of a Shakespeare play exists in relationship to scripts we will never have, to a series of revisions and collaborations that start as soon as there is a Shakespearean text.'[34] If this is so for Shakespeare, it is equally true for Jonathan Goldberg, who wrote these words, and for all authors whose drafts are revised, copy-edited, and who rely upon the help of others in their research. What results in the final printed version is nonetheless the author's even if it includes misprints or other errors, or, as in the case of a play by Shakespeare, may have been subject to censorship. The texts of *Hamlet* and *King Lear* are more problematic in that both were revised, but this in itself does not diminish the authorship of Shakespeare, if it can be established that the revisions were made by him, any more than the three versions of Wordsworth's *The Prelude*, or the revisions of their work by James Joyce or D. H. Lawrence or Harold Pinter, affect the question of their authorship. The problem raised is not one of authority, but rather of what grounds there may be for (a) conflating the texts, as most editions of Shakespeare have done; (b) giving one text preference over another; or (c) regarding all variations as of equal status, and the text as process rather than achieved product.

Of the three major editions of *Hamlet* published in the 1980s, one, the New Arden (1982), prints the traditional conflated text, amalgamating Q2 and F with corrections from Q1; a second, the New Cambridge (1985), includes those passages from Q2 omitted from F, but places them in very discreet square brackets for the observant reader; the third, the Oxford (1986), relegates the lines peculiar to Q2 to an appendix, and prints substantially the Folio text. All three procedures can be defended, though the first especially has now come under fire. A composite text that includes the 220 or so lines of Q2 not found in F, and the seventy or so lines in F not found in Q2, is open to the criticism that it is not the play as it existed at any stage for Shakespeare. On the other hand, for a reader it preserves all the lines we know of that Shakespeare wrote at some time or another for *Hamlet*. The second kind of edition gestures towards presenting the texts in process, but in fact offers an electic text except for putting lines not in F in brackets, and logically should in some way mark also lines not found in Q2. The third sees the cuts and additions in F as made by Shakespeare as part of a 'definite policy designed to make the play more accessible to theatre-goers' by clarifying the action,[35] and therefore omits lines found only in Q2, except where these supply what the editor regards as accidental omissions in F.

The case of *King Lear* is more difficult because the differences between the texts cannot so easily be reduced to so many lines added or omitted. The alterations affect the play in both large and very minute ways (but see pp. 110–11 below), as, for instance, on the one hand, in the omission in F of some passages and reworking of others that in Q refer to a French invasion of England in relation to the return of Cordelia; and on the other hand, in such small but significant changes as reassigning in 1.4 'This is nothing, Fool' (Lear's in Q, Kent's in F), and 'Lear's shadow' (Lear's in Q, the Fool's in F). The traditional conflated edition seeks to preserve all the uncorrupted words of Shakespeare by selecting what seems to the editor best from Q or F, but we now realize that the result is not so much an approach to an ideal text as at times a muddying of the play in such a way as to build in contradictory signals, as in III.1, where Kent reports in Q that a French force has landed in England, but in F speaks only of a civil war in England between Albany and Cornwall, and of their servants who are acting as spies for France, and making their affairs known abroad. Thus it has been claimed that there is no longer any case for an edition of *King Lear* that seeks to combine both texts, and editors will need to choose between Q and F. *The Complete Oxford Shakespeare* (1986) includes both the full Q and F texts, which is one solution; another is to present all textual variants as a process of development, as Michael Warren has done (1990) in an inevitably expensive and not very readable format.

In principle there is no difference, as far as authorship is concerned, between the problems raised by revision in *Hamlet* and *King Lear* and those raised by revision in a poem or novel; but in practice the matter of the staging of plays does affect the issue, because the play as scripted for a performance is likely to differ from the published text, as a director may cut or rearrange it. This brings about, for instance, the paradoxical situation that the senior editor of the Oxford Shakespeare, Stanley Wells, has affirmed that 'future criticism must acknowledge the existence of two authoritative texts' of *King Lear*, when he is committed to the idea that 'plays written for performance are not fully realised until they reach the stage'.[36] He thus simultaneously supports the concept of the authority of the text, and the notion that the play is only realized on the stage. Yet we cannot recover from Shakespeare's time the acting versions of *King Lear*, but only versions of the full authorial text. At the same time, post-structuralist and new historicist criticism offers a different paradox: in dismantling the authority of the author, and rejecting the idea of establishing a text, they appeal to theatre practice, to the play-script as a collaborative work of all those involved in a production, as if its 'only genuine and acceptable realization takes the form of action on the stage'.[37] Yet their concern is with the production of 'cultural meanings', with interpretation as a 'knowledge-seeking activity';[38] and it is not possible to retrieve meaning from acting scripts as such, since we have none from Shakespeare's age except in such a garbled form as Q1 of *Hamlet*. For all their appeal to the theatre, such critics are dependent on non-theatrical texts, the full reading versions of *Hamlet* and *King Lear* they study in the editions they use; and it is not altogether suprising to find them sharing that sense of the theatre as contaminating for which they reasonably criticize some textual scholars; the same anxiety seems to inform the argument of the textual scholar who says that when the play began to be prepared for the

stage, 'what one can only call degeneration began',[39] and the critic
who writes of the 'scandalously indeterminate status' of the play-
text, or argues that 'Shakespeare's work comes into being in that
highly suspect institutional mise-en-scène of fluid, shifting, and
meretricious representation, the theater.'[40]

The differences between Q2 and F have been documented and
analysed in detail by textual scholars and editors,[41] but their
significance is still a matter of debate. Q2 lacks three substantial
passages found in F; these are (a) the sequence at II.2.239–69 in
which Hamlet calls Denmark a prison, and Rosencrantz and
Guildenstern introduce the topic of ambition; (b) the commentary
in II.2.337–62 on the rise and success of the 'little eyases', or
companies of boy-actors; and (c) thirteen lines at IV.2.68–80, where
Hamlet apologizes to Horatio for quarrelling with Laertes. The first
of these passages could have been excised from a Quarto issued in
·1604–5 by censorship, in order to avoid giving offence to the Queen
of England, Anne of Denmark,[42] and the last passage could have
been omitted inadvertently, since the text breaks off at 'is it not
perfect conscience', leaving the sense incomplete, and resumes with
the entry of Osric addressing Hamlet; it seems unlikely that Osric
would interrupt Hamlet in mid-sentence. The second passage, on
the companies of children, is harder to account for, and it has been
regarded as an 'afterthought', a 'later addition', by Shakespeare,
and defended as 'a means of strengthening the analogy Hamlet
draws between the public reaction to the new players, the Children
of the Blackfriars, and to the new king, Claudius'.[43]

Most of the other brief passages found in F but not in Q2 can be
explained as accidentally omitted from Q2, or as 'playhouse interpolations', or as expansions that enrich the mood or strengthen the
'signal' given by the Q2 text.[44] Since Shakespeare worked in the
playhouse as an actor as well as author, there is no reason not to
associate such alterations with him – including Hamlet's cry 'Oh
Vengeance!' at II.2.581 in F, and his dying groan 'O,o,o,o' at V.2.358.
And for some small additions, like Hamlet's important comment,
'What, frighted with false fire' (III.2.266), the presence of a similar
phrase in Q1 confirms that this was in an acting version. The crucial
passages, then, for an explanation of the additions to F (or

omissions from Q) are the two substantial sequences in II.2. For the moment let me simply note that they expand what is already a very long scene.

About 230 lines that appear in Q2 are omitted from F, and these are now regarded by textual scholars as deliberate cuts, made so skilfully in a number of places as to provide strong evidence that Shakespeare himself was the reviser responsible for them. The most substantial, accounting for 205 of the omitted lines, include (a) I.I.108–25, Horatio's lines on omens preceding the fall of Julius Caesar in ancient Rome; (b) I.4.17–38, Hamlet's expansion of his comments on drinking in Denmark, and his 'vicious mole of nature' speech, on the corrupting effects of a single weakness in a man, a speech that seems equally applicable to Claudius, the apparent subject, and to Hamlet himself, and that was used in voiceover to introduce Laurence Olivier's film, applying the words specifically to Hamlet; (c) III.4.71–6, 78–81, 161–6, 169–72 and 202–10, all passages omitted from the long scene between Hamlet and his mother, the most notable lines being those in which Hamlet begins to take delight in 'knavery', and to relish the 'sport' of counterplotting against Claudius; (d) IV.4.9–66, Hamlet's conversation with the Captain of Fortinbras's army, and his last major soliloquy, 'How all occasions do inform against me . . .'; (e) IV.7.68–81, 100–2, 114–23, shortening the dialogue between Claudius and Laertes about duelling; (f) V.2.106–35, 137–43, a considerable part of Hamlet's conversation with Osric; and (g) V.2.195–208, the dialogue between Hamlet and a Lord who summons him to the duel with Laertes.

All these changes have been seen as 'parts of a definite policy designed to make the play more accessible to theatre-goers in general by giving it a more direct and unimpeded action, pruning away some of its verbal elaborations, and smoothing out its more abrupt transitions',[45] but they are not all of the same kind. The first is a narrative passage that is not essential, and slackens the tension of the opening scene, so that cutting makes theatrical sense. Passage (b) also may have been cut to speed up the action and not delay any longer what has been well prepared for, the entry of the Ghost in I.5; but it could have been excised because of its muddled thinking, and the way it comes near to excusing both Hamlet and Claudius, if their actions can be attributed to something 'in their birth, wherein they are not guilty'. The lines omitted in passage (c) are in the main skilful abbreviations of Hamlet's arguably over-long diatribe against his mother, removing some of the more clotted or repetitive sentences, while neatly maintaining the verse pattern. The last passage in (c) however, affects the action:

> There's letters seald, and my two schoolfellows,
> Whom I will trust as I will adders fang'd,
> They bear the mandate, they must sweep my way
> And marshal me to knavery: let it work,
> For 'tis the sport to have the engineer
> Hoist with his own petar[d]; and[d]'t shall go hard
> But I will delve one yard belowtheir mines,
> And blow them at the moon: ô, 'tis most sweet
> When in one line two crafts directly meet.

These lines show how far in Q2 Hamlet has accommodated himself to the ways of Claudius's world; his cold-blooded contemplation of knavery, of getting rid of Rosencrantz and Guildenstern, and his enjoyment in the prospect of outfoxing his opponents, mark him as tainted indeed. Their omission from F leaves Hamlet's state of mind, his intentions as far as his revenge is concerned, and his perception of Rosencrantz and Guildenstern undefined.

The fourth passage is especially interesting, for it includes the Norwegian Captain's cynical account of the pointlessness of Fortinbras's expedition against Poland, and Hamlet's soliloquy, 'How all occasions do inform against me . . .', which brings out the irony of Hamlet's perception of Fortinbras in relation to himself. Recent editors of the play observe that this passage does not advance the action or reveal anything new about Hamlet, merely duplicating the self-laceration of his earlier soliloquy, 'O what a rogue and peasant slave am I.' There is no trace of the sequence in Q1, and this would tend to confirm that the passage was cut in performance. But in drafting it Shakespeare brought out some deeper significances, firstly in relation to Fortinbras, for in exposing the contrast between what Hamlet sees as 'divine ambition' and the trivial and empty nature of what Fortinbras is actually fighting for, the soliloquy demonstrates for us what Hamlet seems not to perceive, the waste and absurdity of fighting for the sake of honour, expressed in the nonsense of

>   Rightly to be great
> Is not to stir without great argument,
> But greatly to find quarrel in a straw
> When honour's at the stake.

Hamlet invokes an heroic ethos, but his twisted judgment is revealed in the way he takes fighting for 'honour' in Fortinbras's expedition to be an inducement to himself to be 'bloody' in revenge; for Fortinbras has in fact forgone his revenge for the death of his father in his planned attack on Denmark, and has settled instead for fighting in Poland. Incidentally, by revealing the senselessness of exposing 20000 men to 'imminent death' for the sake of 'fame', Hamlet also casts a shadow on his father. For Fortinbras is a kind of reincarnation of old Hamlet, seen here by Hamlet as a warrior-hero, and going, like old Hamlet, to make war on the Poles. The sequence thus effectively reveals the limitations of warrior-kings who settle everything by combat. In so far as Fortinbras represents the same values as old Hamlet, we are made to recognize the gap between Hamlet's image of his father and what old Hamlet was really like. The omission of most of this scene leaves the analogy between Fortinbras and Hamlet's image of his father undeveloped, though still to be inferred from the way Fortinbras invades Poland, in what appears to be a repetition of old Hamlet's actions in smiting the Poles.

In the second place, the omission of Hamlet's extended soliloquy from IV.4 realigns the sequence of soliloquies in the play, so that Hamlet's last major soliloquy becomes 'To be or not to be' in III.1, and the last major soliloquy in the play is Claudius's wrestling with his sense of guilt in III.3. The cutting of 'How all occasions do inform against me' may thus strengthen the role of Claudius, while Hamlet's last speech to the audience then becomes ''Tis now the very witching time of night' (III.2.388–99), the time when the play began, and when Hamlet encountered the Ghost in I.5; he is, of course, to see or hallucinate the Ghost again, and his mood as he goes to his mother seems in tune with the midnight hour, as he is prepared to 'drink hot blood' and be 'cruel'. A third feature of IV.4 in Q2 is its renewed emphasis on revenge. Since Hamlet revealed his intentions to Claudius in the 'Mousetrap' scene, then almost stabbed him at prayer, then killed Polonius, and plainly threatened Claudius in IV.3, the action has gathered momentum in its approach to a final showdown with Claudius. Another soliloquy that would break this momentum with yet more self-questioning on the theme of spurring his dull revenge seems out of place. Furthermore, Hamlet is about to go off to England, and technically Rosencrantz and Guildenstern are in charge of him here, escorting him aboard ship, so for them to abandon him while he soliloquizes would seem odd. Perhaps Shake-

speare's first thought was to give Hamlet a big speech before he
departs the stage for a long absence – he returns about 500 lines later
in IV.1 – but another speech on revenge undercuts the impact of
Laertes arriving in IV.5 to seek immediate vengeance for the death of
his father. Those who see Hamlet as having a 'duty' to revenge[46]
tend to want to keep the soliloquy in the play as relating to what
they see as Hamlet's central objective; but if it is omitted, Hamlet is
sent off to England after an enigmatic and effective exchange with
Claudius and Guildenstern:

HAMLET For England?
CLAUDIUS   Ay Hamlet
HAMLET   Good.
CLAUDIUS So is it, if thou knew'st our purposes.
HAMLET I see a cherub that sees them [him F]. But come, for England.
        Farewell dear mother   (IV.3.46–9)

These lines follow directly from Hamlet's killing of Polonius and the
games he plays with the body, and from his outburst against
Claudius in the closet scene with his mother. Throughout the
sequence he maintains something of the note of hysteria generated in
the scene with his mother, and his scornful refusal to acknowledge
Claudius as 'father' also carries over from his denunciations of
Claudius to his mother. Thus Hamlet leaves for England in F after a
striking confrontation with Claudius; and in F Claudius has the last
word, for the scene ends with a short soliloquy for him in which he
explains he is sending Hamlet to his death. So Claudius strikes back
at Hamlet after the killing of Polonius, and the stage is prepared for
the final settling of scores. In this sense, Hamlet's 'How all occasions'
soliloquy is unnecessary dramatically; but it reveals something of
Shakespeare's vision, how critically he saw old Hamlet, and how
confused Hamlet becomes in justifying his revenge.

The action certainly moves more directly and more rapidly if most
of IV.4 is cut, and the fifth omission, of lines from the long exchange
between Claudius and Laertes in IV.7, also seems designed, as
Hibbard suggests, to 'speed up the action'. Two passages (68–81,
100–2) merely embroider the account of Laertes' skill with his
rapier. A third (114–23) includes Claudius's lines on acting without
hesitation, 'That we would do / We should do when we would', and
his anxiety at possible 'abatements and delays' recalls Hamlet's
concern, and the Player King's lines,

> What to ourselves in passion we propose,
> The passion ending, doth the purpose lose. (III.2.194–5)

But Claudius is worrying needlessly, and Laertes at once offers to cut the throat of his father's murderer in church, so that Claudius's lines here may have been cut as confusing the issue, since both Claudius and Laertes are prepared to act without hesitation, however much their speeches here may relate to what Harold Jenkins sees as an important motif', 'the failure of resolution to translate itself into action'.[47] The image of Hamlet as a disease in Claudius's lines here continues a motif present in IV.3 ('like the hectic in my blood he rages'), but this is well established anyway. So again, omitting the lines speeds up the action, and loses nothing of consequence. The last substantial omissions, of thirty-three lines of Hamlet's dialogue with Osric in V.2, and of fourteen lines involving the Lord who enters at V.2.194 to announce that Claudius and Gertrude are 'coming down', also concentrate the action. The Lord's role is unnecessary, and Osric is sufficiently characterized as a 'waterfly' in the dialogue left to him, which focusses on the King's wager and on the weapons to be used in the match between Hamlet and Laertes.

If the omissions speed up the action, their main effect is on the last two acts, and the first three in any case have roughly twice the number of lines of Acts IV and V. As far as Claudius is concerned, the changes throw more weight on his soliloquy in the prayer scene, III.3, and also highlight the way he changes on the news of the death of Polonius to see Hamlet as a disease that must be cut away at any cost. In relation to Hamlet, the omission of the 'vicious mole of nature' speech and his last soliloquy in F reduces significantly the number of his meditative speeches, and leaves out what has become unnecessary. The cutting of most of IV.4 also leaves Hamlet's intentions less clear, and we have to wait until his return from England in V.2 to find him justifying sending Rosencrantz and Guildenstern to their deaths. It is striking that some of the passages omitted from F (the 'vicious mole of nature' speech; Hamlet's 'marshal me to knavery' lines, and the 'How all occasions' soliloquy) have been used as key passages for interpreting the play by a number of critics and directors. But the 'Denmark's a prison' sequence, added in F, has also functioned as a central image for other critics and scene designers; and this passage may be a deliberate addition to provide a focus for all the watching of and by Hamlet in the play,

and for the sense of claustrophobia generated in a court where he is
the 'observed of all observers'.

The omissions from F, then, can in the main be explained as cuts
made purposively to revise and reshape the play, and especially to
sharpen the flow of the last two acts. At the same time, some, notably
the 'vicious mole' lines (1.4), the 'marshal me to knavery' lines (III.4),
and the 'How all occasions' soliloquy, may be seen as revealing
important stages in the process of the play's development into the
revised form printed in F. What then of the passages added in F? Q1
shows traces of two of them, the 'little eyases' dialogue (II.2.337–62)
and Hamlet's apology for his behaviour to Laertes (v.2.68–80), so
that these may have been in the acting version, since Q1 apparently
derives from the text behind F. The third passage, the 'Denmark's a
prison' sequence, has left no trace in Q1, and if it was censored in
print (Q2) and on the stage (Q1), its recovery in F seems on the face
of it odd. A possible reason for the addition is mentioned above; but
it has to be said too that 'in each case Q2 makes good sense as it
stands',[48] so that the additions are not necessary. Yet those who
defend basing their modern editions on F and relegating to an
appendix lines found only in Q2 'because we believe that, however
fine they may be in themselves, Shakespeare decided that the play as
a whole would be better without them',[49] also defend retaining the
Q2 only passages:

The first of them brings out more fully the evasiveness of Rosencrantz and
Guildenstern, which the Prince, fresh from his encounter with Polonius, so
quickly detects in Q2. In the second, Shakespeare seizes on the War of the
Theatres as a means of strengthening the analogy Hamlet draws between
the public reaction to the new players, the Children of Blackfriars, and to
the new king, Claudius. As for the third, its evident purposes is to provide
more reasons than does Q2 for Hamlet's readiness to take part in the
fencing match . . . [50]

These passages are said to 'provide more explanation' and make
transitions less abrupt; but why would Shakespeare revise in such a
way as to make transitions more abrupt in Acts IV and v, and less so
in Act II? And why would he add substantially to an already very
long scene in Act II, while reducing IV.4 to a fleeting glimpse of
Fortinbras?

There does not appear to be an overall logic, and so editors are
driven to defending the retention of 'additions' in F for the same sort

of reasons that one might use to defend preserving lines found only in Q2. The presence of additions in F contradicts, as it were, the explanation for the cuts, if these indeed show Shakespeare revising the play. The evidence we have does not permit a simple sequential interpretation of the development of Hamlet without some special pleading, such as the argument that Shakespeare added the 'little eyases' passage as an afterthought. This being the case, it would seem more rational, and more in accord with the ambiguous and conflicting nature of the evidence, to regard Q2 and F as showing stages in a process of evolution. It is reasonable to suppose that the lines cut or added are by Shakespeare, or, in the case of so-called actors' interpolations, approved by him. On the other hand, there is little reason to regard Q2 or F as a version that was acted as it stands in Shakespeare's time, when Q1 approaches more to a normal length for performance. What we have in Q2 and F is evidence of a process of change; and if in the end I share the view that F represents the latest revision by Shakespeare, I think there is also a case for presenting all the lines found in Q2 and F in a reading version, with those peculiar to Q2 and to F marked off in some way to show the reader that they are unique to one version.

TEXTS OF *KING LEAR*

The texts of *King Lear* has been analysed at length in *The Division of the Kingdoms* (1983) by a group of scholars all of whom reject the long tradition of regarding Q as a bad Quarto, and F as a text that suffered cuts by theatre personnel or contamination by actors – a tradition that led Kenneth Muir to say, in his introduction to the Arden edition (1952), 'A modern editor will, of course, restore these omitted lines, whether his text is based mainly on the Quarto or the Folio.'[51] The new orthodoxy persuasively argues that the text of Q derives from an authorial manuscript, and that F represents Shakespeare's revision of the text printed in the Quarto.[52] The authors of *The Division of the Kingdoms* therefore reject the universal practice of editors until very recently of conflating both texts, as taken for granted in Muir's 'of course'. As in the case of *Hamlet*, it seems to me that the case for revision has been established, short of external proof, but that the significance of the changes between Q and F needs further investigation. Some changes in the *Lear* texts, as in those of *Hamlet*, are evident errors introduced in the printing-house, and the Quarto of *King Lear* is very carelessly printed;[53] some of these errors will be apparent in quotations from the plays, but they do not greatly affect the general arguments for revision, and they will not be considered here.

The conclusion to which the various analyses of particular changes have led is that 'conflation muddies our understanding of Shakespeare's artistry', and that there are 'two authoritative texts' of the play; however, as a corollary to this must be added the assumption by most commentators that the authorial intention to improve is an important factor, and that the Folio text 'is the better play'.[54] This assumption perhaps should be questioned, and as in *Hamlet*, the significance of the changes between Q and F is still a matter to be debated. Q has nearly 300 lines not found in F, which in turn has getting on for 100 not found in Q. Some minor differences could be accidental, caused by compositors overlooking a phrase (as at II.I.78, where Gloucester's 'I never got him' is missing from F), or due to eyeskip (as at 1.4.98, where '*Kent*. Why Fool?, becomes '*Lear*. Why my Boy?' in F; the Fool's response is directed to Kent, and the compositor in F may have picked up Lear's 'Why my Boy?' from line 106, where this phrase appears in both Q and F). Other omissions from F could have been due to censorship of passages that might have given offence to King James I,[55] before whom the play was performed on St Stephen's Night, 1606 (26 December) at Whitehall, according to the entry of the play in the Stationers' Register in November 1607. The Fool's satirical reference to monopolies (1.4.140ff.), Edmund's account of 'menaces and maledictions against king and nobles' (1.2.144ff.) and the references to war with France, all found in Q but not in F, could have been omitted to avoid displeasing a king who was known for granting monopolies to favourites, and who liked to see himself as a peacemaker in his foreign policy.

There are difficulties with the idea of censorship, which has to be inferred from cuts in the text. If passages were excised in 1606, the F text must have been available for performance then, but there is evidence not only that F was in part based on Q, but that the revisions in F were made about 1609–10. Furthermore, if a contemporary critic can see the representation of Lear as 'perilously close to presenting a fictional portrait of the king himself',[56] then James I himself and his officials would surely have seen a general analogy with himself in 'an elderly monarch whose hobby was hunting, whose retinue was distinctive in its foregrounding of a Fool, who during the central acts is evidently insane, and whose authoritarian views ultimately destroyed himself and his entire family'.[57] James did not go insane, or destroy himself and his family, and we have no evidence that he was disturbed by seeing the play; but it does not seem likely that a censor would overlook the larger analogy and merely tinker by removing a few passages and references to France. Therefore, while keeping the possibility of such factors as compositor interference and censorship in mind, I shall consider the more important changes between Q and F as intentional revisions. Both texts, it is now generally agreed, offer full versions of the play, however much they were affected by misreadings, corruption, or incompetence in the printing-house.[58]

There are, it seems to me, six aspects of the Q text that especially characterize its differences from F.

The Fool

The Fool's dramatic weight in the play seems much greater than the limited role of a character who speaks only 225 lines in six scenes, fifty-four of these lines changed in F. Critics agree on his importance, but vary enormously in their conception of the character. So at one extreme he has been seen as half-witted, a natural whose wisdom is a kind of instinctive clairvoyance, and at the other extreme as a sage rationalist, shrewd and thoughtful; also he has been envisaged alternatively as a mere boy, or androgynously as a kind of alter ego of Cordelia (as in 1990 productions at the Royal Shakespeare Theatre and by the English Renaissance Company, in which the Fool was played by a woman), or as a mature adult. He has been portrayed as embodying the conscience of the King, as a voice of social protest, and as a court fool who loses his part and 'shrivels into a wretched little human being on the soaking hearth'.[59] No other character in the play has given rise to such varying and contradictory interpretations. Two notable embodiments of the Fool illustrate the problem. In the Royal Shakespeare Theatre production of *King Lear* in 1982 the Fool was played by Anthony Sher as 'a clown – a Charlie from the late Victorian circus with Dan Leno boots, a Grock violin and a red button nose on a length of elastic'.[60] In other words, he was a mature and skilled entertainer, staging cross-talk acts with Lear, an artist enjoying his rapport with the audience on and off stage. He lost his partner as Lear went mad, and perhaps in response

to this, the director, Adrian Noble, had the Fool stabbed to death by
the old King at the end of III.6. The Fool retreated downstage
holding a cushion to escape Lear's wild fit of rage against his
daughters; the King, stabbing repeatedly at the cushion as if it were
Regan, bloodily speared the Fool as he jumped into a tub. This
treatment of the Fool was the very opposite of Grigori Kozintsev's
presentation of him in his majestic film version (1970). Kozintsev,
fascinated by clowns and fools, read all he could find about them,
and then, he said, realized that 'One must take away from the role of
the Fool everything that is associated with clownery.'[61] Rejecting the
traditional trappings of the clown or fool, Kozintsev turned him into
a simpleton, a man regarded as 'a village idiot', who is laughed at for
speaking the truth. He was represented as a boy with a shaved head,
costumed as a beggar, and distinguished only by the soft sounds of
the bells tied to his legs. The Fool also had a pipe on which he played
melancholy notes, which are heard at the end of the film, for
Kozintsev's Fool remained alive, his music, like the flowing water
associated with Cordelia, intended to suggest continuity and the
possibility of renewal.[62]

These treatments of the Fool, one as a professional circus clown
killed in Act III, the other as a simpleton kept alive through Act V,
both take liberties with the text, in which the Fool goes off in III.6
and is not seen again, or heard of, until Lear's comment 'And my
poor fool is hang'd' (v.3.306). These two interpretations, on stage
and in film, radically different as they are, have obvious analogies
with the extremes of interpretation by critics, and might appear, like
them, to be understandable responses to the confusions of editions
that conflate Q and F. Indeed, John Kerrigan has argued that in the
Folio, 'the Fool is consistently a wise and worldly jester, more urbane
and more oblique than his precursor' in the Quarto.[63] The Fool in
Q, he thinks, could be seen as a natural, but in F he becomes cool
and rational, in pointed contrast to the insanity of the King and the
affected madness of Edgar. He is right to point out that Q and F give
conflicting signals about the Fool, but the contrast between the texts
is by no means as clear cut as he claims.

The Fool is established for the audience in long exchanges with
King Lear, from 1.4.95 to 188, and in 1.5. In 1.4 F omits the Fool's
answer, 1.4.140–55, to his own question to Lear, 'Dost thou know the
difference, my boy, between a bitter fool and a sweet one?', leaving a
loose end, some think because of a cut made by censorship, for the

question is not directly answered. Kerrigan sees here a deliberate jump or dislocation 'working to distance' the Fool from the King,[64] but Shakespeare may have cut the scene simply to tighten it and make it more economical. The Fool is well established by this point, and his teasing of Lear plays variations on the same theme. However, the omission here leaves the audience to think of the Fool as bitter, whereas in Q he presents himself as a sweet fool in contrast to the lord who counselled Lear to give away his land, and this fits in with the general shift detected by Kerrigan, and marked also in the conversion of Lear's 'Who is it that can tell me who I am? Lear's shadow'(Q) into a dialogue with a mocking retort by the Fool: '*Lear.* Who is it that can tell me who I am? *Fool.* Lear's shadow' (F). 1.5 is essentially the same in both versions, continuing the Fool's close involvement with Lear.

The major changes in II.4 and III.2, the next two scenes in which the Fool appears, are the addition in F of two rhyming jingles for him to speak or sing. At II.4.46–55 the addition provides a speech addressed to Lear in a long sequence in which in Q the Fool's speeches are entirely spoken to Kent until line 123. Lear is already troubled by the 'climbing sorrow' (line 57) that leads to madness, and he does not respond to the Fool's sallies, which in both texts provide a sardonic running commentary on what is happening to Lear and Kent. Kerrigan argues that in F 'the King and his jester are on different wavelengths. They are beginning to drift apart, something which never really happens' in Q;[65] but they are in fact just as far apart in Q as in F, for in both texts Lear ignores the Fool until his exit line, 'O fool, I shall go mad' (II.4.286), and this remark is ambiguous, for it could be addressed to himself, marking his recognition of his own folly, or taken as a cue to show he goes off with the Fool. In III.2, in both versions, Lear resumes a dialogue with the Fool at the end of the scene, with his 'Poor fool and knave, I have one part in [of Q] my heart / That's sorry yet for thee.' F, however, adds a final soliloquy for the Fool, his rhyming parody of a Chaucerian prophecy:

> This is a brave night to cool a courtesan:
> I'll speak a prophecy ere I go:
> When priests are more in word than matter;
> When brewers mar their malt with water;
> When nobles are their tailors' tutors,
> No heretics burn'd, but wenches' suitors;

When every case in law, is right;
No squire in debt, nor no poor knight;
When slanders do not live in tongues;
Nor cut-purses come not to throngs;
When usurers tell their gold i'th'field,
And bawds, and whores, do churches build,
Then shall the realm of Albion,
Come to great confusion:
Then comes the time, who lives to see't
That going shall be us'd with feet.
This prophecy Merlin shall make, for I live before his time

(III.2.79–95)

Some have regarded these lines as spurious or irrelevant, while Kerrigan sees them as dramatizing the Fool's 'growing sense of his own irrelevance' in F, as here, he says, 'the F Fool begins to leave Lear'.[66] The first part of the prophecy relates to things as they are in Albion, though riddlingly, and not in a way that lends much conviction to the pursuit of topical allusions here,[67] and the latter part concerns things as they will never be; but as a whole it is consistent with the bitter Fool of F, extending his ironic commentary on selfishness and greed. I see no warrant for asserting that the Fool here senses his own irrelevance or is leaving Lear; the effect in F of foregrounding the Fool with a kind of epilogue or farewell speech, 'I'll speak a prophecy ere I go', is to give him a greater prominence here than in Q; and his prophecy symbolizes the topsy-turvy world Lear has brought about.

The rhyming jingles added for the Fool in F in II.4. and III.2 sharpen his role as satirist, even as he is beginning to be distanced from Lear by the King's incipient madness and preoccupation with his daughters. In both Q and F the Fool becomes a more marginal figure in III.4, where Edgar appears as Poor Tom, and at once takes Lear's attention as a visible projection of his own sense of grievance and loss. The Fool's voice is heard occasionally, punctuating the mad dialogue between Lear and Edgar, and the anxious comments of Kent, with brief pointed sallies of wry common sense, such as 'This cold night will turn us all to fools & madmen' (III.4.78–9), and 'Prithee, nuncle, be contented [contect Q], 'tis [this is Q] a naughty night to swim in' (III.4.110–11). F adds two lines to mark Lear's continuing concern in his lucid moments for the Fool, in which he insists that the Fool go before him into the hovel, 'In boy, go first . . .'

(III.4.26), whereas in Q Lear appears to ignore the Fool throughout this scene.

This last small addition is significant in relation to III.6, which in Q includes the mock-trial of his daughters conducted by Lear, with Edgar, the Fool and Kent acting as judges. The mock-trial has obvious links with many other passages and scenes in a play much concerned with justice, and notably anticipates another mock-trial later, when Lear himself 'becomes' a judge: 'I pardon that man's life. What was thy cause?' (IV.6.109). But it flattens out the distinction between the roles of Edgar and the Fool, who inevitably seem much alike here. Both for the moment are equated as 'judges', and the Fool is restored in Q to a prominence he lacked in III.4. In F the Fool has only three short speeches in III.6, two of them additions to Q, and both extend his role as sardonic commentator. The first is the Fool's retort to Lear's answer to his question, 'Prithee nuncle tell me whether a madman be a gentleman, or a yeoman?'; Lear replies, 'A king, a king' and there the exchange stops in Q, but in F the Fool adds, 'No, he's a yeoman, that has a gentleman to his son: for he's a mad yeoman that sees his son a gentleman before him' (III.6.9–14). This seems to be another biting allusion to Lear's division of his kingdom, giving rule and possessions to his daughters and 'sons' Albany and Cornwall. The second addition gives the Fool an exit line, 'And I'll go to bed at noon' (III.6.85), appropriate to the confusion in Lear's world.

What then is the effect of the differences in the Fool's part between Q and F? The changes in F are generally consistent in reinforcing the general sardonic commentary of the Fool, but they do not, in my view, transform a 'blathering natural' in Q into a 'canny rationalist' in F.[68] It would seem rather that from the beginning Shakespeare had a many-sided conception of the Fool, and that there is a complexity in both texts allowing a range of perspectives on him. In I.4 the Fool is welcomed by Lear as 'my pretty knave' and 'my boy', suggesting an intimacy that is reflected too in the Fool's habit of calling Lear 'Nuncle' as if he were an elderly relative. This has encouraged some to see a mutual devotion between them, as between the childishness of a boy, or of a man who has remained childish, and an old man who has returned to childishness.[69] If Shakespeare had this relationship in mind, he seems also to have intended from the beginning that the Fool should twist the knife in Lear's wounds, and be a 'pestilent gall' to him (I.4.114). The passage about the sweet and bitter fool in Q, omitted from F, makes the Fool plainly call Lear a fool, and also shows that Shakespeare thought of him as wearing motley:

> The sweet and bitter fool
> Will presently appear,
> The one in motley here,
> The other found out there.   (1.4.144–7)

The text of Q here shows that the Fool was conceived from the start as a professional court fool, a clear-sighted analyst of Lear's condition, not simply as a sort of village idiot.

In 1.4 and 1.5 the Fool is close to Lear, and for most of these scenes acts as a partner in a savagely comic duologue in which Lear is the 'feed', providing cues or answers to questions which enable to Fool to score off him. In 11.4, when Lear is preoccupied with his daughters, Kent becomes the Fool's 'feed':

KENT Where learn'd you this, fool?
FOOL Not i'th' stocks [fool F].   (11.4.86–7)

In this scene Lear appears oblivious to the Fool; here, and in 111.2 and 111.4 (Q), there is nothing in the text to indicate that Lear attends or responds to anything the Fool says, until the end of 111.2, when he notices the Fool in a burst of sympathy: 'Come on, my boy. How dost, my boy? Art cold?', and responds to his song 'the rain it raineth every day' by saying 'True boy' ('True, my good boy' Q). The omission of the mock-trial in 111.6 diminishes the Fool's role in this scene in F, and the brief added lines, like the rhyming jingles added in 11.4 and 111.2, enhance his function as a kind of choric commentator. At the same time, the Fool stays with Lear, and two lines were added in 111.4 to renew Lear's sympathy for his 'boy'. The changes made in F thus continue to suggest varying perspectives on the character. On the one hand, he can be seen as a devoted, humble attendant on Lear, perhaps a youth (Lear calls him 'boy', 'knave' and 'lad', though anyone under fifty would perhaps seem a boy to the old King), who might be thought of as frail, easily cowed, perhaps a little feminine (like Cordelia; the same actor could have played both roles[70]), and hence a reflection of Lear's conscience, a mirror or screen on which Shakespeare 'flashes, as it were, readings from the psychic life of the protagonist'.[71] On the other hand, the Fool can be seen as a sharp, rational, mature professional, turning

Lear's language back on him ('Do'st know the difference, my boy, between a bitter fool and a sweet one?'), a figure who establishes through his generalizing comments a note of social protest in the play.[72] The Fool's early scenes (1.4, 1.5) tend to emphasize the first set of images, while the later scenes (II.4, III.2, III.4, III.6) bring out the other range of possibilities; but Shakespeare took pains by small additions in F to keep alive the King's tenderness for his 'knave' even as the Fool is displaced by Edgar to become a more marginal figure.

The 'sage natural, covetous of his Nuncle's attention' Kerrigan finds in Q, and the 'court jester' he sees in F,[73] are combined in both versions of the play. F makes the part more consistent by displacing the Fool from Lear's immediate concern in the later scenes, and expanding his social satire, but does not diminish the complexity of the character. So varying, even conflicting, interpretations of the Fool are to be expected, if a director or critic chooses to stress, or only perceives, one aspect of the Fool's role. The main structural alteration involving the Fool is the omission of the mock-trial in III.6 in F, which goes together with the added lines at IV.6.165, 'Place sins with gold . . .' (so F; usually emended in modern editions to 'Plate sin'; see below, p.204). These lines enhance the dual role of Lear here, where he takes over, as it were, the role of the Fool, both personal and general, at once mad or simple-minded and lucidly rational and satiric, speaking 'matter, and impertinency mixed', as Edgar observes (IV.6.174); and as first Lear, then Kent acted as 'feeds' to the Fool, so now Gloucester takes on that function, cueing Lear's commentary. There is no need for the Fool in the last acts, and Shakespeare allows him to dirft out of existence, incidentally, and in Lear's last speech, even as the old King himself passes away. The opening words of Lear's last speech, 'And my poor fool is hang'd', are usually taken to refer to Cordelia, 'fool' being used as a term of endearment, but they also remind us of the character, and gather him into Lear's overwhelming sense of loss, 'No, no, no life'.

Goneril and Regan

I have commented at length on the Fool because the changes in his role are complicated and affect a puzzling character. The other main differences between Q and F are also significant, but can be dealt with more briefly. Some adjustments to the dialogue of Goneril and Regan in Acts I and II are important in modifying their roles. In

1.3.16–26, Goneril's uncomprising stance towards her father in Q is qualified in F by the omission of her insulting lines (printed as prose in Q) beginning

> Idle old man
> That still would manage those authorities
> That he hath given away, now by my life
> Old fools are babes again . . .

The softening of her personal hostility towards Lear here allows more prominence to her complaint about the riotous behaviour of his retinue of knights, a complaint with which this scene opens. When she enters to encounter Lear in 1.4, her anger is directed in Q and in F against Lear's 'insolent retinue' (line 202), and his disordered and debauched train (241–9); but F adds another two speeches not in Q for Goneril at lines 322–33, who again protests about the hundred troublesome knights. A further speech on the 'riots' of Lear's followers is added for Regan at II.4.141 in F, so that the overall effect is to provide Goneril and Regan with more reasonable cause for their attitude towards their father, since they perceive his retinue as a real threat to peace and order. Their added lines emphasize the kind of behaviour reported in 1.3 ('Did my father strike my gentleman . . .?'), and shown in 1.4, where Lear does strike Oswald, and Kent trips him up.

The war with France

In Q Kent reports as early as III.1.30–42 that the French have secretly invaded England: 'from France there comes a power / Into this scattered kingdom', and they are ready to 'show their open banner'. Gloucester refers to a force as 'landed' at III.3.13, pointing again to a French invasion (the word is changed to the more ambiguous 'footed' in F). At IV.2.56 Goneril calls on Albany to fight because 'France spreads his banners in our noiseless land', and in IV.3 Kent reports that the King of France has returned home leaving his Marshal in charge of his forces in England. Again, in Q, Albany distinguishes between the French as invaders and Lear, and leads his army against the French, not the old King: 'It touches us, as France invades our land . . .' (V.1.25). All these references were changed or omitted in F, and this led Gary Taylor[74] to argue that in effect we have two different versions of the war in *King Lear*, the Quarto firmly stressing an invasion of England by French forces, the Folio clouding the issue and giving more prominence to the war as civil dissension between rival British factions. Although some notable references to France are omitted from F (as by the excision of the entire scene, IV.3), enough remain still to make it clear in F as well as in Q that Cordelia arrives at Dover at the head of a French army. In both Q and in F Cornwall says at III.7.2 that 'the army of France is landed'; at IV.4.25 (IV.3.25 F), Cordelia, responding to a report that 'the British powers are marching hitherward', tells us that 'great France' has taken pity on her sorrow for Lear, and provided her with an army; Oswald refers to Edmund at IV.6.250 (IV.5.250 F) as being with the 'British party' (Q) or 'English party' (F); and Lear wakes at IV.7.76 (IV.6.76 F) to imagine he is in France. The stage directions in F, but not in Q, call for a display of 'Colours' to accompany not only the entry of Edmund and Regan with their forces (V.1.0), and the arrival of Albany, Goneril and their army (V.1.17), but also the entry a little later of Lear and Cordelia leading their army (V.2.0). In the entry at V.2 in Q it seems that Cordelia, holding her father by the hand, follows on after her 'powers' have marched over the stage, whereas in F Lear and Cordelia are at the head of their 'Soldiers', and the 'Colours' shown by them would presumably be those of France, perhaps echoing a display of a French coat of arms or banner when the King of France enters in the opening scene. Thus the loss of some references to France in F does not bring about a radical change; indeed the omission of some verbal allusions is perhaps more than compensated for in the use of colours to provide a visual emphasis as the various armies march over the stage in the last act.

Pathos

In the second half of the play Q has much more emphasis than F on suffering and the generation of pity. Lear's mock-trial of his daughters is followed by the commentary (III.6.97–115) of Kent and Edgar on suffering and fellowship in misery:

> When we our betters see bearing our woes,
> We scarcely think our miseries our foes.
> Who alone suffers, suffers most i'th'mind,
> Leaving free things and happy shows behind . . .

Attention is focussed on the 'pain' of Lear, with Edgar's quasi-choric rhyming lines soliciting our pity for him. In III.7 the lines expressing the sympathy of the servants who seek to help the blinded Gloucester are present only in Q, as is Albany's denunciation of Goneril and Regan in IV.2.31–50, 'Tigers, not daughters, what have you per-form'd . . .' The whole of IV.3 is found only in Q, a scene in which Cordelia is described as weeping 'The holy water from her heavenly eyes' in pity for her father, as opposed to the cruelty of his other 'dog-hearted daughters'. Then Q alone has the lines (V.3.205–22) in which Edgar expatiates on the sufferings of Kent and reports Kent's 'piteous tale' of Lear and him. In all these passages unique to Q we are invited to have compassion for suffering, as our sympathies are channelled and pity roused for Lear, Gloucester, Kent and Cordelia. They may have been omitted in revision because they are emotion-ally coercive in a way the play generally is not.

Edgar, Albany, Kent

All these characters have larger roles in Q than in F, with more stress on moralizing and quasi-choric commentary by them. Albany has a special importance at IV.2.31–69 in Q, where his vision of potential anarchy ('Humanity must perforce prey on itself / Like monsters of the deep') as the consequence of the barbarity of Goneril and Regan, tempered by his faith that 'the heavens' will punish human offences, creates a sense of horror, turning Goneril into a 'fiend'. Albany's role is also enhanced in V.1, where he announces in Q that he fights only against the French, not against Lear, and where Edmund defers to him – 'Sir you speak nobly', and 'I shall attend you presently at your tent' (V.1.28,33) – in lines present only in Q. In Q too Albany is given the last speech in the play, appropriately since in relation to the French invasion he is the surviving prince in England by right of marriage. His status in F is less clear, since he is there embroiled in what looks more like a civil war, and the final speech is given to Edgar. In Q Edgar has an expanded role notably in III.6, in the mock-trial and in his lines on Lear's suffering, and in V.3, in his long account of his meeting with Kent. This speech (V.3.205–22) draws extra attention to Kent, whose role in Q is much enlarged by the dialogue he has with a Gentleman in IV.4.3, a scene omitted in F.

Lear and Cordelia

F makes significant changes to Lear's opening speeches in Act I, and to this final words in Act V. At the beginning of the play F adds a few lines for Lear which explain his motives in dividing the kingdom; in these lines (1.1.40–5; 49–50), Lear announces his retirement, his intention to 'Unburthen'd crawl toward death', and his desire to prevent 'future strife' as he divests himself of 'rule, / Interest of territory, cares of state'. All of these remarks are ironic in relation to his subsequent inability to relinquish authority, but might be seen as softening a little the impression of absolute domination and arbitrary use of power conveyed more strongly by the text in Q. The additions in F here also announce the underlying potency of the theme of death, which is what Lear and Gloucester have in mind, and indeed, later on actively desire. This desire is sustained at the end in Q, where the line 'Break heart, I prithee break' (V.3.313) is spoken by Lear, as it were, to himself, whereas in F it is given to Kent. Moreover, in Q Lear's previous speech ends, 'pray you undo this button, thanke you sir, O,o,o,o', as, groaning or sighing, he faints, and recovers only to wish for death. In F by contrast Lear's last spoken lines are

> Do you see this? Look on her? Look her lips,
> Look there, look there.

Here he appears to think that after all Cordelia may be alive, so that his final moments have a quite different emphasis, allowing for the possibility that he dies in the joyful delusion that Cordelia remains alive; so the F text makes his death more richly nuanced than in Q, though in both Q and F death comes as a release from suffering, a kind of bitter benefit. Lear's seeking death in Q may be linked with the passage, also found only in Q, in which Kent anticipates his life's end at IV.7.95–6:

> My poynt and period will be throughly wrought,
> Or well, or ill, as this day's battle's fought.

The revisions to the part of Cordelia in the opening scene are small but significant, exacerbating the force of the confrontation between her and her father, and diminishing somewhat the sense that she is his best-loved child. F adds '*Lear.* Nothing? *Cor.* Nothing' to the dialogue between them, and changes 'Although the last, not least in our dear love' (Q) to

> Although our last and least: to whose young love
> The vines of France, and milk of Burgundy
> Strive to be interest. (F)

Later scenes also diminish the impact of Cordelia in F, notably the omission from F of v.3, which includes Kent's report of her weeping for her father. It has been claimed that the Cordelia who 'exerts a powerful and active presence in the Quarto is revised to become incidental and subordinate in the Folio',[75] and this is largely true in Acts III and IV; but it does not then follow that in Act v 'the active Cordelia becomes the passive companion in the Folio, led by her father rather than leading him by the hand', for it is Cordelia who insists on pushing her father into fighting, under the colours of France (see below, pp. 206–7).[76] The Cordelia of the Folio is a less prominent figure than in the Quarto, but also stronger and tougher, and not likely to be thought of simply as an emblem of holinesss and pity.

If we acknowledge that there are numerous small changes that seem indifferent in their effect, and are not easily explained, in *King Lear* especially, and if we allow for errors creeping in in the printing-house, it is still reasonable to suppose that such careful splicing as if often shown in the changes made in *King Lear* and *Hamlet* must have been done by the author. In *King Lear* such minute but deliberate alterations as reassigning the two words 'Lear's shadow' to the Fool instead of to Lear himself also would seem to point to authorial intervention. In the case of *Hamlet*, the changes made in the F text speed up the action, and give it more directness and force, and the omission from the later part of the play of a long soliloquy and of other speeches in which Hamlet explains his motives results in the loss of some interesting lines, but enhances the sense of mystery about Hamlet himself, and complicates the pattern of relationships. In *King Lear* the changes in F are more detailed and more extensive, and some may be the kind of indifferent variants that tend to occur when any author goes over his writing, such as 'Shut your mouth' (F) for 'Stop your mouth' (Q), or 'Thou hast spoken right' (F) for 'Thou hast spoken truth' (Q), both in v.3. Many of the changes, however, work to effect a coherent reshaping of some aspects of the play, such as the omission of the mock-trial episode in III.6, avoiding duplication with another mock-trial in IV.6, where additional lines are neatly interwoven to strengthen Lear's new sense of injustice in the

world. One small modification here is in the line 'Through tattered
clothes great vices do appear' (F), a revision of 'Through tattered
rags small vices do appear'(Q), a change that clarifies the point that
the vices of the poor are treated as great, while the rich and powerful
escape; it also connects with the added lines, where the word 'rags' in
Q is given a new context in F that strengthens the whole passage:

> Place sins with gold,
> And the strong lance of justice, hurtless breaks:
> Arm it in rags, a pigmy's straw does pierce it.

At the same time, the reworking of *King Lear* is not so thorough as to
mean that we have to think of two plays; some characters, notably
the three daughters, Cordelia, Goneril and Regan, are made more
complex, less simply good or bad; a good deal of choric commentary
is omitted, reducing the moralizing effect that Edgar, Albany and
Kent have in Q; some revisions again streamline the action and
avoid duplications; and some subtle changes, like those to Lear
himself at the beginning and end, complicate the mood and enrich
the significance of events. I therefore prefer the Folio text of both
plays, while recognizing that what we have are reading versions of
both plays, and that there is good reason for readers to be interested
in the process by which the plays developed as this is reflected in the
Quarto texts.[77]

CHAPTER 5

Hamlet, King Lear *and art*

LET'S RESTATE THE PROBLEM

Hamlet and *King Lear* raise in an acute form the question whether it is possible to think of either play in aesthetic terms, since both exist in two versions that appear to have 'authority'. Criticism as usually practised at the present time is almost entirely concerned with meanings or interpretation, and a good deal of effort has been expended on differentiating between the meanings of the two texts of *King Lear*; Shakespeare's revision of this play, it is claimed, has given us in effect two different plays, in which the roles of Albany and the Fool, for example, change considerably between Quarto and Folio, and a French invasion of England in one text is said to turn into a civil war in the other, and the changes could drastically affect interpretation. Many other authors have, of course, revised their work, and the existence of more than one version of a poem like Wordsworth's *The Prelude*, or variant endings of a novel like *Great Expectations*, or a play like *Rosencrantz andGuildenstern are Dead*, raises questions about the integrity of these as works of art. On what grounds may one version be privileged over another? The author's latest reworkings may in each case seem to some critics inferior to an earlier version. The change of the ending, as in the reworking by Dickens of the last pages of *Great Expectations*, or the cutting of the last two pages or so from all editions of *Rosencrantz and Guildenstern are Dead* after the first, might seem especially important in relation to the shaping of the work, and the reader's sense of closure: do Pip and Estella come together for good, or part for ever? Does the cycle of events come to an end in Stoppard's play, or start all over again? The question is relevant to *King Lear*, which likewise has variant endings.

From the perspective of the sheer scope of a novel like *Great Expectations*, a change in the final pages may not, on the other hand, seem all that significant, compared with the problem of Wordsworth's poem, which evolved from a two-book version through a recension in five books to a thirteen-book manuscript and a fourteen-book posthumously published text. In modern editions, like the Norton Critical Edition, it can be studied as a text in process of becoming. The very idea of a text in process, as presented at its most complex in the Gabler edition of James Joyce's *Ulysses*,[1] may marginalize, if not jettison altogether, the idea of the novel or poem as a work of art, since it focusses attention on often minute differences between versions and shifts in nuances of meaning, so distracting attention from the work as a whole. The case of a play is still more complicated by its nature as a basis for a script to be used in the theatre; the novel or poem exists for most people only as words on a page to be read in private. Indeed, it has become a commonplace of recent post-structuralist criticism to deny, especially in relation to Shakespeare, the authority of the dramatist as creator of a play, and to claim that 'a piece of Elizabethan theatre was a collaborative creation' between the author, the company of actors, those who worked for the stage, and the audience.[2]

Consideration of a play as art has been sidetracked further by the post-structuralist attack on the authority of the text. So the text of a play may be conceived in Barthesian terms as a 'score', inviting the reader to bring it into being; or we may be told that the critics in effect creates the text by putting its meaning into play, so that post-structuralism 'grants readers the right to ring endless changes on a text', and no text is complete in itself: 'No longer are readers expected to stand back before the accomplishments of a remote and godlike author; instead they must enter in, fully and responsibly, to render intelligible a text that remains deliberately unfinished.'[3] The literary work, it can then be claimed, exists only as the 'collective interpretation of successive generations of readers'.[4] It is a short step from this position to the assertion that all forms of literary activity, whether fictive or critical, 'become indistinguishable and are experienced only as forms of production'.[5] If all texts are indistinguishable in value, and the work of literature has no privileged status, then there is no possibility of an aesthetic of literature. As far as Shakespeare is concerned, the recognition that he probably revised some of his most powerful plays might seem to go far to re-establish the authority of the dramatist and make it possible to consider his intentions in revising; but in fact it has provided further ammunition for those who would dismantle the authority of the text. The possibilities for reworking in the playhouse, the idea of Shakespeare collaborating with the company in making alterations, perhaps cutting a soliloquy because Burbage was overburdened, or allowing actors playing clowns to improvise and add material of their own, and the sense that each performance was different from the previous one, have all contributed to the current enthusiasm for treating a play-text not as a work by a dramatist, but as a product of cultural forces. In this view, a play is to be thought of as made actual in a social event, a theatrical performance, which is always collaborative:

Shakespearean texts are produced by a multitude of determinations that exceed a criticism bent on controlling the text or assigning it determinate meanings or structures. Although all we have to go on are the texts, we must go on knowing that they do not make the Shakespearean text proper. No one can own the text. No one can clean it up.

The printed Quartos and the Folio, it follows, in attempting to 'monumentalize and stabilize Shakespeare offer instead the counterfeit properties of the Shakespearean text'.[6]

This is a somewhat startling pronouncement, given that the printed texts are the only traces of the plays we possess; but if the implied claim for a radical indeterminacy be allowed, then critics who argue in traditional ways for a 'determinate structure' of a play as a work of art come under attack as seeking to control, or, in current jargon, to 'police' the text. A corollary to this kind of argument is the abolition of the authority of the dramatist, who becomes a function, in Foucaultian terms, by which discourses are known, an ideological product of society.[7] The idea of the author is displaced behind the concept of the work as produced by cultural forces, so that it becomes possible to dismiss the very idea of the author, and to deconstruct the 'Shakespeare myth'.[8] The effort to do this proceeds by exposing the way Shakespeare has acquired a special cultural authority in Britain and the United States over the last two centuries as a teacher and philosopher. It also examines the way certain of his plays have been used in the past as instruments of educational policy or political propaganda. Older criticism may then be presented as engaged in a kind of conspiracy to maintain this cultural authority; and textual critics and editors who have sought to establish texts of the plays are presented as engaged on 'A project which seeks to award those texts the status of holy writ'.[9]

The story of the application of modern bibliographical and textual criticism to Shakespeare is thus part of a larger narrative in which Shakespeare was transformed from a popular author, whose plays were part of the staple fare of the popular theatres that provided entertainment for the growing populations of the nineteenth century, into the supreme poet of an élitist culture centred in specialized theatres for the educated located in larger cities, in colleges and universities.[10] But the two-pronged attack on the idea of the Shakespearian text, firstly by deprivileging it in general terms as no more significant or valuable than any other form of discourse, and secondly by treating it as a product of collaborative social forces in the theatre of Shakespeare's age, has opened the way to demonizing textual critics who have sought to tease out an accurate text of the plays. If plays are to be thought of as 'routinely adapted and rewritten against a horizon of ephemeral theatrical performances',[11] then the idea of establishing a final text may be pilloried as 'pathetic and perhaps downright ludicrous'.[12] Such demonization ignores the fact that editors during the twentieth century, especially in such landmark editions as the New Arden and now the Oxford and New Cambridge editions, have sought to do away with the accretions, interventions, errors and bowdlerizations of earlier editions, in the effort to achieve not an ideal text, but one as accurate as possible, and based on the earliest printed versions. For many of Shakespeare's plays, there is only the text as printed in the Folio, and for all the emphasis now on the plays as ephemeral productions collaboratively staged, hardly any traces remain of performance for most of the plays, except in occasional notation of actors' names, or in some kinds of stage direction, or in small textual interventions, like Hamlet crying 'Oh Vengeance!', that may derive from the playhouse;[13] and all these traces were first pointed out by editors and textual critics.

The recognition that the surviving texts of a handful of plays that were printed in Quarto and in Folio versions show evidence of Shakespeare revising his work makes no essential difference to the question of textual authority. It is true that for a long time textual critics were seduced by the mirage of a single text that would be closest to the lost original of the author, and so supposed that printers' errors or playhouse interpolations and cuts could alone

account for the differences between the variant texts of plays like
Hamlet and *King Lear*, not merely corruptions, substitutions, misreadings and the like, but also substantive changes that are neatly
dovetailed into the verse pattern, as well as what look like major
authorial cuts or additions. Now most editions of such plays still
conflate the available texts, since editors are reluctant to omit
anything that seems authentically Shakespearian. It is probably no
coincidence that the realization that Shakespeare revised these
works emerges at roughly the same time as post-structuralist attacks
on the concept of the author and the text. Both the emphasis on
revision and the dismantling of the author and text became fashionable as there was a pronounced shift to extreme right-wing governments in Britain and in the United States, and perhaps we may see
here a transference into the realm of literary criticism and theory of a
deep anxiety about and resistance to all forms of external authority.
In relation to this shift, there is a certain irony in the cultural
authority now accorded to figures like Barthes and Foucault, who
energized the devalidation of the concept of the author, and even
greater irony in the care those who are most dismissive of the notion
of establishing the text of a play lavish on establishing the texts of
their critical theories.

If the author and the work are seen as constructs, constituted and
endlessly reconstituted by successive critics, or alternatively envisaged as products of a particular set of historical conditions, then
again there is no place for an aesthetic criticism. For either formal
considerations become an aspect of social and political concerns, or
they are devalued along with the author and the text. But if there is
not something in the notion of the 'exceptional subject' and in
'artistic values',[14] why, we may ask, do those who pour scorn on the
Shakespeare myth, and who are most concerned to devalue the
author and dismantle the authority of the text, devote so much
attention to Shakespeare? In their efforts to decanonize Shakespeare, they help to re-establish him at the head of the canon; and in
their efforts to dismantle his authority as a writer, they in effect
substitute claims for their own authority as critics, but still with
reference to Shakespeare. If all texts are equal in value, and none are
privileged, then the critic has no reason to give more attention to
Shakespeare's plays than to any other works; but the critics who
strenuously argue for levelling all texts as products of cultural forces,
or dismiss the idea of the author as a construct, thereby privileging

the critic over the dramatist, often focus their attention exclusively on Shakespeare. Evidently there must be some other factor that makes Shakespeare's plays so important.

Here it might seem possible to appeal to the idea of complexity of meaning, if it were not that this notion has been undermined in several ways. The analysis of the critical reception of *Hamlet* and *King Lear* in Chapters 2 and 3 shows that critics do to some extent produce the meanings of the plays in the context of their own age, and can switch rapidly, for instance, from seeing *King Lear* as a play of redemption in the 1950s to reading it as a play of despair in the 1960s. Post-structuralist theory underscores the importance of the reader or critic as creator of meaning by demolishing the concept and authority of the dramatist. The current emphasis on the play-text as a script for performances which change all the time, and are only realized in the ephemeral and shifting conditions of the stage, further tends to weaken any notion of a body of meanings inherent in the text. Then again, the destabilizing effect of a recognition that Shakespeare might rework a play to create more than one version would also seem to do away with the idea of the play as embodying a determinate set of meanings.

Yet I think the issue of artistic value, and its relation to meaning, needs to be reconsidered, for through all the changes in critical fashion and through all the reinterpretations of Shakespeare's plays, one constant feature has been the unstated assumption that Shakespeare deserves special attention; and this implies that his plays are notable artistic achievements. Recent onslaughts on long-cherished critical practices have only confirmed the importance of Shakespeare. The same arguments that have undermined the idea of a play as possessing inherent meanings could also be applied to the concept of artistic quality or value, and these arguments need to be countered. In addition, there is a problem in relation to works of art that have been reworked, some many times, by artists or writers, in determining whether one version is superior to another, and whether the very existence of multiple versions does not further undermine any consideration of a literary work in terms of art. In the case of a play, there is a further problem in that if it is to be thought of as a performance script – and all productions differ from one another – then there could only be an aesthetic of each performance. I am arguing, however, that the printed texts of *Hamlet* and *King Lear* exist as works to be read, and that they were not originally performed in their entirety, as far as we know, and have rarely been since they were written, so that we do not have Shakespeare's 'performance scripts'. I would therefore like to consider whether any claim can be made for an artistic shaping of these plays that allows for the possibility of varying concepts of their form in relation to the possibility of varying, even contradictory, interpretations of their meaning.

SHAKESPEARE UNDER ATTACK

Until recently little attention was given to the elevation of Shakespeare into a massive cultural authority in Britain and America towards the end of the nineteenth century. As early as 1848, H. N. Hudson advised his hearers in his popular lectures that Shakespeare's works provided 'a far better school of virtuous discipline than half the moral and religious books which are now put into the hands of youth'.[15] Hudson anticipated the later institutionalization of Shakespeare in schools, colleges and universities as a great moral teacher and philosopher, whose works needed to be studied for their educational value, but could only be understood through special training. In Britain, according to Ian Hunter,[16] the rise of English studies 'produced an ethical technology directed to forming the moral attributes of a citizenry, but a technology also capable of forming a stratum of ethical exemplars from this citizenry: the teachers of English'. Subsequently, 'from the 1920s, criticism as it had been practised by Johnson and Coleridge, Kames and Arnold, began to be taught in colleges and universities as a means of training teachers'.[17] If the response to literature so cultivated was aesthetic in so far as the literary text was conceived as autonomous, allowing 'the discipline of an aesthetic self-culture to enter the pedagogical apparatus',[18] the aim was moral, as the critic or teacher offered a normative way of reading the text against which the student could measure and correct his ethical understanding. The teaching of Shakespeare also had a political colouring, in so far as it was related to the teaching of history and geography, which remained imperialist and patriotic in Britain until well after the Second World War.[19] In the United States, the teaching of Shakespeare had a political significance as well as an ethical one, as a force to weld together into a nation a diverse mass of immigrants; so J. Q. Adams commented in his dedication speech at the opening of the Folger Shakespeare Library in Washington in 1932:

Fortunately, about the time the forces of immigration became a menace to the preservation of our long-established English civilization, there was initiated throughout the country a system of free and compulsory education for youth ... As a result, whatever the racial antecedents, out of the portals of the schools emerged, in the second or third generation, a homogeneous people ... On the side of the humanities, that schooling concerned itself mainly with the English language and literature ... in our fixed plan of elementary schooling, [Shakespeare] was made the cornerstone of cultural discipline ... the chief object of their study and veneration. This study and veneration did not stop with the grammar and high schools; it was carried into the colleges and universities, and there pursued with still more intensity.[20]

If criticism 'first entered the pedagogical domain not as the ... vehicle of "man's" cultural realisation, but as the source of a special social personality – the ethical exemplar – required by the tactics of moral administration',[21] it has become a self-sustaining industry within the universities. Shakespeare criticism is produced by academics for consumption by their colleagues and students, and is not merely a function of their pedagogy, but a means of obtaining professional esteem and career enhancement. Post-structuralist criticism has, of course, abandoned any notion of a normative reading of a text, since it claims that 'interpretation is the source of texts, facts, authors, and intentions';[22] so Stanley Fish can congratulate himself: 'No longer is the critic the humble servant of texts whose glories exist independently of anything he might do; it is what he does, within the constraints embedded in the literary institution, that brings texts into being and makes them available for analysis and appreciation.'[23] If what Fish calls the 'interpretive community' is the source of meaning in a work, rather than the text itself, so that 'the literary work exists only as the collective interpretation of successive generations of readers',[24] then the authority of both author and text vanishes, and the critic is freed from a humility towards the text as a source of ethical or political guidance, or even of aesthetic pleasure. Post-structuralist criticism has used this freedom as a means of invading and taking over other disciplines, using techniques drawn from sociology, social and political history, philosophy, cultural anthropology and psychoanalysis to energize its activities. The interpretive communities thus established, such as the deconstructionist, new historicist, cultural materialist and feminist, have opened up new perspectives on Shakespeare, but they each tend to write as if possessing a special access to truth. What they have in common is a rejection of textual authority and of aesthetic principles, since 'whatever they do, it will only be interpretation in another guise because, like it or not, interpretation is the only game in town'.[25]

The demolition of Shakespeare as a cultural idol has in many ways been healthy, as through it we have been enabled to realize the extent to which Shakespeare may have been used in the United States as 'an instrument of WASP cultural domination', and in Britain as a cultural authority associated with an imperialist ideology.[26] Post-structuralist criticism is sensitized to and problematizes issues such as gender, power, patriarchy, misogyny, and the treatment of the mob in Shakespeare's plays. Older critics wrote with a confidence that they were correcting the inadequacies of their predecessors in a process of paring away error in order to arrive at an always deferred final determinate reading. Their teaching was often coercive in exerting pressure on students to accept one interpretation as superior to others, if not definitive. This is exemplified in recent critical editions of *Hamlet*, for instance, such as that by Harold Jenkins (1982), who takes it for granted that the play 'imposes on its hero the duty of revenge', and that Hamlet can be categorized as 'a man with a deed to do' who fails to carry it out. Jenkins is a learned and sensitive editor, and my concern is not to attack his edition, but rather to illustrate by reference to it the presuppositions of critics who assume that a determinate reading is possible. Jenkins writes with the confidence that he can know what the play is about: 'The essential subject of *Hamlet*, suggested by and focussed in the old story of a son's revenge, is, then, as I see it, the intermingling of good and evil in all life.'[27] The tone of certainty is striking; he has no doubts about what Hamlet's 'duty' is, and he knows what the play is about, what its 'essential subject' is, though this turns out to be rather platitudinous; the mingling of good and evil in life is a commonplace of all kinds of writing. If post-structuralist criticism has abandoned this form of coercion, it has introduced another in that 'interpretive communities' such as the new historicists implicitly seek to persuade that their mode of inquiry is superior to others. Older critics took for granted a traditional post-Kantian concept of a play as possessing an organic artistic unity, but said almost nothing about it, and concentrated on meaning. Post-structuralist critics have, on the whole, dismissed aesthetic issues as irrelevant, and continue to concentrate on interpretation, which is what colleagues and students have come to take for granted as their proper business. Shakespeare as ethical guide has been displaced by Shakespeare as purveyor of knowledge, whether conservative or potentially subversive, as involved in articulating, or questioning, or failing to deal adequately with issues relating to what Stephen Greenblatt calls the 'circulation of social energy'.[28]

One group of critics, the marxists, have continued to grapple with aesthetic questions, which, to their credit, they have always recognized as an important matter. For them a central problem has been to reconcile the conflicting notions that literature 'refracts the generating socio-economic reality',[29] and at the same time possesses some 'trans-historical substance'. Herbert Marcuse, for example, defined aesthetic form 'as the result of the transformation of a given content (actual or historical, personal or social fact) into a self-contained whole'; so art is somehow autonomous in transforming specific social relations, and yet as ideology 'opposes the given society'.[30] Stylization is said to 'reveal the universal in the particular social situation',[31] but how this revelation of the universal is achieved remains a mystery. Terry Eagleton resolves this difficulty by abolishing literature as a category: 'Literature, in the sense of a set of works of assured and unalterable value, distinguished by certain shared inherent properties, does not exist.'[32] For him no work has value in itself, but only as it is construed and interpreted by its readers; and he uses this argument as a starting point for expanding literature to include other 'cultural and social practices'. He also denounces departments of English in universities (meaning presumably that at Oxford where he was teaching, since his description suggests he knows little about what happens elsewhere) as places where Shakespeare's texts 'are hermetically sealed from history, subjected to a sterile critical formalism, piously swaddled with eternal verities and used to confirm prejudices which any moderately enlightened student can perceive to be objectionable'.[33] His swashbuckling polemic is directed towards re-connecting the symbolic with the political, so that his widening of the scope of literature and of criticism aims at the 'development of a counterpublic sphere within which opposition to the administered culture and politics of late capitalism might be nurtured and developed'.[34] He says 'Every literary theory presupposes a certain use of literature', and his use is overtly ideological; the construction of meanings and values by criticism is at the heart of his argument.[35]

Eagleton sees himself as restoring the traditional role of the critic, which, he says, had 'diverse preoccupations' before a narrow and impoverished canon was established; the pursuits of criticism thus 'have no obvious unity beyond a concern with the symbolic processes of social life, and the social production of forms of subjectivity'.[36] Literature would seem then to be restored to its function in the Arnold/Leavis tradition of acting as a 'moral technology', instilling 'specific kinds of value, discipline, behaviour and response in human subjects'.[37] In escaping from one contradiction, that exposed by Marcuse between ideology and aesthetic form, Eagleton reveals another gap: for, on the one hand, he argues that criticism should have political aims, and re-connect 'the symbolic to the political', and, on the other hand, he sees the nature of literature (a term that he allows has to be used for want of a better) as 'a set of ideas, which organises the experience of the subject' to make him 'sensitive, receptive, imaginative, and so on'.[38] Sensitivity, imagination 'and so on' have no necessary connection with political ends. So Eagleton is caught in paradoxes: from his position in one of the élite institutions of the English-speaking world, he excoriates élitism; and though he wants to expand literature to include a range of cultural practices in the media, as well as working-class and minority writing, and though he claims that Shakespeare 'is great literature because the institution constitutes him as such',[39] he nevertheless has contributed to the continuing cultural authority of Shakespeare as a 'great' author by writing two books about him.

If most post-structuralist criticism has no interest in aesthetic issues, since text and author are seen as 'products of interpretation' and interpretation is 'the only game', marxist criticism has trouble in reconciling a recognition that art gives pleasure with a conviction that the function of criticism is political, to 'struggle against the bourgeois state'.[40] Thus its central concern is inevitably with meaning, because 'our judgements on the individual work of art are ultimately social and historical in character',[41] and form is therefore a function of content. Consequently there can be no concept of greatness in literature: Shakespeare is great only because 'the institution constitutes him as such' and 'there is no such thing as literature which is "really" great, or "really" anything, independently of the ways in which that writing is treated within specific forms of social and institutional life'.[42] So there is no room for the idea of a play as a work of art, or as having artistic 'value', and it becomes easy to sneer at the notion of 'priceless artistic values', even if some marxist critics seek to retain a precarious hold on the concept of a literary work as an 'autonomous whole'.[43] Effectively post-structuralist criticism has deconstructed the idea of literature as such by showing that it is impossible to define its boundaries, and by claiming that texts only exist as constituted by readers or by institutions. By absorbing all kinds of writings, and indeed cultural practices in other media, into its critical and pedagogical province, it has, on the one hand, demolished all frontiers and made all writings available as literature; and on the other hand, it has taken over techniques of other areas of study, notably in philosophy and the social sciences, in formulating modes of interpretation that equate all texts as the products of cultural forces.

If all texts are equal, Shakespeare's plays should lose their special status, but in spite of the levelling arguments of those who would abolish the canon and all distinctions between works of literature, his works remain as strongly entrenched as ever in the standard syllabuses of colleges everywhere. No doubt a sense of self-preservation ironically encourages many of those graduate students who are excited by post-structuralist criticism, and who seek a career teaching Renaissance literature in the academy, nonetheless to bring Shakespeare into their dissertations, because they need to be qualified to teach courses on him. But the fact is that Shakespeare retains his wide impact outside the schools and universities, if his plays are not now popular in the sense in which they were in the early nineteenth century. Numerous festivals worldwide draw large audiences to see performances of the plays every year, and filmmakers keep coming back to them, as shown in the recent success of Kenneth Branagh's *Henry V* and Franco Zeffirelli's *Hamlet*. What is it then that gives plays like *Hamlet* and *King Lear* an appeal that so far has proved permanent in our culture?

The attack on Shakespeare in the academy has come from two directions: on the one hand, from critics and theorists who have found a way to establish their superiority to authors and texts, and so enhance their status by colonizing other disciplines for an expansion of their critical activities; and on the other hand from left-wing critics who see in Shakespeare 'the badge of cultural élitism and the instrument of pedagogical oppression',[44] and who, for different reasons, want to abolish the canon and relocate the study of literature as part of wider 'cultural and social practices'.[45] Claims for critical authority are now at issue, rather than for the authority of Shakespeare. As noted earlier, the argument about such matters is conducted in writings by members of a body of teachers and graduate students in colleges and universities for circulation mainly among people like themselves. Theirs is more accurately the 'badge of cultural élitism', for the subject of attack, Shakespeare, remains accessible to and popular among a much wider audience of play-goers and readers. At the same time, it has to be admitted that to go far beyond an immediate enjoyment of the powerful plot-lines of his tragedies demands a level of education and a response to nuances of language that are constitutive of a cultural élite, if a much larger segment of the population than the small intellectual élite within the universities.

'Great' literature tends to appeal to an élite in the sense of an educated minority, and Western societies will continue to have cultural élites who prefer Shakespeare to sitcoms and grand opera to pop music. It is a pity that the word 'élite' has gained currency as a mark of cultural snobbery, and has been invested with a notion of superiority, in opposition to a term like 'popular' (or in a parallel way, 'highbrow' in opposition to 'lowbrow'), signifying inferiority. This is what gives leverage to post-structuralist critics as cultural politicians to attack élitism. But the issue is not really whether Shakespeare's plays are superior to 'popular' art-forms, and there is no reason why both cannot be enjoyed and valued by the same person. It is not élitist to claim for Shakespeare a richness of texture and an emotional and psychological depth that make his plays exceptional among works of literature. Beyond this is the question of what claims can be made about Shakespeare's artistry, a matter which is disregarded as more or less irrelevant in much current criticism. It may be that 'The attempt to locate the power of art in a permanently novel, untranslatable formal perfection will always end in a blind alley',[46] but this formulation is a typical manoeuvre of recent criticism, to set up an Aunt Sally as an easy target, as in the notion of 'formal *perfection*', or 'assured and *unalterable* value', or '*priceless* artistic values.'[47] The language of such phrases betrays an element of contempt, and is deliberately tenden-tious, but nonetheless, their emphasis on concepts of permanence, on unalterable values, etc., invites consideration of the possibility of an aesthetic that would not be locked into immanent or eternal values.

INWARD ILLUSION

Post-structuralist criticism not only dismisses the concept of artistic value, but effectively denies also the concept of mimesis or imitation.[48] If a literary work such as a play is constructed by its readers or viewers, and endlessly reconstituted in this way, then it cannot be pinned down as an art of representation or imitation. The commonplace of Shakespeare's age, that a play was 'the imitation of life, the glass of custom, and the image of truth', would seem irrelevant.[49] This is Thomas Heywood's formulation, but the idea, attributed to Cicero and known from Donatus, was echoed by many others. Cicero's three terms are not equivalent, but they tended to coalesce in a common emphasis on a play as a picture or image reflecting life as a mirror: 'View but his picture in this tragic glass', says the Prologue to Marlowe's *Tamburlaine*, and there were no doubt many then who assumed unthinkingly that this is what plays made possible. The most famous expression of the idea occurs in Hamlet's advice to the Players, where he describes the purpose of playing as to 'hold as 'twere the mirror up to nature; to show virtue her feature, scorn her own image, and the very age and body of the time his form and pressure' (III.2.22–4). Hamlet's neo-classical standards, however, are presented ironically in relation both to his own behaviour and to that of the Players who are about to present 'The Mousetrap'. For on the one hand, Hamlet does not follow his own recommendations; he objects to actors who strut and bellow, and to clowns who speak more than is set down for them, but he struts and bellows himself when, for instance, he falls to 'cursing like a very drab' in denouncing Claudius (II.2.588), and if anyone in the play within the play speaks more than is set down for him, it is Hamlet, who takes on the role of clown, and intervenes boisterously. On the other hand, the Players performing 'The Mousetrap' do not follow Hamlet's advice, and Lucianus, making his 'damnable faces' (III.2.253) at the audience, ostentatiously disregards it. Moreover, the play within the play fails to frighten Claudius by mirroring his deed; he watches the dumb-show and much of the playlet with indifference, and is alarmed finally, it seems, less by the image it presents of what happened in the past, the murder of old

Hamlet, than by the image it offers of what as yet is hypothetical, when Hamlet identifies Lucianus as nephew to the king, and 'The Mousetrap' suddenly seems to embody Hamlet's threat to kill his uncle, Claudius.[50]

It can be shown from other of his works that Shakespeare did not simply accept the common formula that plays imitated and reflected life. If some characters think of painting or art as mirroring nature, and providing 'a pretty mocking of the life', or 'the life as lively mock'd as ever',[51] Shakespeare also understood that the artist need not merely reflect or rival nature, but could outdo her:

> Look when a painter would surpass the life
> In limning out a well-proportioned steed,
> His art with nature's workmanship at strife,
> As if the dead the living should exceed,
>   So did this horse excel a common one,
>   In shape, in courage, colour, pace and bone.
>
> (*Venus and Adonis*, 289–94)

Similarly, the Painter's portrait of Timon of Athens is 'artificial', yet 'livelier than life' (*Timon*, I.1.37–8); but the dramatist's perception of art goes beyond 'life' here, for Timon is depicted in the presence of the wholly imaginary goddess Fortune, so that the painting is doing something more than improve on life.[52] Perhaps Shakespeare's most sophisticated expression of artistic possibilities occurs in *The Rape of Lucrece*, where Lucrece studies a painting of the Greeks and Trojans confronting each other before the walls of Troy. In this 'skilful painting' (line 1367), the dead are given 'liveless life' (1374), and the painter 'laboured with his skill / To hide deceit' (1506–7) in depicting Sinon, so that he both expresses and conceals, leaving much to the imagination:

> For much imaginary work was there, –
> Conceit deceitful, so compact, so kind,
> That for Achilles' image stood his spear
> Gripped in an armed hand: himself behind
> Was left unseen, save to the eye of mind:
>   A hand, a foot, a face, a leg, a head
>   Stood for the whole to be imagined.   (1422–8)

Here Shakespeare shows an understanding of the 'necessary incompleteness of all two-dimensional representation', and of the stimulus to the imagination of what is partially displayed, a notable effect of illusion in art, for, as E. H. Gombrich has shown, even the most naturalistic of paintings leaves something to the imagination.[53] Shakespeare also had a lively sense of the possible uses of illusion in what he called 'perspective', or what we would now call anamorphosis, as when Duke Orsino in *Twelfth Night* is surprised to encounter Viola and Sebastian as look-alikes: 'One face, one voice, one habit, and two persons, / A natural perspective, that is and is not' (v.1.216–17).

In Shakespeare's age it was common for actors and dramatists to be praised for representing characters to the life, as in the well-known elegy on Richard Burbage:[54]

> Oft have I seen him leap into the grave,
> Suiting the person which he seemed to have . . .
> So lively that spectators and the rest
> Of his sad crew, whil'st he but seemed to bleed,
> Amazed, thought even then he died indeed.

In eulogy an actor's highest achievement might be represented as an ability to delude the audience into thinking 'the Personator were the man personated';[55] and the dramatist too might be lauded, as John Fletcher was, for making the audience 'feel / The Players' wounds were true, and their swords, steel!', so that 'the Spectators ran to save the blow'.[56] If such hyperbolic images of audiences confusing a play's action with real life gave vigour to praise of actors and defences of the stage, they also provided those hostile to the theatres, the city authorities and puritan apologists, with ammunition. The Lord Mayor of London complained in 1597 that plays were tainting young people, who copied the 'corruption of manners' they represented and were drawn into 'imitation and not to avoiding the like vices'.[57] The circularity of such arguments, which are still sometimes heard, passed unnoticed. Plays, it was said, represent vices by copying from life, and so the actors are corrupted, 'The *actors*, in whom the earnest care of lively representing the lewd demeanour of bad persons doth work a great impression of waxing like unto them'; and in turn the spectators are corrupted by watching performances, 'the *spectators*, whose manners are corrupted by seeing and hearing such matters so expressed'.[58]

In such attitudes to acting and the stage, the idea of imitation in the drama is taken literally as meaning to copy, picture or mirror life, and there is no room for a play of imagination, for the fantastic, or the exercise of what Shakespeare called the 'conceit deceitful'. Such a naive and unthinking concept of stage-illusion assumes that spectators are taken in by the spectacle, and that the illusion is

complete. The notion that the drama holds the mirror up to life or
nature, and that the audience is deluded into thinking what they see
is real, has had a long life, and survives tenaciously, notably among
would-be censors of the stage.

At the same time, actors in plays do in some sense imitate and
represent imagined personages, so it is worth attending to the efforts
of a philosopher and a critic who has sought to revive a concept of
mimesis in relation to drama. Kendall Walton is concerned with
representational art in general, including verbal representation in
fiction or drama, and he claims[59] that 'It is the function, in any
reasonable sense of the term, of ordinary representational works of
art to serve as props in games of make-believe'; appreciation of art,
then, is largely a matter of playing games with them, and understanding 'what fictional truths it is their function to generate'.
Children who play games are subject to the rules of the game,
whereas onlookers, 'observing the game from without do not think
of themselves as subject to the rules'. Thus 'Appreciation of representational works of art is primarily a matter of participation',
but a participation that has to be psychological or contemplative,
not physical; this is to say that participation stops short of intervention.[60] But it is not clear why the viewer or reader recognizes or
accepts restrictions on participation, and Walton has difficulties
with the notion of the aside to the audience, or direct address to the
reader, techniques that deliberately suspend or violate 'appreci-
ators' participation'. Asides, indeed, are disconcerting in Walton's
argument, as they make for 'moments of interaction, within the
appreciator's game world, between him and one or more of the
work's characters. But only moments. The interaction remains
severely limited.' Indeed, he seems to say that it may be better not
to admit asides at all, even if they constitute one of the 'limitations
on participation' that give the appreciator a 'kind of objective,
"distanced" perspective on the world of his game'.[61] Walton wants
to claim at once a ground for empathy with fictional characters on
the part of the viewer or reader, and an objective perspective that
will enable him to 'concentrate on fictional truths about what the
characters are up to'.[62]

Such a brief summary of part of Walton's argument hardly does
justice to the scope of his book, but serves to indicate some of the
problems it raises. His emphasis is on rational explanation and on
'fictional truth' in art, but it is not clear how this 'truth' relates to

cognition: are we gaining some kind of knowledge through this access to truth, or is a fictional truth merely imaginary? He says early on 'What is true is to be believed; what is fictional is to be imagined', so that a 'fictional truth' appears to be a contradiction in terms. He has trouble with asides or authorial interventions, which contribute to distancing and enable the viewer to consider 'fictional truths', but might seem to disable the notion of empathy; and he hardly considers other built-in distancing features of works of art: the surround or frame in painting, the sequence of chapters bound up in a book one closes at the end, the fixed extent of time in a play – aspects that in their nature cut works of art off from life, and might be thought to disengage them from any form of make-believe. In pursuing the matter of representation in art he is dealing with an important issue, but he seems uninterested in aesthetic questions; for him,

The experience of fictionally facing certain situations, engaging in certain activities, having or expressing certain feelings in a dream or fantasy or game of make-believe is the means by which one achieves insight into one's situation, or empathy for others, or a realization of what it is like to undergo certain experiences and so on.[63]

Here he suggests a cognitive function for art that does not depend on 'fictional truths', though the alternatives proposed leave it uncertain whether the appreciator gains 'insight' about his own self, or merely a fellow-feeling for others.

Some of the same issues are addressed by A. D. Nuttall, who writes from the point of view of a philosopher-critic who is disturbed by the claims of post-modernist criticism. In response to critics who deny any relationship between the text or language and the real world, Nuttall has attempted to construct a sophisticated new theory of imitation, asserting that 'Mimesis successfully conveys the real object in a manner which deepens our experiential knowledge of that object or of like objects.'[64] He avoids the naive assumption that an audience is deluded into supposing an imitation of life is the same as reality by arguing 'not that literary works have nothing to do with knowledge but rather that they have to do with experiential knowledge',[65] so that although he is committed to a concept of 'mimetic truth', he qualifies his claims for realism as reflecting an objective reality by defining this 'truth' as relating to probabilities rather than to facts: 'So long as we remember that fictions involve mediated truth to probabilities rather than immediate truth to specific facts, Shakespeare's plays may properly be seen as a continued feat of minute yet organized accuracy.'[66] But accuracy to what? Can 'accuracy' apply to probabilities? If 'experiential knowledge' relates, as Nuttall says it does, to 'people and things',[67] it would seem that it would have to be measured against some specific reality. His argument is subtle and complex, but fails, as it seems to me, to resolve this problem of the relation of objective 'truth' or 'reality', and of 'knowledge', to works like Shakespeare's plays.

These are large issues, and my concern is more limited. In some sense, the post-structuralist claim is unanswerable, that there is nothing outside the text, that we compose our history and sense of reality in language, and that the 'work' such as a play by Shakespeare has no ontological status, since it exists only as it is realized in performance on the stage or in the mind; equally Nuttall's claims for verisimilitude and the representation in Shakespeare's plays of some kind of objective reality are unanswerable. Perhaps a bridge between these apparently contradictory positions, or at least a deeper understanding of Shakespeare's artistry, can be developed by attending to the nature of dramatic illusion. Nuttall himself says, 'If the critic never enters the dream he remains ignorant about too much of the work',[68] but he does not go on to consider what he calls the 'dream', or how this might affect his theory of mimesis.

I take 'dream' here to point to dramatic illusion, which became an important topic of debate at the end of the eighteenth century, even as major changes in technology were making possible exciting new effects of scenic illusion in the theatres in London through advances in scene-painting and stage lighting, and through such inventions as the eidophusikon, an advance on the magic lantern introduced in 1781, the panorama, invented by Robert Barker in 1796, and the diorama, introduced in 1823.[69] These new techniques made it possible to suggest motion, as in the passage of clouds across the sky, and to create illusions of depth, which, with a new accuracy in scene-painting and use of sets, seemed to one contemporary witness to perfect 'the deception of the scene'.[70] Earlier eighteenth-century writers had been much occupied with the rules of drama, and the validity of the three unities celebrated in French theorizing, rules which seemed superficially to correspond to a concept of drama as a mirror of life. But perceptive critics recognized, even while condemning excessive irregularity or defiance of the rules, that all plays

are likely to contain, in the words of Farquhar, 'several Improbabili-
ties, nay, Impossibilities'.[71] His essay on comedy is especially interesting because of his defence of that master of irregularity, Shakespeare, whose plots, he said, were 'only limited by the Convenience
of Action'.[72] There were others who rejected slavish attempts to obey
the rules, but it was left to Dr Johnson to stimulate real advance in
the concept of illusion.

In his *Preface to Shakespeare* (1765), he was especially severe upon
the unities of time and place, attacking the inadequacy of a simple
conception of imitation as a copy of life:

The objection arising from the impossibility of passing the first hour at
Alexandria, and the next at *Rome*, supposes, that when the play opens the
spectator really imagines himself at *Alexandria*, and believes that his walk to
the theatre has been a voyage to *Egypt*, and that he lives in the days of
Antony and Cleopatra.[73]

If the spectator is so deluded, then, Dr Johnson argued, he can
accept anything, and this struck him as so implausible that he
rejected altogether any possibility of stage-illusion: 'The truth is,
that the spectators are always in their senses, and know, from the
first act to the last, that the stage is only a stage, and that the players
are only players.'[74] This categorical position provoked an immediate
response from William Kenrick, who saw the contradiction in Dr
Johnson's argument, that Shakespeare's plays do not convince the
viewer that he is watching a representation of reality, and yet that
Shakespeare remains the 'poet of nature'.[75] Kenrick tried to distinguish between delusion affecting our belief, and delusion affecting
our emotions, and claimed that 'the deception goes no farther than
the passions, it affects our sensibility but not our understanding'; this
was a more supple argument, but it led him to conceive of the
audience as merely passive, and to think that our 'convulsions of
grief or laughter are purely involuntary'.[76]

Others, like Lord Kames, who thought of the audience in the
theatre as in a 'waking dream', attempted to develop a better
understanding of stage-illusion,[77] and Erasmus Darwin took the
debate a stage further in the prose interludes in *The Botanic Garden*
(1789), by introducing the idea of a voluntary participation by the
audience in what they watch; he wrote, 'if any distressful circum-
stance occur too forceable for our sensibility, we can voluntarily
exert ourselves, and recollect, that the scenery is not real'. So he
thought that we 'alternately believe and disbelieve, almost every

moment, the existence of the objects represented before us' on the stage.[78] It was left to Coleridge, who had read Kames and Darwin and many others who touched on the question of illusion in perception, to develop what remains perhaps the most searching analysis of the issue. In 1808 he wrote two drafts of an introduction to a lecture in which he rejected the common notion that the audience at a play was in a state of 'actual Delusion', and dismissed also Dr Johnson's view that the audience is never deluded. He distinguished between the aim of a painting by Claude, in which, he said, the artist imitates a landscape at sunset, 'but only as a Picture', and the aim of a scenic artist representing a forest in the theatre: 'a Forest-scene is not presented to the Audience as a Picture, but as a Forest'; the first only delights us if we are not deceived into thinking it is real, whereas the second has as 'its very purpose . . . to produce as much Illusion as its nature permits'.[79] All the same, he argues, though children may sometimes be 'deceived by Stage-Scenery', adults are 'no more *deceived*' by it than they are by paintings. It was from this consideration of stage-scenery that he went on to develop his theory of stage-illusion as a 'temporary Half-Faith', which the spectator enters into voluntarily by an act of will, 'because he knows that it is at all times in his power to see the thing as it really is'.[80]

Coleridge came at the problem on the one hand from his reading of earlier critics, and on the other hand from the new developments in stage-scenery and lighting effects in the theatres of his time. It was a concern with stage-scenery that prompted Charles Lamb to write his essay called 'Stage Illusion' (1825), in which he confuses terms and issues even as he starts from what was evidently for him a commonplace: 'A play is said to be well or ill acted in proportion to the scenical illusion produced.'[81] In his writing he seems to use the terms 'stage illusion', 'scenical illusion', and 'dramatic illusion' interchangeably, and his essay is primarily concerned with the effect of the scene presented on the stage, and the way actors should play roles in tragedy and comedy – whether they should break the illusion or not, and what degree of credibility they should seek to maintain. Lamb's confusion of terms persists to this day; it was reinforced by the claims of naturalism in the late nineteenth century to be creating a theatre of illusion, a claim which in turn provoked the attacks on illusion by, for example, Bertolt Brecht, who demanded the 'Removal of Illusion',[82] and by Peter Brook, who appeared to J. L.

Styan to be creating in his 1970 production of *A Midsummer Night's Dream* a theatre of non-illusion.[83] Lamb, Brecht, Brook and Styan were all primarily concerned with scenic illusion, and appear not to have thought much about their use of the term.

The confusion of terms troubled Coleridge, however, who constantly sought to desynonymize them. In a letter written in 1816 he offered an abbreviated and somewhat changed account of what he had said in 1808, proposing what he called a 'true theory of Stage Illusion': he now affirmed that, as in dreams, images and thoughts 'possess a power in and of themselves, independent of that act of the Judgement or Understanding by which we affirm or deny the existence of a reality correspondent to them'.[84] So what started in 1808 as an explanation of the effect on the audience of scenery and scene-painting becomes more ambitiously defined in terms of images and thoughts, and prepares for the famous formulation in *Biographia Literaria* (1817), where, describing his own proposed contribution of 'persons and characters supernatural, or at least romantic', i.e., imaginary or ideal, to *Lyrical Ballads*, he defined his aim as being 'to transfer from our inward nature a human interest and a semblance of truth sufficient to procure for these shadows of imagination that willing suspension of disbelief for the moment, which constitutes poetic faith'.[85] Here Coleridge reworked ideas developed in relation to his continuing concern with the drama of Shakespeare, and applied them more generally to literature. His insistence that we transfer 'from our inward nature' human interest and a semblance of truth is very important as an elaboration of his rebuttal of Dr Johnson, who is again criticized in the 1816 letter for trying to 'persuade us that our Judgments are as broad awake during the most masterly representation of the deepest scenes of *Othello*, as a philosopher would be during the exhibition of a Magic Lanthorn with Punch & Joan'. Coleridge argued here that we voluntarily lend the 'Will to this suspension of one of its own operations (i.e. that of comparison & consequent decision concerning the reality of any sensuous Impression)';[86] in other words, he is concerned to differentiate between scenic illusion, as what painters and actors strive to create on stage, and dramatic illusion, as a process in the mind of the spectator. But he saw too that stage-scenery only produces what illusion 'its nature permits', and that the effect is created by what, in the peroration of a lecture he gave in 1813, he called the 'inward Illusion' in the imagination of the viewer:

O blest is He who not only in the theatre, but in the probationary Play of Human Life, possesses a life & creative joy in his own Heart, which by the Strength of the inward Illusion can supply the defects of the outward scenes – O happy that Actor on the Stage of real Life, for whom the becoming Warmth & honest Fervor of his own Part the daubed Landscapes on the wormeaten Canvas, bloom as a Paradize, & whom the shiftings of the scenes awakens not out of his delightful Vision.[87]

Perhaps too much weight should not be placed upon this flourish at the end of a lecture on *Hamlet*, but it suggests a further dimension to Coleridge's theory of dramatic illusion. In reading or watching a play we fill out and energize in an activity of the imagination the inevitable incompleteness and artifice of the representation, while always remaining aware of the play as play, and as distinct from life.

This 'inward illusion' or temporary half-faith through which the reader or viewer contributes to the recreation of an imaginary world provides a basis for recovering an understanding of Shakespeare's artistry. Each reader or member of the audience transfers an interest from herself in composing her own imagined world, thus accounting for the construction of a variety of meanings, the play of signification dear to post-structuralist criticism; but the idea of 'inward' poetic or dramatic illusion also allows for a text or script, a structure of words, which is objectively there in *Hamlet* and *King Lear*. The play is not merely an 'anthology of performances' without a 'text'; rather each performance or reading of a play requires of the actor, viewer or reader an active involvement and creative input which round out through an activity of mind the dramatist's words and directions. So each enactment or reading will be different, but each will be constructed, with the aid of the 'eye of mind', from the same materials, the reading texts, with theatrical markings in stage directions and the like, which are the source of all interpretations and concepts of Shakespeare's artistry. Coleridge's idea also allows for the delight we take in the breaking of stage or scenic illusion, as in the device of the play within a play, or when characters step out of their roles to speak directly to the audience, as the Fool does with his bawdy joke at the end of 1.5 in *King Lear*:

> She that's a maid now, and laughs at my departure,
> Shall not be a maid long, unless things be cut shorter.

We are not disturbed by such features because we are not committed to 'fictional truth', as Walton conceives it, or to experiential knowledge, in Nuttall's terms, and can accept the playfulness of what Shakespeare called a 'natural perspective'.[88] I use the terms 'playful' or 'playfulness' rather than Walton's word 'game' to indicate not something played according to rules or requiring a notion of make-believe, but rather an active mental involvement by the viewer or reader in a drama or work of art as a recreation that is a source of pleasure and does not involve responsibility on his or her part. We take delight in the breaking of stage or scenic illusion, in the aside to the audience, as we do in discovering that the strange object in Holbein's 'The Ambassadors' can be identified as a skull; for it is part of the playful nature of our relation to a representational work of art that we have a quasi-anamorphic sense of it, as it is both what it seems to be and is not. It is by our own mental activity that we 'complete' the text, the words on the page, the actor's limitations, or the spatter of brushstrokes on the canvas. Because texts need to be 'completed' in this way, they do not need to be thought of as final and permanently fixed in themselves. Works of art have frequently been revised or reworked by the artist, and may exist in several versions, but if the basic structure remains roughly the same, these versions are rightly considered as variants of one work. *Hamlet* and *King Lear* are works on a huge scale, in which the alteration of details, the addition or omission of lines or passages, or a soliloquy, or even in one case a whole scene, may significantly affect the details of interpretation, as such matters as the role of the Fool and the war with France have provoked debate in relation to *King Lear*; but though the changes between Q and F modify the presentation of some characters and events, their impact on the shaping of the play can be seen as one of emphasis or balance. It is often a matter of tightening up or speeding the action, or of giving characters more (Goneril and Regan in F) or less (Kent, Albany and Edgar in F) weight and prominence. Whereas interpretation builds up from particular passages or incidents or images in order to construct an overall meaning, which is inevitably partial, for the play, a concept of artistry begins from the whole as structure or pattern, in which the details may vary considerably, as in variants in a large narrative painting or a long novel, so that it is nuanced differently, but not essentially changed.

Merely in copying out a text writers will change words or phrases, as in copying out his 'Ode to Autumn' Keats alternately wrote 'Drows'd', 'Doz'd' and 'Dased' with the fume of poppies, variants that hardly affect the poem as a whole. Literary texts are, as art, a special case, being made up of words – in the case of a play, thousands of words; and numerous indifferent variants, of the kind represented by the example from Keats, may be found in plays with two early printed texts, like *Othello* and *Troilus and Cressida*.[89] These variants may make, so to speak, subtle differences of shading, but have little effect on the work as a whole. We do not know what led Shakespeare or his associates to make the more substantial revisions in *Hamlet* and *King Lear*, but these too affect possibilities for interpretation more than they do the overall design. Some of the changes are baffling, but the omissions in the Folio *Hamlet* generally streamline the play's narrative flow, while leaving the reasons for Hamlet's behaviour less explicit, and so giving more scope to the imagination of reader or viewer. The changes in the Folio *King Lear* sometimes clarify, as in the opening scene, sometimes seem designed to make the balance of sympathies more even, as in the exchanges between Goneril, Regan and Lear, but more often remove passages that coerce the audience's emotions, so again leaving more to their imagination (see Chapter 4).

Whatever sense we may have of artistic coherence or quality is an aspect of the 'inward illusion' in which we fill out the play's signals in our imagination. Just as we contribute to creating meanings, and may differ in our interpretations, so we contribute to creating a sense of artistic coherence, which is not immanent or inherent within the text,[90] but only exists as perceived by the viewer or reader through his or her active involvement with it. This explains why some find coherence in works which others see as artistically unsatisfactory, as frequently happens in responses to new plays or works of art. Our sense of unity in a play like *King Lear* is fostered by our imaginative recreation of the trajectory of an action that unfolds in time, and of the way the narrative shape seems to gather momentum as it leads to a conclusion that in retrospect seems inevitable. It was this sense that Romantic critics transferred to the play itself, in claiming organic unity as a property of the text. Coleridge in fact had a more complex concept of artistic unity; while he followed Schlegel in attributing 'organic form' to Shakespeare's plays,[91] at the same time he internalized the sense of unity as a mental experience in the viewer or reader. It was a concept he developed in relation to his thinking about dramatic illusion, which led him to argue that 'the aesthetic experience depended upon a willing and active awareness of illusion as illusion'.[92] Hence the idea of the 'beautiful Whole' is in 'the mind of the spectator'.[93] Unity is thus what the reader or viewer capable of experiencing the play is enabled to perceive. I say 'capable of experiencing the play' because some general understanding of the language of the play is necessary for anyone to experience it.

KNOWLEDGE, MEANING, ARTISTIC FORM

What then is the relation between meaning and unity if both are in some measure constructed by the reader or viewer? Before I deal directly with this issue, something needs to be said about the problem of knowledge. Ian Hunter has shown how the teaching of English literature developed by taking on 'the role of a repository of ethical experiences, and thereby absorb[ed] the key functions of moral training';[94] but as criticism took over the function of moral training, and has tended to displace literature at the centre of literary pedagogy, so criticism 'is pulled in one direction by its role as a moral discipline, and in another by its mission to take its place as a knowledge alongside the other human sciences'.[95] Post-structuralist criticism in the academy has sought to validate itself as one of the human sciences, invading others in the process, in order to substantiate a central role for departments of literature as concerned with the same sort of knowledge as other sciences. The position is stated with a certain crude vigour by Robert Scholes:

interpretation is not a pure skill but a discipline deeply dependent upon knowledge. It is not so much a matter of generating meanings out of a text as it is a matter of making connections between a particular verbal text and a larger cultural text, which is the matrix or master code that the literary text both depends upon and modifies.[96]

For the marxist, the role of criticism becomes more specifically that of 're-connecting the symbolic to the political',[97] and thus it seems necessary to achieve a 'radical contextualising of literature which eliminates the old division between literature and its "background", text and context'.[98] The pursuit of theory and of context converts the study of literature into philosophy, history or cultural studies, and so establishes a claim that it deals in knowledge. In his spirited attempt at a critique of post-structuralism, A. D. Nuttall would reinstate a concept of mimetic realism and focus on the text, but he still wants to claim that literature conveys knowledge, specifically what he calls 'experiential knowledge' of the 'real object'; but the drama deals in fictitious persons, and he goes on to say 'Even where, as in Shakespeare's Roman plays, the characters are drawn from history, we do not claim, in calling them realistic, that they closely resemble their specific originals; we mean only that they behave as such people would in real life.'[99] This argument seems to trip over itself; if we measure fictitious persons by asking if they behave as people would 'in real life', then we are not gaining knowledge, but only confirming what we already know. In a 'post-marxist' analysis of the problem, Tony Bennett argues that 'aesthetic discourse ... constitutes a really useless form of knowledge', and rejects the idea of the study of literature as leading to 'ethical self-shaping'; he would substitute instead an epistemological and political 'self-formation':

Unlike its Romantic forebear, the aesthetic reading is not a vehicle for reconciling the antinomies of personality as part of a technique of character formation. Nor is the critic an ethical exemplar. Rather, reading is organised as a process of learning again the difference between science and ideology, of disentangling oneself from the latter, and heading towards the former (but without ever actually arriving there) under the guidance of a critic who is refashioned, here, in the image of an epistemological exemplar – one whose activity, in placing him constantly on the road which leads from illusion to knowledge, allows him to function both as spur and guide to those who would plot a similar course across the epistemologised contours of the literary text.[100]

In this somewhat opaque passage, what is being rejected is more clear than what form of knowledge is to be gained, but it would seem that literature is to function by exposing ideologies while guiding the reader to a surer knowledge of history or 'science'. But there is no certain road from illusion to knowledge. Even in those extreme cases in Shakespeare's age where a play was based on topical matters, like Thomas Middleton's *A Game at Chess*, or claimed to be presenting the truth, like *Henry VIII*, subtitled *All is True*, spectators brought their common knowledge of the people and events concerned to the theatre for the pleasure of witnessing an imaginative recreation, that is to say it was their knowledge that led them to illusion. It seems to me that it is impossible to show that the study of literature leads through art to ethical self-improvement, or to the acquisition of experiential or political knowledge. We may acquire knowledge of various kinds, through learning how an author perceives people, places and events, through mastering his or her referential framework and range of discourse, but this knowledge would appear not to be dependent on the experience of a text as a work of art, which is why recent criticism has been able effectively to abandon the aesthetic aspects of literature altogether to concentrate on interpretation or meaning.

It is understandable that academic critics should wish to show that the study of literature is productive of knowledge, so that such study will be valued in the academy as having the same cognitive claims as other subjects. The mistake has been to try to absorb aesthetics into a theory of literature as knowledge. The study of literature certainly is involved with various kinds of knowledge, but a play like *King Lear* opens up imaginative vistas and possibilities for human interaction that most of us can never 'know' from real life, or test against what we see around us. In studying and commenting on literature we are concerned with knowledge of the cultural context, the meanings of words, the ideas being canvassed, the historical sources, the nature of the texts; but in experiencing the play we are not acquiring knowledge in the sense of anything that can be tested against evidence. In order to teach the interpretation of a literary text, we must be prepared to teach the cultural context; but the ordinary viewer and reader, if such there be, is concerned with understanding and appreciation, not with interpretation in this sense. Here it is necessary to distinguish between understanding and interpretation. The action of *Hamlet* and *King Lear* is both visual and verbal, and the viewer or reader who is capable of the 'inward illusion' necessary for experiencing the play must have some basic appreciation of both aspects of the action, which means that he or she must be able to respond to the flow of dialogue. The level of understanding necessary for such response, however, is very different from that required for a full scholarly interpretation of the nuances of meaning in the dialogue. The difference can be illustrated by reference to passages that defy understanding on the stage or by most readers, such as, for instance, Macbeth's lines:

> Come, seeling night,
> Scarf up the tender eye of pitiful day,
> And with thy bloody and invisible hand,
> Cancel and tear to pieces that great bond
> Which keeps me pale! Light thickens, and the crow
> Makes wing to the rooky wood . . .   (III.2.46–51)

Editors have provided a mind-boggling variety of glosses on this passage, which, of course, defies a final explanation. The commentator can explain the implications of 'Come, seeling night' in relation to falconry, and explore some of the connotations of 'seeling' as a pun on 'sealing' (binding to secrecy? stamping with approval and authority? echoing and inverting the New Testament use of the word to mean pledged irrevocably to the service of God, as at 2 Corinthians, 1.22, '[God] Who hath also sealed us, and given the earnest of the Spirit in our hearts'?), and so on; but he will not exhaust the possibilities of interpreting these lines. The image of the crow making wing to the rooky wood has provoked much debate as to precisely what the implications of 'rooky' are. William Empson thought he had solved the puzzle at the end of a page and a half of discussion, when he proposed that Macbeth is the solitary crow making wing to the gregarious rookery to which he would like to belong, in spite of his plan to murder Banquo. This does not do justice to the subtlety of his detailed explanation, but the point of mentioning this is to note the satisfaction with which, finally, he congratulates himself: 'Personally I am pleased and given faith by this analysis, because it has made something which seemed magical into something that seems to me sensible.'[101]

This is what editors and commentators feel required to do, in order to help their readers and please their students, namely to reduce magic to sense. Macbeth goes on to say to Lady Macbeth, 'Thou marvell'st at my words', and we are meant to marvel too, at what is an invocation of the powers of darkness, a kind of magic incantation, not reducible to 'sense'. Many other such passages in a number of Shakespeare's plays, such as the rages of Othello or the tortured self-questionings of Angelo or Leontes, suggest extremities of emotion, or a failure by the character to understand himself, and their speech conveys this failure. The Arden editor, Harold Jenkins, has about two pages of footnotes and about ten pages of additional notes on Hamlet's soliloquy 'To be or not to be',[102] about which there is a basic disagreement: is Hamlet thinking of suicide, or of taking arms against Claudius? The language of Lear's curses, or of his ranting speeches that attempt to outfrown the storm, or of his mad dialogue with Gloucester, is beyond the grasp of most auditors of the play, but it is not beyond the experience empowered by inward illusion, since in such cases the intricacies or impenetrabilities of the surface meaning are configured as a sense of inner discord in the character, an expression of mood or atmosphere, or of conscious or repressed feelings of desire, disgust, love, fear, outrage, pity, pain, and as contributing to the design of the whole.

Interpreters may zoom in on images like 'Come, seeling night' in *Macbeth*, or 'Do thy worst, blind Cupid; I'll not love' in *King Lear* to show how these connect with other passages to create thematic meanings in the contrasts between physical blindness and spiritual insight, the 'eye' of sight and the 'eye' of mind, and such meanings can be generated by the studious reader, which is to say the critic or graduate student in the academy. It is a processing of the text that can be taught. However, it is possible to learn how to interpret in this way without ever really living through the play, or yielding to that inward illusion that enables us to half-create and share in the emotions and anxieties of the characters without ourselves being required to act upon them or to judge; an illusion that allows us to experience the working out of a coherent dramatic action that seems inevitable. Interpreters or academic critics always push to find new meanings, to differ from their predecessors, to look for richer intertextualities, focussing on particularities to the point where the play itself may as a whole be marginalized. Where the central concern is with what can be taught, or with impressing colleagues, the work of the critic becomes more important than the play itself. But *Hamlet* and *King Lear* are more than all the meanings that can be attributed to them, and their value arises as much from the emotional and formal qualities we perceive in them as from meaning.

To put this another way, post-structuralist criticism has rejected any notion of determinacy in a text, and relishes demonstrating that 'any "objective" statement can be deconstructed and revealed as "subjective"',[103] so that all texts, it is claimed, are unstable, cannot be closed off, and overrun their apparent borders into an infinity of context, an endless play of signification. But, as Juliet Sychrava has pointed out in an analysis of the way aesthetics in the Romantic tradition has focussed on *how* we perceive, which is related to the category of the 'sentimental' in Schiller's usage, rather than on *what* we perceive, which is related to his concept of the 'naive',[104] this is to read a text

'reflectively' or outwards, from text to context, to context-of-context – and this will always reveal the instability of meaning. But it is possible to read 'determinately' or inwards, from context-of-context, to context, to text, and this is perhaps more like the way in which we usually – as readers, not critics

– read. In this sense, such 'determinant' reading could be called 'naive' and would provide what we think of as specific, stable meanings. This model of two possible directions can, it seems, be a way of combining or at least holding together the naive and the sentimental awareness.

What I am proposing is analogous to her position, in seeking to allow for the operation of 'inward illusion' in a simultaneous subjective and objective relation to Shakespeare's plays: 'Such a reading will at once consider the text as a post-structuralist might – a web to be unwoven and revealed as process, as the activity of reading, writing, interpreting – and as a more unsentimental critic might – as the finished product of those activities: the patterned cloth.'[105]

Since words signal meanings, and plays and other forms of literature are made out of language, then it would seem that the 'patterned cloth', the formal qualities of a play like *Hamlet* and the pleasure it gives, are necessarily bound up with meaning, and that an aesthetic account of the play would therefore involve processes of cognition. I suggest that the knowledge acquired in appreciating *Hamlet* as a work of art is different from the knowledge gained by unweaving the play, making connections with its 'larger cultural text' or context, or by explication or reducing the magical to sense, in the manner of Empson (see above, p. 140). This knowledge gained through appreciation is not, however, experiential in Nuttall's sense, but hypothetical, in the sense that in experiencing *Hamlet* we enter imaginatively into the curve of the action, its shaping of characters and events, and so gain insight into, for example, clashes of value-systems, the problematics of revenge, the potential provocations to violence in human beings, the difficulty for those in power of matching ethical and political behaviour, the controls that may be exercised over people by events in the past, and the cruelty that can emerge as the flip side of love. Such 'knowledge' as is gained in this way may have little immediate relation to the ordinary lives of most readers or viewers, and will be interpreted differently by each in relation to his or her experience and mores. Knowledge of this kind is not a form of moral technology, instilling values and ethical discipline, nor does it 'organize the experience of the subject' (see above, p. 122), but it does, I trust, have an effect in widening the sensitivity, the moral and political awareness, and the imaginative range of those who respond to the artistic shaping of the play.

I have been arguing that artistic form, like meaning, is not an immanent value, eternally present, but is generated through the interaction of subject and object, reader and text, to the extent that he or she recreates a sense of pleasure and formal satisfaction in experiencing it. As meanings are both there and not there, so form is both there and not there: each reader or viewer, and each new generation of readers and viewers, may interpret the play differently from others, and may perceive different formal qualities, if both meaning and form are 'completed' from the signs on the page, or from performance on the stage, in the imagination of the reader or beholder. The value of a work of art, that is to say its artistic value, develops out of the interplay between meaning and form. There are dramatists who seriously engage with important issues, but whose plays are, for the most part, stillborn for want of an adequate formal and emotional appeal. But value also depends upon some notion of a canon, since we only recognize the scale of a high peak in a mountain range as we measure it against other lesser peaks. Those postmodernists who appear most anxious to abolish the canon of literature in fact need such a concept: 'Some workable notion of canon, some examined idea of history, though like most human arrangements they may be represented as unjust and self-serving, are necessary to any concept of past value with the least chance of survival, necessary even to the desired rehabilitation of the unfairly neglected.'[106] Value we construct from a combination of factors, meaning, form and history, and it is not a fixed or eternal property of the work of art itself. The 'great' work of art is constituted as such both by its power to generate in the reader or viewer for the time being a sense of profundity, usually combined with complexity of meaning, and at the same time an experience of emotional power in a satisfying sense of formal shaping and closure; and the idea of 'greatness' is validated by its historical placement in relation to other works in the same genre. But this is not to locate any of these features as immutable properties of the text itself; I would suggest again that a play like *Hamlet* or *King Lear* presents a kind of natural perspective that is and is not – is really there in that in some sense it imitates people as if they were real, yet at the same time causes things to appear other than in reality they are, through a sense of artistry that is activated by our playful engagement with it, or our input of what Coleridge called inward illusion.

The next two chapters seek to draw together the various threads of the argument so far in focussing on *Hamlet* and *King Lear*. The accounts of the reception of these plays in Chapters 2 and 3 show that criticism of Shakespeare's plays has been inescapably involved with social and political conditions at the time when the critic was writing, however much the individual critic may claim impartiality or believe that 'a critical discovery will present itself as the *whole* truth of a work, a provision of its total meaning'.[107] They also show the extent to which criticism has been mainly devoted to interpretation and the search for meanings, rather than to considerations of Shakespeare's artistry. Current critical theories have tended to canonize the treatment of literature as a body of discourse indistinguishable from other forms of discourse, including criticism itself; and criticism is much preoccupied with the local and tangential, and little concerned with overall dramatic shaping. The chapter on 'Plays and texts' relates post-structuralist theories to textual criticism, in order to show that, however isolated from or hostile to critical theory textual critics may be, their work has been especially important in destabilizing both the authority of Shakespeare as a dramatist and the authority of texts that were probably revised, demolishing the idea of recovering an original text embodying the author's intentions. Their specific arguments about revision therefore need to be interrogated. In the present chapter I have been addressing the issue of revision in relation to the concept of artistic form, and proposing a concept of artistry that is not tied to the author or to his authority.

Those who have considered form in Shakespeare's plays have differed in the methods and units of design they have attributed to the dramatist. For instance, Emrys Jones argued that Shakespeare worked with 'scenic units' in what he called – using an analogy from music – 'movements', and that the tragedies 'gain in clarity if they are considered as plays conceived in two unequal movements'.[108] Mark Rose independently at the same time proposed that Shakespeare designed plays in groups of scenes, the number varying 'according to Shakespeare's purposes in each play', so that in *Hamlet*, for example, he finds eighteen scene-units, each usually of three to five segments, forming two roughly equal 'movements' separated by the 'Mousetrap' scene, the play within the play, which becomes the 'central emblem'.[109] Jean Howard also used a musical analogy in the term 'orchestration', in a more ambitious attempt to define Shakespeare's intentions. She sought to show that Shakespeare was constantly looking beyond 'the visual design of individual scenes to the meaningful orchestration of groups of scenes and entire plays';[110] but she rejected the possibility of revision in *King Lear* because the Folio text conflicted with what she took to be Shakespeare's purpose.[111] For Ruth Nevo, on the other hand, the phases of tragic development 'exhibit a very high correlation indeed with the Folio act divisions', so that she sees five phases articulating the traditional, which is to say Aristotelian, components of tragedy, fall, suffering, knowledge and death.[112] A different view is presented by Charles and Elaine Hallett, who argue that units of action are more important than scenes, and that the structure of Shakespeare's plays should be thought of as based on sequences of actions, which may embrace 'two or more scenes', a sequence being 'that unit of action in which Shakespeare raises a single dramatic question and answers it'.[113] What all these books have in common is the assumption that Shakespeare's design, what he planned and purposed, can be identified within the text.

Accepting that the destabilization of literature has made it impossible both to retain the idea of artistic form as fixed and immanent in a work and to keep recycling the notion of organic unity as deployed by Coleridge and others, I argue that we can use another formulation of Coleridge's, that of 'inward illusion', to help in generating a concept of artistic form not as determined by the author, but as constructed at any given time in relation to meaning as then perceived. I differ, then, from these formal critics both in my general approach, which is concerned with the overall structure rather than with a search for units of design, but also and more importantly in recognizing that we invent the dramatic designs we attribute to Shakespeare, and it is our purposes that govern our perception of Shakespeare's purposes. In the following chapters on *Hamlet* and *King Lear*, I seek to integrate a reading that is conscious of general social and political resonances affecting our age with a defence of the Folio texts as embodying the best reading versions we have of these plays. These readings and the defence of the Folio texts in turn are enmeshed with and support a clarification of the dramatic design of the plays that is also necessarily partial and a product of the present time. Quotations are generally modernized but retain Folio or, where specified, Quarto punctuation.

CHAPTER 6

A design for Hamlet

In this account of *Hamlet* I am concerned to shift attention from Hamlet himself to the larger conflicts and issues that now seem important to me in shaping the action. It is almost impossible to comment on a drama without treating the characters as if they were human beings acting in full autonomy, and it would be rather absurd to preface every remark by noting that the characters only exist as we produce them from Shakespeare's words on the page. Furthermore, as critics have shown over and over again, the characters and the play take on a life of their own in relation to the world of the critic, a life that Shakespeare could not have imagined. But all we have to work from is the text as printed in the Quartos and Folio, and the aim of the analysis of the dramatic action that follows here is to bring out what for convenience I call Shakespeare's artistry as it can now be reconstructed from that text. In other words my aim is to bring out the ways in which the play may be seen as shaped and patterned, through the conflicts generated between characters and the working out of the larger issues raised. So attention is focussed less on details or nuances of language than on varieties of perspective, on the way the past is used to frame characters and events, and on the development of patterns of events, values and ideas that are brilliantly completed in the final act, however much meanings may continue to reverberate beyond our immediate experience of the play. In accordance with the analysis of the text in Chapter 4, quotations are from the Folio text, but modernized, and with significant variants from Q2 added in brackets.

HAMLET SENIOR

Accounts of *Hamlet*, especially those tinged with Hamletism, give much weight to the soliloquies, and to Hamlet's relations with

Ophelia and with his mother, but above all focus on him, often as if his point of view is all that matters. Performances likewise tend to emphasize Hamlet and cut minor roles like those of Marcellus or Horatio. The reading texts we have, however, in Q2 and F, show that Hamlet's father, as a topic of concern in all but one of the scenes in Act I, and as a striking presence on stage in four appearances, was crucial to Shakespeare's design in the unfolding of the action. The first act is dominated structurally and in atmosphere by the Ghost. Its appearance is prepared for each time it stalks on stage in a manner that generates a maximum of tension and excitement. The Ghost is a central image from the past, a past that exerts a constant pressure on characters and events in the play. Hamlet's idea of his father, our sense of what he was like, his war with Norway, his marriage to Gertrude, his death, his appearances as a ghost, are matters that bear upon almost all the play's action. *Hamlet* is a play in which the past is recalled again and again, in memories of what was, in changes that have taken place, or in dealing with the consequences of past actions or events, as in the negotiations with Norway reported in II.2. The Ghost is difficult to stage convincingly in an age of disbelief in apparitions, but seems to have been conceived as an important emblem, a figure in whom the past is momentarily revived.

Greg's argument (1917) that the Ghost in *Hamlet* is a liar so troubled J. Dover Wilson that he found it necessary to refute it at length in *What Happens in Hamlet* (1935); and Eleanor Prosser's claim that the Ghost is really a devil likewise roused critics to defend the Ghost as belonging 'to a cleaner and more wholesome world than the Denmark of King Claudius'.[1] If Greg and Prosser do not finally convince, they succeed in bringing out an anxiety even the most sympathetic reader or spectator of Act I is likely to feel, an anxiety of the kind Hamlet himself expresses when he says in his soliloquy in II.2,

> The spirit that I have seen
> May be the [a Q2] devil, and the devil hath power
> T'assume a pleasing shape.   (II.2.598–600)

This anxiety is generated in part by what has often been noticed, the ambiguity about the nature of the Ghost – whether it comes from heaven, purgatory or hell, and why, if it is a Christian and an 'honest' or trustworthy figure (as Hamlet says at I.5.138), it calls for revenge, which is expressly forbidden by Christian teaching, and can, like a devil, be 'Hic et ubique', above and below, and everywhere at once in the cellarage beneath the stage.

Shakespeare's presentation of the Ghost is, I think, designed to arouse a deeper anxiety than that concerning its nature, though this is important. In F the twenty-five lines exchanged between Barnardo and Horatio after 1.1.107 are omitted, lines which stress the 'portentous' aspect of the Ghost, and link it with the apparitions and ghastly sights that preceded the fall of Julius Caesar. It has been suggested[2] that these lines were cut because they do not advance the action, but a more important reason may be that they powerfully suggest to reader or audience that the Ghost is essentially a portent, a 'prologue' to disasters yet to come, as Horatio puts it. There are other links with ancient Rome in a play composed soon after *Julius Caesar*, which some would see as a source for *Hamlet*,[3] but here they merely distract attention from what is much more important, the immediate past in Denmark. The Ghost has a dual aspect for Horatio, Barnardo and Marcellus: it is indeed, as they assume, an 'apparition', and 'illusion' (1.1.28, 127), constantly alluded to by them as 'it'; and at the same time it is old King Hamlet, as like him 'As thou art to thyself' (1.1.59), in Horatio's words to Marcellus.

The 'dreaded sight' (1.1.25) that appears to startle them just as they have sat down, relaxing, to hear Barnardo's story, harrows Horatio 'with fear & wonder' (1.1.44) not least because the Ghost is in armour, and ready for battle. No other ghost in the drama of the period shows up armed in this way,[4] and if the obvious reference is to the preparations in Denmark for defence against a threatened attack from Norway, the Ghost also provides the immediate stimulus for Horatio's recollection of historical events that are made to appear as if they took place in the very recent past. We learn in the next scene that Horatio has just returned from Wittenberg, where he was presumably Hamlet's fellow-student, but he speaks of old Hamlet's fight with the Poles as if he had seen it with his own eyes. Only in Act v do we learn that Hamlet was born on the day his father fought with old Fortinbras (v.1.144–8), and audiences and most readers have by this time forgotten the inconsistency by which Horatio is made here in the opening scene to give what could be an eyewitness account of events that took place, so to speak, before he was born.

The effect is to give these events a powerful immediacy, as the past seems about to repeat itself in young Fortinbras's preparations for an

attack on Denmark to recover the lands his father lost, and gain
revenge. Horatio is quite specific, even though he cannot have been
present at an event that took place thirty years previously: the Ghost
wears the very armour old Hamlet had on when he fought old
Fortinbras; and on his first entrance with 'martial stalk' he frowns as
he did when, in an angry confrontation,[5] he 'smote' the Poles, a
biblical usage meaning he destroyed them (as in Judges 15.8,
Authorized Version, 'And he [Samson] smote them hip and thigh
with great slaughter'). When the Ghost appears for a second time,
Horatio addresses it, pointing to three reasons why it might have
appeared to them:

> If there be any good thing to be done,
> That may to thee do ease, and grace to me;
> Speak to me.
> If thou art privy to thy country's fate
> (Which happily foreknowing may avoid)
> Oh speak.
> Or, if thou hast uphoarded in thy life
> Extorted treasure in the womb of earth,
> For which, they say, you[r Q2] spirits oft walk in
>   death,
> Speak of it. Stay, and speak.   (1.1.130–9)

All three reasons relate to common beliefs that were held to account
for the appearance of ghosts in Shakespeare's age, and suggest that
Horatio thinks of the Ghost as guilty of some wrongdoing and/or as
possessing secret knowledge it would reveal about its own guilty past
or about Denmark. The Ghost's actions, in spreading its arms (as
though to take off, or fend off Horatio?) confirm that it is responding
to what is around it, and begin to turn it into a character.

The Ghost thus in the opening scene embodies at once an ancient
and a recent past. It seems to belong to an earlier, more primitive
age than the present, a time when men went to war rather than to
university, and fighting was a normal way to conduct international
affairs. At the same time, Horatio's eyewitness account of the duel
with old Fortinbras makes this immediately present to reader or
audience, just as the appearance of the Ghost serves to bring old
Hamlet to life again. In describing to young Hamlet what he and his
colleagues have seen, Horatio again impresses both the Prince and us
with the immediacy of the presence of the old King. When Horatio
says, 'I think I saw him yesternight', Hamlet replies,

Sāw? Who?

HOR.   My lord, the King your father.   (1.2.189–91)

Horatio again is witness to what he can scarcely have known; he claims to have seen old Hamlet 'once' (1.2.186), and yet can say, 'I knew your father: / These hands are not more like' (1.2.211–2). The effect that Shakespeare seems to have sought in using Horatio so inconsistently (at 1.4.7 he seems to know nothing of life at the Danish court) is brillantly gained: the Ghost becomes at once an apparition and the actual figure of Hamlet's father, just as it becomes at once representative of an ancient heroic warrior ethos that seems located in a Classical or medieval context, and a participant in a fight that is described as if seen very recently by an eyewitness.

Horatio reports the Ghost as having an expression more of sorrow than of anger, and it is no surprise that a ghost so lifelike, gesturing emotionally, bearded, armed and carrying his marshal's truncheon, should indeed 'assume' the person of old Hamlet. All we have seen and heard about the Ghost prepares for his encounter with Hamlet in 1.5, when he visibly turns into Hamlet's father as soon as he opens his mouth to speak. One reason for the omission from F of Hamlet's speech expanding his comments on drinking in Denmark was no doubt that it delayed too long the Ghost's appearance on stage. The action has mounted to 'its first great climax' at the moment when the Ghost speaks with the 'threefold authority of supernatural being, King and father'.[6] Well, yes, but these three forms of authority sit uneasily together, and directors face a problem in staging the scene. If the Ghost begins as supernatural being in his stiff lines, he very much becomes the father later on, so that a director might be tempted to make him take his son by the arm on the line, 'If thou didst ever thy dear father love . . .'(1.5.23), and address him as man to man.

For from this point on the Ghost speaks as, and indeed becomes visibly for the audience, Hamlet's father. After referring to himself intially in the third person ('Revenge his foul and most unnatural murther'), he shifts rapidly into the first person, 'I find thee apt', and proceeds to call for revenge on Hamlet's uncle (lines 7, 61), which is to say his own brother (74), but not on Hamlet's mother (85–6). Much attention has been given to what the Ghost demands of his son, but usually in the context of the question of the nature of the Ghost. Is he an 'honest' ghost, laying upon his son a demand that in

effect imposes a duty which Hamlet has an obligation to carry out
(not least because there is no other way to obtain justice for his
father's murder when Claudius himself embodies the law)? Or is he a
'devil' (II.2.599) leading Hamlet astray in clamouring for a revenge a
Christian knows is forbidden, and even giving his son false information? Even those who acknowledge the ambiguity of the Ghost's
nature, and the sceptical attitude to ghosts in Shakespeare's own
age, frequently take Hamlet's immediate reaction to the Ghost's
imperatives as simply authoritative: 'He now also has his directive, a
commission that is also a mission. His reaction to the Ghost is like a
religious conversion.'[7] It is important therefore to notice what the
Ghost says in relation to the character presented here – for as the
Ghost becomes Hamlet's father, so he becomes also an actor playing
a character and inviting our attention as such.

In the first place, the Ghost's command to revenge, or in other
words, to kill Claudius, is contradicted by his reflection on his own
death as 'Murther most foul, as in the best it is'. The manner of his
death rather than the murder itself is what seems to obsess the Ghost,
as when he describes at length the way he died as if he were an
observer standing outside himself. What especially grates on him is
the effect of the 'leperous distilment' of the poison, that caused an
eruption to break out over his smooth skin 'with vile and loathsome
crust'. His horror at the manner of his dying, of being instantly
transformed into a leper, modulates into his anxiety about being
denied the sacraments, and together these reactions are focussed in
the line 'Oh horrible, Oh horrible, most horrible'. The physical
disfigurement merges into the moral disfigurement of 'Cut off even
in the blossoms of my sin'. The foul eruption on the body is a kind of
bloom of sin, that of both Claudius and old Hamlet, who acknow-
ledges his 'foul crimes' done in his lifetime. The Ghost's moral horror
is compounded with a physical revulsion. So it is in his account of
Claudius and Gertrude, an account that bears little relation to what
we have seen of them. Claudius is said to have seduced Gertrude to
his 'shameful lust', and the Ghost as Hamlet's father goes on:

> So lust [but Q2], though to a radiant angel [angle Q2] link'd,
> Will sate [sort Q2] itself in a celestial bed,
> And prey on garbage.   (I.5.55–7)

Here 'lust' is apparently transferred to Gertrude as once an 'angel',
but because the word stands free, it seems to embrace all lusts,

Claudius's also, as in the final disgust of 'prey on garbage'. Again
there is a sense of physical revulsion. If the Ghost is, as he says, a
spirit, here he becomes flesh indeed, and his preoccupation is with
himself, and with the lust (luxury) and incest he sees in the 'royal
bed' of Denmark. Like father, like son: his perception of Claudius as
an 'adulterate beast', and his horror at the idea of incest in marriage
with a brother's widow, officially proscribed by the table of kindred
and affinity in the Book of Common Prayer, echo Hamlet's own
words in his first soliloquy (1.2.129–59). The Ghost adds two points:
the additional accusation of adultery, that Gertrude has slept with
two brothers, and the account of the manner of his death. The sense
of moral outrage combined with physical disgust is common to
father and son, and the Ghost's words confirm and expand Hamlet's
own jaundiced view of Claudius and disgust with his mother, so that
the Ghost's words – he speaks only to Hamlet – may legitimately be
seen as a projection of Hamlet's own imagination.

This is perhaps why the appearance of the Ghost not in armour,
but in 'his habit, as he lived' (or night-gown, i.e., dressing-gown, if
the stage direction in Q1 may be trusted) at III.4.101 does not seem
inconsistent. Here the Ghost is not visible to Gertrude, and so can be
taken as hallucination on Hamlet's part, a reminder to himself in the
midst of his angry outburst against his mother that he is neglecting
the Ghost's 'dread command'. The Ghost's imperatives in 1.5,
'Revenge', 'bear it not', 'Taint not thy mind' and 'Remember me',
all merge in Hamlet's immediate response into the single word
'commandment', a word combining the military authority of the
marshal with an echo of biblical injunction, as in the Ten Com-
mandments; and this seems to refer primarily to 'Remember me',
twice echoed by Hamlet here, and to revenge, though the idea of a
commandment has its irony in its reminder of the Sixth Commandment in Exodus, 'Thou shalt not kill.' Hamlet's immediate response
in III.4 is likewise to recall the 'command' of his father; but when he is
away from the Ghost's influence, the idea of a command slackens
into at best the sense of being 'prompted' to revenge (II.2.584).

The Ghost crystallizes for Hamlet and externalizes for him and for
the audience what he has already felt or suspected, and gives
sanction to the idea of revenge. But the contradictions in the Ghost's
utterances, and the uneasy relation between moral and physical
outrage, are focussed in his third imperative, 'Taint not thy mind',
since Hamlet's 'mind' is already 'tainted' in the sense that his moral

and physical disgust at his mother's remarriage has already led him
to contemplate suicide; and the whole effect of the Ghost is to taint it
further by urging him to carry out another murder by way of
revenge. The Ghost, indeed, may be said to express in 'Taint not thy
mind' Hamlet's own yearning for a 'cleaner and more wholesome
world' than the one in which he finds himself, possessed as he sees it
by 'things rank and gross in nature'. But inasmuch as the Ghost, in
his character as Hamlet's father, resembles Hamlet and confirms his
fantasies and fears, the Ghost can hardly be regarded by readers and
audiences as a representative of that better world. There is a vital
difference between the image Hamlet has of his father and that
shown on stage and described in the text.

From the beginning Hamlet idolizes his father as a godlike figure,
as Hyperion, Hercules, Jupiter, Mars or Mercury; images of Classical
deities or great heroes like Hercules seem to spring readily into his
'mind's eye' as he 'sees' his father. One might attribute his liking for
Classical figures to his education in Wittenberg, as reflected in his
choice of Aeneas' account of Pyrrhus avenging the death of Achilles
upon Priam when he would have a 'taste' of the 'quality' of the
visiting players, but it affects Hamlet and the play in important
ways. Hamlet associates his father, and himself incidentally, with an
heroic ideal, even if he disparages himself in saying Claudius is 'no
more like my father / Than I to Hercules'. The heroic image for
Hamlet seems bound up with the idea of martial honour, with
something of the idea of a great soldier as simple, good and truthful;
but by distancing the idea of his father into a Classical context, he
invokes the ethos of a pre-Christian world in which 'what are
required are actions. A man in heroic society is what he does.'[8] And if
we ask what old Hamlet has done, we know little more than that he
has, in a fit of anger, slaughtered Poles in winter, and that he slew
old Fortinbras in single combat.

Old Hamlet is known to have had personal courage, appears in
armour in his 'fair and warlike form', but all that report speaks of are
his martial victories (even if a domestic touch is added by the Ghost,
that at home he was accustomed to sleeping in his orchard in the
afternoon). In the account Horatio gives of him, he seems to belong
to a more primitive order, a medieval world where challenge and
combat are important because the hero is only known by his
prowess; and in Hamlet's usual imagery, his father is located in a
Classical heroic world in which courage is the central virtue, and

every time the warrior fights, he courts the death that lies in wait for him: 'in heroic societies life is the standard of value. If someone kills you, my friend or brother, I owe you their death and when I have paid my debt to you their friend or brother owes them my death.'9 In that simpler, masculine world revenge would be required as a virtuous act. But the old Hamlet his son imagines and we hear about is not the same as the figure embodied in the Ghost, who confounds these simplicities by combining an heroic stance which assumes revenge as normal and necessary with a Christian morality that defines virtue primarily in terms of sexual relations. So the Ghost explicitly opposes virtue to lust ('virtue, as it never will be moved, / Though lewdness court it in a shape of heaven'), rather than to cowardice. The Ghost demands revenge, as is appropriate to an heroic code, but preaches a morality that focusses on sexual relations and expressly forbids revenge. 'Leave her to heaven' for appropriate punishment, he says of Gertrude, and if of her, why not of Claudius too, since, according to St Paul, 'Vengeance is mine. I will repay, saith the Lord'?

Hamlet would simplify his father into an heroic figure associated with an ancient world, but just as the Ghost reveals as soon as he speaks that he relates to a Christian framework of heaven, hell and purgatory, so Hamlet reveals his own Christian indoctrination the first moment he is alone, in his concern

> that the Everlasting had not fixed
> His canon 'gainst self [seal Q2]-slaughter.

Thus another form of slaughter embodied in the idea of revenge loses the clear moral imperative it had in heroic societies, and takes on a barbarous and hellish aspect, as is seen in the First Player's speech about Pyrrhus. The revenge of Pyrrhus for the death of his father Achilles is throughout the speech described in an epic manner recalling Virgil and Marlowe's *Dido and Aeneas*, but also in terms that associate Pyrrhus and his actions with hell and horror, culminating in the image of Hecuba being forced to witness the way he makes

> malicious sport
> In mincing with his sword her husband['s F] limbs. (II.2.513–14)

The subtle connections here with old Hamlet and Gertrude re-inforce the sense of horror in the very idea of murder and revenge.

Pyrrhus, 'o'er sized with coagulate gore', recalls the image of old Hamlet dying coated in a 'vile and loathsome crust'. It is as if he has come to life in the figure of Pyrrhus, 'Roasted in wrath and fire', the fire of burning Troy linking with the fires of purgatory; and the weeping and clamour of Hecuba, watching the brutal slaughter of her husband, seem to comment on Gertrude's lack of feeling about the death of hers.

The Pyrrhus speech displays the horror from a Christian point of view of a revenge carried out in an ancient heroic context, and in calling for the Player to repeat this passage, one he especially 'loved' (II.2.446), Hamlet represents to himself, unintentionally as it appears, the conflict between the heroic ethos he idealizes in his father and the Christian values the Ghost invokes, and which are assumed as a common frame of reference by other characters in the play. The ironies in Hamlet's situation are, of course, compounded by the behaviour of Laertes, who rushes to his revenge, already providing himself with poison before the idea of an arranged fencing match with Hamlet is mentioned, and who would undertake

> To cut his throat i'th church.
> KIN.   No place indeed should murder sanctuarize;
> Revenge should have no bounds.   (IV.7.126–8)

In rejecting the Christian attitude to murder and revenge, Laertes, applauded by Claudius, here offers, in the manner of an ancient hero, to commit sacrilege (as Pyrrhus did, according to Virgil (*Aeneid* II.550–1), dragging Priam on to an altar to kill him) in respecting his obligation to exact a death for the death of his kinsman. Laertes is like Pyrrhus in his view that the pursuit of revenge disables all other considerations.

Old Hamlet calls for vengeance, but qualifies that call in such ways ('Murther most foul, as in the best it is'; 'leave her to heaven') as to confuse the issue for Hamlet. Pyrrhus and Laertes as revengers illustrate the reasons why Hamlet would in a Christian context be inhibited from carrying out his revenge because of ethical and religious considerations. The other potential revenger in the play, whose father has, like old Hamlet, Achilles and Polonius, been slaughtered, forgoes revenge ironically while enacting in other ways the role of ancient hero. Fortinbras, strong in the arm, revives the image of old Hamlet, in that he is known only for his warlike deeds, and it would have made sense for the same actor to have doubled the parts of the Ghost and Fortinbras. His invasion of a part of Poland, repeating the attack made by old Hamlet, is launched to enhance his status as warrior, for the sake of fame, and in other respects is pointless, as is implicit in the text in F and made explicit in Q2 in Hamlet's dialogue with the Norwegian Captain and in his soliloquy in iv.4.

The ironies multiply in the final scene, when Fortinbras returns 'from the Polack wars' with his army apparently unscathed in an expedition in which they courted death, to find 'so many princes' dead at the court of Elsinore. He claims rights in Denmark, encouraged by Hamlet's dying vote, and gives Hamlet's body a military send-off, with a march and the sound of gunfire. At the end, then, Fortinbras revives the image of the warrior-hero, arrives costumed as a soldier, and is about to take over the rule of Denmark, recovering, as it might seem, the heroic ideal Hamlet longed for. But that ideal has been so tarnished and eroded by the exposure of the mindless violence involved in war and in the code of revenge, and its limitations as an ethos have been so emphatically shown up by contrast with the Christian values against which it is continually measured, implicitly or explicitly, that we can have no confidence in Fortinbras restoring a simpler and better order to Denmark. If this is especially true for the late twentieth century, when Western countries have learned to regard military dictatorships with repugnance, the play itself continually qualifies the heroic ideal, so that there is no reason at the end to imagine things will be better under Fortinbras, however different they may be.

GERTRUDE AND OPHELIA

The first act of the play establishes Hamlet's idealization of his father as a Herculean hero, and his own sense of difference and inferiority. Freud and his followers have shown that Hamlet's relation to his father, Claudius and Gertrude can be understood in Oedipal terms, but Shakespeare's primary design seems to have been to make us see Hamlet enthralled by the Ghost as representing a male ethos, and making demands in terms of that ethos. It is an ethos that has no place for women other than as loyal and pure, subservient to men, breeders of more heroes. Hamlet's misogynistic attacks on the two women he loves are directly related to his attempts to adapt himself to this male ethos in a world where women are breeders of sinners. As

Hamlet idealized his father into an immaculate hero, so, it seems, he assumed his mother also had no flaws. Gertrude appears to have existed in the shadow of old Hamlet, enveloped by his love, having no independent existence, or at least being known only as his consort. Hamlet's opening soliloquy is shocking in several ways, not only because of his expressed death-wish, his transformation of personal feelings into a condemnation of the whole world, and his misogynist denunciation of women in general, but also because of what it shows about his relation to his mother. He expected her to fulfil the role he had projected for her, of old Hamlet's totally devoted dependant, whose mourning for her dead husband would continue indefinitely. Hamlet's perspective is powerful because he has a dominant voice in the play, but the Gertrude we see is not the one he imagines as demurely hanging on his father. The death of old Hamlet may indeed have been a kind of liberation for her, a release from a suffocating subservience, and from the need to embody an ideal of womanly virtue. Hamlet is shattered by her refusal to mourn as he does, but evidently in 1.2 she does not begin to understand why he persists in seeking for his father in the dust. Old Hamlet seems to have had no real knowledge of his 'most seeming virtuous queen' (1.5.46), whom he in turn appears to have idealized as a 'radiant angel'.

The Gertrude we see appears liberated, in the sense that she seems able to speak freely in the court, and her concern is chiefly with her son. She does not understand him, or why his grief is so particular, any more than he understands her, but her concern for him is vividly registered in her first scene, and then again in 11.2, when Rosencrantz and Guildenstern arrive at the court, and Polonius reports what Ophelia has told him of Hamlet's love for her. A striking feature of this scene is the way Gertrude intervenes at will, and Claudius defers at times to her. So, when Polonius apparently whispers privately to him,

> And I do think, or else this brain of mine
> Hunts not the trail of policy, so sure
> As I have [F; it hath Q2] us'd to do: that I have found
> The very cause of Hamlet's lunacy,   (11.2.46–9)

Claudius sends him off and immediately reports what he has said to Gertrude,

> He tells me my sweet Queen, [my dear Gertrude Q2] that he hath found
> The head and source of all your son's distemper.

A little later, after Polonius's long explanations of Hamlet's madness, Claudius turns to Gertrude to ask 'Do you think ['tis F] this?' before agreeing to follow Polonius's advice. Also Gertrude herself questions Polonius, rebukes him by calling for 'More matter, with less art', and is a full participant in the debate. Gertrude has often been accused of 'too much sexuality', as if she were the cause of all the ills of the play, largely because of Hamlet's passionate assertion of her guilt; but, as Jacqueline Rose observes, 'What requires explanation, therefore, is not that Gertrude is an inadequate object for the emotions generated in the play, but the fact that she is expected to support them.'[10]

What we see is not her sexuality, but her constant concern for her son and for her husband; her behaviour is decorous, and she has no idea what is going on in the play within the play, though her line, 'The lady [doth protest Q2] protests too much methinks' has been wrenched out of context to become a 'cliché for the sexual "inconstancy" of females'.[11] About a third of all her lines in the play occur in the closet scene, when Hamlet diverts attention from his own bloody deed in killing Polonius by his verbal onslaught on her; and it is here that for the first time he accuses her of an excess of sexuality, and forces upon her a self-scrutiny that makes her see the 'black and grained [greeued Q2] spots' in her own soul (III.4.90). But quite what spots she sees we never know, for the Ghost appears to Hamlet leaving her to think he is mad, and the scene is devoted to what Hamlet sees or thinks he sees; and his sexual fantasies, his images of her in 'the rank sweat of an enseamed bed' (III.4.92) have prompted directors of the play to present him here as half-suppressing an incestuous sexual desire for his mother. F cuts about nineteen lines of the long tirade in which Hamlet dwells on the sexual relations of her with Claudius, but still the stress is on his obsessive attribution of guilt to her, and by implication to all women ('Frailty, thy name is woman'). Hence his astonishing assumption of moral authority in charging her:

> Confess yourself to heaven,
> Repent what's past, avoid what is to come,
> And do not spread the compost on [or F] the weeds
> To make them rank [ranker Q2]. Forgive me this my virtue ...
>   (III.4.149–52)

The echo here of the image in his first soliloquy of the world as an unweeded garden full of things 'rank and gross' carries over his sense of women as the source of corruption, and allows him, here with the

blood of Polonius fresh on his hands, to preach to her and claim
'virtue' for himself as an attribute of the male. The scene certainly
makes her aware of her own, unspecified, sins (IV.5.17), but brings
no similar awareness to Hamlet.

Hamlet's 'frailty' includes also Ophelia, who was for long roman-
ticized as 'a girl who feels too much, who drowns in feeling', and who
more recently has become symbolic in feminist criticism of the
madwoman as heroine registering 'protest and rebellion . . . against
the family and the social order'.[12] In the play it is her want of feeling
for Hamlet that is striking, or we might say the suppression of her
feeling; her overt emotional attachment is to her brother and father.
In her obedience to Polonius, her acceptance of his guidance ('I do
not know, my lord, what I should think', 1.3.104), she ironically
embodies the 'virtue' Hamlet wishes his mother possessed; but in
Ophelia it is a shrinking virtue, afraid of feeling. She 'did repel his
letters, and denied / His access' to her, and is 'affrighted' by his
farewell visit to her. We only have her account of this last visit, and it
is an account dominated by her fear:

OPH.   with a look so piteous in purport
  As if he had been loosed out of hell
  To speak of horrors: he comes before me.
POL. Mad for thy love?
OPH.   My lord, I do not know:
  But truly I do fear it.   (II.1.79–83)

Does she fear his madness or his love, or perceive his love as madness?
If Hamlet perceives in his mother passion without virtue, in Ophelia
he encouters virtue without passion. This makes it easier for him to
distance himself from all that women symbolize for him, and to
suppress the feminine part of himself; his verbal lashing of Ophelia in
III.1 is also a lashing of himself for ever having yielded to the
weakness of loving Ophelia: 'We are arrant knaves all.'

'I think nothing, my lord', says Ophelia to Hamlet in the 'Mousetrap' scene, apparently in innocence;[13] yet in her madness she reveals
that she is not so ignorant of sexual innuendos. Her songs amalga-
mate lover and father, grief for Polonius with sexual desire and fear:

        Young men will do't, if they come to't,
           By Cock they are to blame.   (IV.5.60–1)

From one perspective, Ophelia can be seen here as able in a
dominant patriarchal society to assert her individuality only in her

madness; from another point of view, she can only express in madness the longings suppressed by one whose very nature seems watery. Death by drowning is appropriate not only because of the association of water with feminity, but because in her fluid, unformed character, relying on others to tell her what to think and feel, she has appeared 'like a creature native, and indued / Unto that element' (IV.7.179–80). At the same time, Hamlet's crushing attacks on Ophelia and on Gertrude make us aware of all that he repudiates in his pursuit of revenge, and confirm his acceptance of the masculine ethos he idealizes in his father.

CLAUDIUS

Greg's representation of the Ghost as a liar, and of Claudius as possibly innocent, was countered by Dover Wilson's return to orthodoxy; and G. Wilson Knight's enthusiasm for Claudius as running a strong and healthy state (see above, p. 34) began to seem perverse in the context of Hitler and Stalin.[14] It is much more usual for the versions of Claudius given us by Hamlet and the Ghost to be taken as true, or at least as giving us the essential Claudius, and often he receives little attention in accounts of the play. So Harold Jenkins sees Claudius as merely 'the bad man', as 'sensual appetite' in opposition to the 'magnanimous soul' of old Hamlet, so that Hamlet's 'task' is 'to rid the world of the satyr and restore it to Hyperion'.[15] Such readings, that see the play through Hamlet's eyes and focus on the delay or failure of Hamlet in relation to his task or duty, miss an important feature of Shakespeare's design, which is brought home by a significant revision in the Folio text, where Claudius's lines as he attempts to pray in III.3 become in effect the last major soliloquy in the play with the omission of Hamlet's 'How all occasions' speech in IV.4; and it is at this point above all that Claudius is shown to be too self-aware and conscience-stricken to be marked down simply as a satyr or embodiment of appetite.

When L. C. Knights found in Claudius's opening speech in I.2 a masterly example of 'the distillation of personality into style', an immediate signal in the 'unctuous verse rhythms' that here was a 'slimy beast',[16] he was over-reacting, no doubt with the hindsight of his later knowledge of Claudius as murderer, to the use of rhetoric as an instrument of power. The carefully balanced phrases suggest a rehearsed speech, and empty out the emotional content of words like 'grief', 'woe', 'sorrow' and 'joy', distancing feeling behind a general blandness:

> Though yet of Hamlet our dear brother's death
> The memory be green: and that it us befitted
> To bear our hearts in grief, and our whole kingdom
> To be contracted in one brow of woe:
> Yet so far hath discretion fought with nature,
> That we with wisest sorrow think on him,
> Together with remembrance of ourselves . . .

But this is a ceremonial court occasion, when Claudius, speaking in the royal plural and addressing his whole council, is making a public announcement by way of introducing the business of the moment. The calm formalities of his opening lines provide a startling contrast to the sense of alarm generated in the first scene by the portentous Ghost, threat of invasion, and preparations for war. Here at court all is under control, ordered, peaceful. The marriage is accepted by everyone, and Claudius claims that he has proceeded all along with general support:

> nor have we herein barr'd
> Your better wisdoms, which have freely gone
> With this affair along.

Claudius presents himself as a democrat within his court.

Hamlet alone is marginalized in this scene, and might be thought to have a grievance against an apparent usurper, since only in Act v do we learn that he was defeated in an election to the throne by Claudius; but this is not raised as an issue, and Hamlet is out of tune with the rest of the court, where it seems affairs are conducted openly and in mutual trust. Claudius deals first with foreign affairs, sending ambassadors to negotiate with old Fortinbras, and then perhaps steps down from the throne as he shifts from the royal 'we' to speak personally to Laertes, relaxing into an almost jocular manner, 'And now Laertes, what's the news with you?' By contrast, Hamlet's sullen response to Claudius's attempt to treat him similarly ('But now my cousin Hamlet, and my son?'), and the intervention of Gertrude, return Claudius to his public manner, and perhaps to the throne, as he publicly calls on Hamlet to remain in Denmark, and announces that he nominates him as his successor in Denmark, 'for let the world take note, / You are the most immediate to our throne.'

If Claudius unbends to Laertes and initially to Hamlet, he enters

and leaves this scene in state as king, but evidently as a very different
king from old Hamlet. His way is not to make war, but to use
diplomacy, to work with words, not weapons. As throughout the
play old Hamlet is associated with war and an heroic code suggestive
of a Classical or medieval order, so Claudius is established on his first
appearance as related to a modern (in Elizabethan and twentieth-
century senses) political way of operating, working with the consent
of the court to achieve his ends by diplomatic means. It may be that
Shakespeare named the King Claudius with a conscious sense of
irony, after the Roman emperor who was noted, like James I, for
shrewdness and learning as well as for ungainliness and gluttony,
and who was no soldier. The world of this emperor (ruled A.D. 41–
54) was far removed from the myths of Hercules or Mars with which
Hamlet links his father.

Claudius of course relies on advice to conduct affairs, and his chief
counsellor, Polonius, takes it for granted that he should pry suspi-
ciously into everyone's business, including that of his own children.
If in one aspect he is a comic busybody, in another he is the
prototype of the director of a Central Intelligence Agency, eager to
find dirt, to gather information he can use to bully Ophelia, confirm
his worst suspicions about Laertes, or reveal the cause of Hamlet's
madness. He is rendered amusing by his naive confidence in his own
perspicacity; and he enjoys hunting the trail of policy so much that
he does not see how his 'wisdom' and 'reach' might be corrupt in
searching out corruption. Polonius's wisdom is not, however, simply
despicable, since it is so much bound up with service and loyalty to
the state:

> I hold my duty, as I hold my soul,
> Both to my God, and [one F] to my gracious king. (II.2.44–5)

The idea of making service and loyalty to the state an over-riding
consideration is anathema to today's liberal critics, as exemplified in
Stephen Greenblatt's account of Shakespeare's *Henry V*, in which he
takes it for granted that Henry ought to let friendship outweigh
other factors in his reaction to his low-life companions: for him,
Henry shows 'every nuance of royal hypocrisy, ruthlessness, and bad
faith – testing, in effect, the proposition that successful rule depends
not upon sacredness but upon demonic violence'.[17] The condemnation of Henry seems deliberately overpitched to draw attention to
itself, but a more radical feature of this argument is its claim that

Shakespeare was testing an idea of rule which I would suggest that
he took for granted. Here, says Greenblatt, 'the founding of the
modern state, like the self-fashioning of the modern prince, is shown
to be based upon acts of calculation, intimidation, and deceit';[18] but
no form of rule shown in the plays of Shakespeare excludes such acts,
which are a function of the very nature of power and the exercise of
controls in the state. The modern state differs from earlier forms of
kingship in the kinds of ruthlessness and terror it employs, but
Shakespeare accepted as a necessity of rule what Greenblatt sees him
as questioning.

I suggest that he finds a reflection of our own times in the mirror of
Shakespeare's drama, and transfers on to *Henry V* his own resent-
ment at the 'acts of calculation, intimidation, and deceit' that have
marked recent governments in the United States and in Britain, in
relation to both external and internal affairs. One has only to think
of the Irangate scandal, the treatment of Nicaragua and the trial of
Colonel North, the lies told about the Grenada and Falklands wars,
the surveillance of citizens, and the manufacturing of 'disinforma-
tion'. The world of *Henry V* is not sleazy in such ways any more than
is the world of *Hamlet*; but the behaviour of governments in recent
times has made it difficult to imagine a society in which it was not
regarded as dishonourable to put loyalty to the state before personal
attachments. There are still situations and countries where such a
stance is approved, as the black Jamaican writer Elean Thomas has
reminded us in saying of her white English husband, 'we both know
that the day he betrays my people is the day I part from him, no
matter how much I love him'.[19] The court of Queen Elizabeth was
such a society, and just as Fulke Greville was proud to have 'Servant
to Queen Elizabeth' inscribed on his tomb, so might Polonius have
described himself as 'servant to King Claudius'.

This is not to justify Henry V or Polonius or Claudius; however,
on the issue of political necessity, requiring at the extreme the
passing of death sentences on friend or kinsman, on the Earl of Essex,
on Mary Stuart, or on ancient Pistol, there is every reason to think
Shakespeare perceived and was troubled by the conflict between its
demands and those of Christian morality and personal loyalties, and
indeed felt outrage at abuses of 'authority' as voiced by Lear; but
there is no reason to suppose he could imagine the sleazy and
pervasive corruptions of the modern political scene. As Elizabeth
maintained her informers and spies, so it is natural for Claudius to

keep a watchful eye on Hamlet, and to employ Polonius, Rosencrantz, Guildenstern and Ophelia to 'sift him' (II.2.58). The need
grows as Hamlet manifests what increasingly appears to be a
'dangerous lunacy'. In III.1 Claudius confirms what hitherto only the
Ghost has asserted, that he carries a burden of guilt for an unspecified 'deed'; not that his guilt is ever in doubt, but it is an important
moment when Claudius drops in an aside the mask of royalty and
becomes a man with a conscience.

As Claudius reveals himself to us, so Hamlet reveals himself to
Claudius. It is ironic that while Claudius's attempts to investigate
Hamlet through his various agents bring forth little more than that
Hamlet has loved Ophelia, Hamlet should show his hand not only in
shouting 'Those that are married already, all but one, shall live'
(III.1.148), but also in the play within the play. When the dumb-
show fails to provoke any reaction on Claudius's part, Hamlet resorts
to interpreting 'The Mousetrap', and in identifying the murderer as
'nephew to the king', changes the story line from one that resembles
the murder of old Hamlet to one that anticipates the murder of
Claudius. When Claudius rises and leaves the stage, Hamlet assumes
he is 'frighted with false fire' (F; not in Q2) in the sense that his guilt
in the murder of old Hamlet has been exposed, but Claudius may
just as well be angry, as Guildenstern reports (III.2.303), or fright-
ened by Hamlet's threat to him. His immediate response is to pack
Hamlet off at once to England in the charge of Rosencrantz and
Guildenstern, in order to rid himself of the danger ('hazard') that
'doth hourly grow / Out of his lunacies' (F; Q2 has 'brows' for
'lunacies'; the change in F may mark a small but significant
authorial revision; it is in Claudius's interest to have Hamlet publicly
regarded as mad).

Hamlet thus provokes Claudius to go beyond investigating him,
and to take action by ridding himself of the threat he now perceives
in his nephew. At this point, before Hamlet's interview with his
mother, and at the centre of the play, comes Claudius's soliloquy, in
which he speaks as man, not as king. Here Claudius drops altogether
the royal 'we', and in the very act of confessing that he murdered his
brother wins a measure of sympathy, since we are made to feel that
the consciousness of his guilt is itself in some measure a punishment
of him, an awareness he is burdened with behind the public face of
kingship. It never occurs to Hamlet that Claudius might be a killer
with a conscience, self-tormented:

Oh, wretched state! O bosom, black as death!
Oh limed soul, that struggling to be free,
Art more engag'd.   (iii.3.67–9)

Claudius finds himself trapped, unable to renounce what he possesses ('My crown, mine own ambition, and my queen'), and unable
as a result to repent or seek forgiveness, however much he tries. The
consummate politician turns out to be a Christian too, condemned
to live in the stink of his one black deed, as he cries 'Oh my offence is
rank, it smells to heaven.' The word 'rank' here links him with
Hamlet, who uses it in denouncing the world in i.i and his mother in
iii.4 (see above p. 158).

   This soliloquy takes on a futher resonance in relation to what
follows almost at once; Hamlet rejects the chance to stab Claudius at
prayer, but then, with an intention to kill ('dead for a ducat, dead',
iii.4.23), thrusts his sword through the arras. The striking feature of
his killing of Polonius is his lack of real concern about it; 150 lines
later he casually says, 'For this same lord, / I do repent' (iii.4.172),
but he shows little sign of repentance, or of any feeling, as he goes off
lugging 'the guts' behind him. The placing of Claudius's soliloquy is
perfect, for on the one hand, Hamlet's rank offence sets off by
contrast his own lack of a sense of guilt for the death of Polonius; on
the other hand, as an indirect consequence of the murder of old
Hamlet, it traps Claudius in further coils, for just as Hamlet cannot
use the law to punish the murderer of his father, so Claudius cannot
use the law to punish the killer of his friend and counsellor, who now
threatens him:

Alas, how shall this bloody deed be answered?
It will be laid to us, whose providence
Should have kept short, restrain'd, and out of haunt,
This mad young man.   (iv.1.16–19)

So Claudius is driven by Hamlet to arrange another murder or
execution by pressuring the King of England to put Hamlet to death
when he arrives there.

   Claudius and Hamlet become open enemies, each seeking the
death of the other, Hamlet announcing his intentions in the killing of
Polonius and in scarcely veiled threats, Claudius concealing his
designs from Gertrude especially. This is brought out in the sharp
confrontation at the end of iv.3, where Hamlet, still high it seems,
the adrenalin flowing after his encounter with his mother, cannot

resist challenging Claudius in response to Claudius's question, 'Where is Polonius?': 'In heaven send thither to see. If your messenger find him not there, seek him i'th other place yourself. But indeed, if [if indeed Q2] you find him not [within Q2] this month, you shall nose him as you go up the stairs into the lobby.' The threat must be obvious to Claudius as it is to the reader, compounded by the deliberate offence given in Hamlet's refusal to acknowledge Claudius as father; but Claudius has the last word in a short soliloquy in which he reveals he has ordered 'The present death of Hamlet'. This scene marks a climax; after it there can only be a conflict to the death between Hamlet and Claudius, and it is appropriate that Hamlet goes off at once to England, returning 500 lines later in v.1. The cutting from F of Hamlet's dialogue with the Captain, and of his soliloquy, 'How all occasions . . .', strengthens the impact of this important clash between the main antagonists in the play.

The death of Polonius is the crucial event in. the action, for it brings Hamlet and Claudius into the open as 'fell and mighty opposites', creates disorder in the court, sends Ophelia mad, and provokes Laertes to return at the head of a rebellious mob. Claudius has little choice but to channel Laertes' passion for revenge into a plot to bring about the death of Hamlet. Having rid himself of one madman, he finds himself confronted with another in Laertes, and has much 'to do to calm his rage' (iv.7.192). Since he cannot proceed in public or by law against Hamlet, both because of his love for Gertrude and her love for Hamlet, and because of Hamlet's popularity with the 'general gender' or common people (iv.7.18–20), he is driven to subterfuge, picking up the idea of poison from Laertes to make trebly sure that Hamlet will not escape death. In retrospect we see that Claudius's attempt to repent in iii.3. was the last moment when he could so, for Hamlet's killing of Polonius forces him to take action against Hamlet and plot another murder, so that indeed in struggling to be free, he becomes 'more engag'd' (iii.3.69). By killing Polonius, Hamlet inadvertently springs a further trap on Claudius.

Claudius's efforts to placate Laertes, and plotting with him to ensure Hamlet's death by rapier or two kinds of poison if the sword fails, may be seen as acts of desperation. Thrown by the death of Polonius, Claudius makes a mistake as king in not giving him a proper funeral, but he faces down the rebellion with courage and aplomb, even if it is easy to point to the irony of his claim to divine protection against treason at this moment, given his own treason against his brother. There is no reason to discredit his avowed love for Polonius, or his devotion to Gertrude:

> She's so conjunctive [conclive Q2] to my life and soul
> That as the star moves not but in his sphere,
> I could not but by her. (IV.7.14–16)

Claudius gained the throne by his one black deed, but for the most part he is a responsible monarch and an affectionate husband, and things go wrong for him only when he is driven into error, and into direct confrontation with Hamlet, by the killing of Polonius. Then he is forced to shrug off repentance for his first offence and compound it with a second, the death of Hamlet. Political necessity over-rides moral considerations, as indeed it tends to in the modern world; in this sense Claudius's attempt to repent, however much it humanizes him, was an aberration, an understandable desire to unburden himself and acknowledge his conscience and sense of guilt, even though it could have no effect on his political conduct, any more than the presidents and governors who now ostentatiously attend church on Sundays allow what is said or happens there to affect their political actions during the week.

HAMLET

The critical fortunes of Hamlet outlined in Chapter 2 show how he has been appropriated as an image of man in the modern world, conceived especially as ditherer and blatherer, as Seamus Heaney puts it, as a failure, unable to take decisive action. This image of Hamlet is derived largely from his soliloquies, and recognizes in him the first fully developed subject in literature in whom interiority is privileged over the external world. Yet as presented in the action, Hamlet is very much a Renaissance figure, who shares that humanist idea of man's potential that seemed to be realized in the brief glory of Sir Philip Sidney's life:

> that immortal spirit, which was deckt
> With all the dowries of celestial grace,
> By sovereign choice from th'heavenly quires select,
> And lineally derived from Angels race.
> (Edmund Spenser, *The Doleful Lay of Clorinda*, 61–4)

Hamlet's familiar speech on man generalizes such an image (I quote the F version; Q2 differs slightly in wording and considerably in punctuation): 'What a piece of work is a man! how noble in reason? how infinite in faculty? in form and moving how express and admirable? in action how like an angel? in apprehension how like a god?' 'It exceeds man's thought to think how high / God hath rais'd man since God a man became', wrote Sir John Davies in *Nosce Teipsum* (1599); the next step from manhood is Godhead, so that even the angels are astonished at man, and it seems a short step from man's 'dying flesh' to infinity. Such extravagant images were not confined to poetic hyperboles, and could be the theme of sermons:

We are to sit at the right hand of God, which is on the throne, the best, and next place to God himself. And by this, we are above the angels; For to which of them said he at any time, Sit on my right hand. No, but stand before me, as ministering spirits all... the Right hand is kept for us. (Lancelot Andrewes, Sermon 7, 1612)

This Christian idealization of man is implicit in Hamlet's transfiguration of his father into a Classical deity or hero:

> See what a grace was seated on his [this Q] brow,
> Hyperion's curls, the front of Jove himself,
> An eye like Mars, to threaten or [and Q] command,
> A station, like the herald Mercury
> New lighted on a heaven [heave a Q2] kissing hill:
> A combination and a form indeed,
> Where every god did seem to set his seal,
> To give the world assurance of a man.   (III.4.55–62)

The attribute of 'grace' suggests graciousness, but also echoes the 'celestial grace' Spenser saw in Sidney. Hamlet prefers to associate his father with an ancient heroic code, as the warrior at home in armour or on the battlefield, but he does not thoroughly disentangle the Christian and the Classical, an aspect of the confusion he suffers and generates. He judges what he sees around him in terms of this heroic ideal, but also in terms of a profound sense of the other side of the Renaissance paradox, that if man is chosen for the right hand of God, he is nonetheless, in Robert Burton's words in *The Anatomy of Melancholy*, 'a castaway, a caitiff, one of the most miserable creatures of the world ... unregenerated man, so much obscured by his fall that (some few reliques excepted) he is inferior to a beast'.[20]

The tragic dilemma of Hamlet may be seen in terms of this paradox, and certainly Hamlet finds an opposite to his father by demonizing Claudius in the image he has of him as a 'satyr', a 'mildew'd ear', or a 'vice of kings'. The Ghost confirms Hamlet's attitude by telling him what he wants to hear, as in some sense a projection of Hamlet's feelings, focussed in the idea of Claudius as 'that incestuous, that adulterate beast'. When the Ghost speaks, indeed, he becomes an actor playing old King Hamlet to the life, not a Classical hero, but the last King of Denmark, with a Polonius-like love of moralizing about virtue and lust, and a habit of sleeping every afternoon in the orchard. He belongs to the Christian world, even if he makes unChristian demands. The speaking Ghost brings to life an old Hamlet who is very much a part of Hamlet's present world, unlike the ideal of his father as warrior-hero Hamlet has elsewhere in the play. Hamlet, so to speak, straddles both worlds, but locates Claudius within the Christian Denmark in which Claudius embodies for him all the worst in man; and implicitly, by the moral distance he puts between himself and his idealized father, Hamlet aligns himself more with the Claudius he so despises: 'no more like my father, / Than I to Hercules'; 'I am very proud, revengeful, ambitions, with more offences at my beck, than I have thoughts to put them in.'

What his father asks of Hamlet is appropriate to an ancient heroic code, and appalling in Christian terms. The 'foul crimes' done in his days of nature by old Hamlet presumably include slaughtering Poles, and the English, whose 'cicatrice looks raw and red / After the Danish sword' (IV.3.60–1). Hamlet's nostalgia for a simpler, heroic world run by men strong in the arm cannot be reconciled either with the violence of that world or with the moral and political demands of modern Denmark. And there is no way the Ghost's demand for revenge can be reconciled with the Christian ethos that is the basis for his condemnation of Claudius. Hamlet does not have a 'duty' to revenge;[21] his Christian duty is to avoid it, and to distrust the demand for it, even though it comes from the ghost of a father he hero-worships. So, after his immediate emotional reaction to the Ghost, in which Hamlet takes the demand for revenge as a 'commandment', with all that word's connotations of martial and biblical authority, it is not surprising that cooler reflection should lead him to question the Ghost's words and seek further evidence of Claudius's guilt.

Hamlet's 'delay' in F is that of someone who feels the need to be certain that a Ghost who enjoins him to a morally outrageous act really is telling the truth about old Hamlet's death. He has one major soliloquy in which he berates himself for not acting like Pyrrhus, and defines why he cannot when he calls Claudius

> Remorseless, treacherous, lecherous, kindless villain!
> Oh, vengeance!   (II.2.581–2)

The first of these lines, except for the word 'lecherous', applies to Pyrrhus as much as it does to Claudius, and the cry 'Oh vengeance', added in F, becomes at once a call for retribution and a reminder that the previous line defines the nature of the revenger much more that it does the Claudius we have seen. Hamlet is, in any case, the odd man out at the court of Denmark, constantly observed as much as he observes, and unable simply to rush to his revenge, even if there were no reason to question the nature of the deed.

My point is that it isn't enough to see in Hamlet 'a struggle between Falsehood and Deception, embodied in the King, and Truth, embodied in the Prince',[22], or to see the play as about a good man perplexed by his inability to carry out revenge without becoming contaminated by the corruption in Denmark, without becoming like Claudius.[23] Nor is it sufficient to see Hamlet as exemplifying the metaphysical predicament of Man as between 'the angels and the beasts, between the glory of having been made in God's image and the incrimination of being descended from fallen Adam'.[24] All these perspectives are helpful, but the play in F also insists on Hamlet's need to acknowledge the beast in himself, and overcome his resistance to the soiled working that is the way of the world. His misogyny, the burden of his first soliloquy ('Frailty, thy name is woman'), later shown in his appearance like a ghost to frighten the wits out of Ophelia, in his harsh dismissal of her in III.1, and in his attack on his mother in III.4, invites psychological speculation as to its possible causes, and two seem immediately relevant. One is his nostalgic longing to be associated with the world of heroic, masculine values with which he identifies his father, a longing which would account for a repression of feminine qualities in himself. The second, as noted earlier, might be a repressed incestuous desire for his mother, which is often allowed to emerge in his behaviour to her in the closet scene in modern productions of the play. But as expressed in the play his misogyny seems rather to function as a kind of release: Hamlet's verbal lashing of Ophelia effects a transference, and it is as if the weakness which has led her to obey her father, deny her love for Hamlet, and return his 'remembrances' with words that echo Polonius in style triggers in Hamlet an insight into his own inadequacies. The central speech of the scene with her exaggerates this awareness to include all men as well as all women: 'What should such fellows as I do crawling between heaven and earth [earth and heaven Q2]? We are arrant knaves [all. F].'

The 'Denmark's a prison' sequence (II.2.239–69), found only in F, relates to this process by which Hamlet releases in himself the potential for the offences his imagination can shape. Denmark is a prison in one sense because Hamlet feels surrounded by spies, as if anticipating a sense of the power of modern society as effected through surveillance,[25] but also because it brings out the criminal in Hamlet: in saying 'there is nothing either good or bad, but thinking makes it so', he invents a morality for the moment that cancels Christian concepts of right and wrong. Hamlet recognizes that notions of what is good can be adjusted. We are made peculiarly aware of this when he comes on Claudius praying, and with sword drawn debates whether to stab him in the back, not in terms of the morality of revenge itself, but rather questioning how he can make sure Claudius goes to hell. Dr Johnson notoriously found Hamlet's lines here 'too horrible to be read or to be uttered',[26] and one can see why: Hamlet thinks if he stabs Claudius here,

> so he [a Q2] goes to heaven,
> And so am I revenged: that would be scann'd,
> A villain kills my father, and for that
> I his foul [sole Q2] son, do this same villain send
> To heaven.   (III.3.74–8)

If Claudius is a villain to kill old Hamlet, what is to be said of young Hamlet contemplating killing in cold blood someone whose damnation he wants to ensure, as if he can play God? Who is good and who 'foul' here, to pick up what may be a felicitous error in F?

The blurring of moral demarcations comes to a head in the scene between Hamlet and Gertrude, when Hamlet turns from stabbing Polonius, marked by this 'bloody deed' as a killer himself, even if the deed was not premeditated, to berate his mother for her 'trespass' in marrying Claudius. Hamlet's sense of physical revulsion at what he imagines goes on in 'the rank sweat of an enseamed bed' echoed the revulsion the Ghost felt at the physical corruption of his body by

poison, and helps perhaps to summon the hallucination, as it may
be, of the last appearance of Hamlet's father, now domestic in a
night-gown (according to Q1), and unseen by Gertrude. The Ghost
revives here in Hamlet the idea of revenge as a 'dread command',
one made easier for him to carry out now that he has killed Polonius.
Hamlet's purpose has hardly been 'blunted', as the Ghost says,
embodying Hamlet's own anxiety no doubt, for in stabbing Polonius
he thought he was killing Claudius. To turn on Gertrude and lash
her for loving 'A murderer and a villain' when he has just slain
Polonius again shows Hamlet adjusting his morality to suit his deeds
and purposes:

> For this same lord,
> I do repent: but heaven hath pleas'd it so,
> To punish me with this, and this with me,
> That I must be their scourge and minister.
> I will bestow him, and will answer well
> The death I gave him: so again, good night.
> I must be cruel, only to be kind;
> Thus [This Q2] bad begins, and worse remains behind. (III.4.172–9)

Hamlet adapts to political necessity, or to craft, double-dealing and
revenge, by claiming the death of Polonius as an act of God, as if
heaven has both punished him and made him its agent of punishment of others, and officer (minister) to chastise, or purge, or bring
comfort (his words here ironically recall 'Angels and ministers of
grace defend us'). In accommodating himself to murder, Hamlet has
to sacrifice his principles, and he saves his self-respect by interpreting
what he is doing as the will of heaven.[27] So he sends Rosencrantz and
Guildenstern to their deaths crying, 'They are not near my conscience', and claims heavenly sanction for killing Claudius:

> is't not perfect conscience,
> [To quit him with this arm? is't not to be damn'd
> To let this canker of our nature come
> In further evil. F]   (v.2.68–71)

Here, in lines found only in F, Hamlet sets himself up as judge and
executioner, as if to fail to kill Claudius would be damnable; and
relieves himself of responsibility for what happens to Rosencrantz
and Guildenstern by saying (in F only), 'Why man, they did make
love to this employment' (v.2.57). 'There is nothing either good or
bad but thinking makes it so': here Hamlet is rethinking the idea of
killing into a good.

Hamlet also in F expresses sorrow for his anger with Laertes, and aligns himself with Laertes as revenger, 'For by the image of my cause, I see / The portraiture of his.' According to Paul Werstine, 'From his first appearance in i.ii, F offers a Laertes who seems stronger and a bit more reflective and therefore more worthy, in his own right, of the respect that he eventually wins from Hamlet in v.ii than the Laertes that Q2 depicts';[28] and certainly the omission from F of Hamlet's lines mocking Osric's description of Laertes as an 'absolute gentleman', and so seeming to mock Laertes himself, puts much weight on the lines just quoted; but the 'respect' Hamlet has for Laertes here is for him as standing to Hamlet in the same way that Hamlet stands to Claudius. So on the one hand Hamlet accepts the idea of revenge as good in itself, and on the other hand sees himself as the agent of it in the hands of Providence ('There's a divinity that shapes our ends'; 'There's a special providence in the fall of a sparrow'). In this way he accommodates himself morally to the violence his revenge requires, before the final reckoning that brings the deaths of Claudius, Gertrude, Laertes and Hamlet himself.

Hamlet is the most ostentatiously Christian of all the tragedies, but its Christian colouring does not make it 'primarily a religious play'.[29] A ghost comes apparently from purgatory, Ophelia is seen at her orisons, Claudius at prayer, and a priest conducts the burial service for Ophelia after the sexton or gravedigger explains scripture to his companion. From 'Angels and ministers of grace, defend us!' on Hamlet's sight of the Ghost, to 'A ministering angel shall my sister be', to 'flights of angels sing thee to thy rest', runs a strong current of Christian allusion. Christian rites, on the other hand, are broken or interrupted: mourning for old Hamlet by the marriage of Claudius and Gertrude; the burial of old Hamlet by the casting up of his spirit from the 'ponderous and marble jaws' of his tomb; Ophelia reads a prayer-book for show, and is interrupted while doing so; Claudius cannot in fact pray in spite of his attempt; and Ophelia's burial rites, like those due to her father, buried in 'hugger-mugger', are 'maimed'. Hamlet's outrage at Gertrude's failure to mourn for old Hamlet beyond a month or two, like Laertes' concern about his father being obscurely buried,

No trophy, sword, nor hatchment o'er his bones,
No noble rite, nor formal ostentation,   (IV.5.215–6)

and his distress at the restricted ceremony for the death of Ophelia, all relate to a deep anxiety that there may be nothing beyond the grave.[30] This is why monuments, memorials and ostentation are so important to commemorate the dead for the living.[31] The dread of something after death troubles Hamlet, who has seen a ghost, but death remains

> The undiscovered country, from whose bourn
> No traveller returns.   (III.78–9)

The graveyard scene shows us skulls of the long dead being thrown about, so that Hamlet can moralize on oblivion, in typical misogynistic fashion directing the bare bone of Yorick at women: 'get you to my lady's chamber [table Q2] and tell her, let her paint an inch thick, to this favour she must come'. This scene symbolically brings in procession to the grave all the main characters of the play, even as Hamlet relentlessly pursues the conversion of Caesar or Alexander the Great into dust, and grotesquely into a bung to stop a beer-barrel, in contrast to Laertes a little later imagining the dead Ophelia as a 'ministering angel'. Whatever pieties may be uttered in relation to heaven or hell, to mercy or damnation for the souls of the departed, the play insists on the brute fact in relation to the dead that they are gone for ever; so Ophelia sings, and whatever the immediate application to Polonius, the song has a generalizing force:

> And will he not come again,
> And will he not come again:
>   No, no, he is dead
>   Go to thy death-bed,
> He never will come again.   (IV.5.190–4)

The Ghost is some sense returns old Hamlet to life for reader or audience, but not for Hamlet, for whom it is a spirit of doubtful nature, whose essential message is 'Remember me' ('Do not forget' in III.4). The living owe the dead remembrance because there may be nothing else:

> Remember thee?
> Ay, thou poor ghost, while memory holds a seat
> In this distracted globe.   (I.5.95–7)

The pun on globe as head, as world, and as theatre, reinforces the sense that only re-enactments in forms of remembrance stand between the dead and oblivion.

If the play is the most Christian of the central tragedies, it is also the most Classical. Even without Horatio's speech in 1.1 on omens preceding the death of Julius Caesar in ancient Rome, the F text is rich in a variety of references to the ancient world. Hamlet's training in and love of the Classics appears in his choice of a speech from a play based on the *Aeneid* for the First Player to recite, in his recourse to Classical deities for adequate comparisons to his father, and in his paraphrase of the familiar definition of comedy, attributed to Cicero, in his advice to the Players ('imitatio vitae, speculum consuetudinis, imago veritatis'; see above, p. 125). In addition to other casual allusions, 'Like Niobe all tears', or Polonius having played Julius Caesar, and formal personifications of Phoebus, Tellus, Neptune and Hymen in the play within the play, we are constantly reminded of the Classical world by the names of characters like Claudius, or Horatio (recalling the brothers Horatii, who defended Rome and defeated the Curiatii?), Laertes (the father of Odysseus), and Marcellus.

There are two ways in which these links are especially important. One relates to war, and, as noted earlier, is especially focussed in old Hamlet and Fortinbras. The play begins with threats of war, and ends with Fortinbras returning victorious from Poland, and ordering a military funeral for Hamlet – the only ritual in the play not broken, and ironically identifying Hamlet at last with the image he felt he fell short of, but treasured, of his father as warrior. Imagery of war is common in the language of most characters,[32] especially Hamlet, who chooses for recitation a story from the Trojan war, and reports a battle at sea with pirates; but even Gertrude, the 'imperial jointress to this warlike state', can describe Hamlet's wild looks in a comparison with soldiers:

> as the sleeping soldiers in th'alarm,
> Your bedded hair, like life in excrements,
> Start up, and stand an end. (III.4.120–2)

War has a double aspect as associated in some measure with honour and chivalry, but more vividly, in the feats of old Hamlet and Fortinbras, with brute violence.

A second especially important link with the Classical world is in the emphasis on fortune in the play, not in the common sense of luck, but as the goddess Fortune, a sort of cross between chance and destiny swaying human affairs. She comes to life in Hamlet's welcome of Rosencrantz and Guildenstern:

GUILD.   On Fortune's cap [lap Q2], we are not the very button.
HAM.   Nor the soles of her shoe?
ROSEN.   Neither, my lord.
HAM.   Then you live about her waist, or in the middle of her favours?
GUILD.   Faith, her privates, we.
HAM.   In the secret parts of Fortune? Oh, most true: she is a strumpet.

(II.2.229–36)

Fortune is proverbially a strumpet who gives her favours or refuses them indiscriminately, at the turn of her wheel (II.2.495), but in this dialogue she becomes something more than a simple personification, almost a personality. She takes on a more powerful presence in Hamlet's praise of Horatio as

A man that Fortune's buffets, and rewards
Hath [Hast Q2] ta'en with equal thanks. And blest are those,
Whose blood and judgement are so well co-mingled [comedled Q2]
That they are not a pipe for Fortune's finger,
To sound what stop she please.   (III.2.67–71)

Hamlet implies that he is a pipe at the mercy of Fortune's finger, and his comment here follows on from his best-known allusion to 'The slings and arrows of outrageous Fortune' (III.1.59), where Fortune herself becomes a warlike figure attacking him.

At the end of the play Horatio offers to carry out his promise to Hamlet to tell his story (he is, of course, the only one who knows it; Hamlet shows his concern to be remembered after his death by three times urging Horatio to report the truth about him, and then preventing him from following the stoic's path like an 'antique Roman' and taking his own life). Horatio's version will tell

Of carnal, bloody, and unnatural acts,
Of accidental judgements, casual slaughters,
Of deaths put on by cunning, and forc'd [for no Q2] cause,
And in this upshot, purposes mistook,
Fallen on the inventors' heads.   (V.2.381–5)

Here it sounds as if most of the play's events might be attributed to outrageous Fortune, to chance, accident, mistakes, and an element of human cunning. The First Player's account of the death of Priam ends with an appeal to the gods to take away the power of Fortune and break her wheel, but it seems that she, of all the gods, holds most sway in the play.

Hamlet, then, is located in relation to two worlds. One is Christian, the modern Denmark ruled over by Claudius, in which numerous protestations, shows, broken rituals attest the lip-service given to religion. What people do in life – plot, betray, spy, practise craft and assays of bias, fight, kill, and commit 'foul crimes' – may have little to do with their apparent beliefs or religious practices. Their ostensible trust in an afterlife is troubled by an anxiety that there may, after all, be mere oblivion in death, and so they are anxious to be memorialized after death. In the bitterness Hamlet pours out on his mother, he accuses her, in marrying Claudius, of doing a deed that 'sweet religion makes / A rhapsody of words' (III.4.48), and we might think of Ophelia with a prayer-book in her hand, or of Claudius praying, and also of Hamlet himself in this scene, shuffling reponsibility for the death of Polonius on to heaven, as indulging in a rhapsody of words. Hamlet makes a series of moral adjustments after he kills Polonius, finding it convenient to ascribe his own violent acts to Providence rather than now blame Fortune; but there is no sign that Providence has a special care of anyone in what Horatio sees as a string of 'casual slaughters'.

The second world is Classical, and predominates in the early part of the play, where the goddess Fortune is more prominent. The main impact on Hamlet is not in the Senecan stoic ideal he attributes to Horatio, or in the sense of a Classical education that informs Hamlet's dialogue, so much as in the simple heroic code he identifies with his father, 'An eye like Mars, to threaten or [and Q2] command'. This is a code that has nothing to do with Christianity or Providence, and accepts revenge as a norm. In his aspect as warrior, old Hamlet appropriately commands his son to revenge his death. The characters in the play speak religion, but do not or cannot practise its lessons, while Hamlet seems not to recognize the gap between the heroic code and the Christian ethic he too makes much of in words, though not finally in practice. From one point of view Hamlet can be seen as shifting towards an adaptation to the world of Claudius, and he is in the end successful in outfoxing his mighty opposite. From another point of view, Hamlet starts with an allegiance to two incompatible codes, one identified with his father, the other with the canons of the Almighty, and ends by adopting the methods of Claudius, while claiming Providence is on his side. No wonder he causes so much anguish and so many deaths.

Hamlet's problem, finally, is one of imperception. For all his self-

absorption, his analysing soliloquies, his superiority in wit over
Polonius and Rosencrantz and Guildenstern, he cannot see what the
play brings home to the reader and audience: namely, that in the
final analysis there is not much to choose between the worlds of old
Hamlet and of Claudius. Both use violence to achieve their ends, one
openly, by challenge and war, the other covertly, by assassination
and diplomacy. Hamlet wants to keep his hands clean, but really
knows he cannot, that 'We are arrant knaves all', and ironically
becomes the cause of more suffering than Claudius has ever been.
The death of Polonius makes Hamlet seem indeed the 'most violent
author / Of his own just remove' (IV.5.80–1), as his verbal violence to
Ophelia and Gertrude turns to physical violence. At the end he gives
his dying vote to Fortinbras, who will make a good military dictator.
So the play concludes without deciding between a corrupt government by consent on the one hand, and a military government by
force on the other. *Hamlet* is most profoundly a political play in
setting against one another the two modes of government that have
predominated in Western history, and through Hamlet's struggle to
reconcile ethical and political imperatives, the limitations of both are
revealed.

This account of *Hamlet* seeks to bring out the general design of the
play as at present I perceive it in the Folio text, and it is bound up
with an overall reading of the play which is necessarily of our time.
The play is haunted from the start by past events: the quarrel
between Denmark and Norway, the deaths of old Fortinbras and of
old Hamlet, the deaths of all fathers, and the hasty marriage of
Claudius and Gertrude. Hamlet himself is haunted by a ghost, and
confronted by a classic dilemma, that his father has been murdered
by someone who as ruler embodies the law, so how can he obtain
justice? But the shaping of the early part of the play, which presents
Claudius as a good ruler, old Hamlet as a questionable ghost, and
Hamlet as already unstable and condemning all women for what by
him alone, and by no one else at court, is seen as his mother's incest
and adultery, ensures that we see more than Hamlet does. Hamlet
himself opens up gaps between past and present, between his yearning for an ancient heroic code he associates with his father, and his
involvement in modern diplomacy and spying; between Christian
morality and politics; and between revenge and justice. But we see
further into these gaps than Hamlet does, and also become aware of
other spaces he does not seem consciously to notice, between Fortune

and Providence; between Classical and Christian, and between masculine and feminine values. In his disgust with his mother, his rejection of Ophelia and his violence towards her, Hamlet represses the feminine qualities in himself, while at the same time idealizing his father ('He was a man'), and the masculine code associated with him (symbolized in the armour the Ghost wears in Act I, where he appears dressed as marshal of an army, not in the clothes he was wearing when murdered, sleeping in his orchard). In committing himself to revenge, Hamlet also commits himself to becoming a killer in turn, and we see the erosion of his ideals as he puts pressure on Claudius, even while Claudius's self-confidence erodes under the pressure of coping with Hamlet's antic disposition.

In seeking to expose Claudius through the play within the play, Hamlet is more successful in revealing his own purposes to Claudius; and in proceeding against Claudius, Hamlet traps himself in accepting a code of violence that can be resisted when it might involve stabbing a man in the back (Claudius at prayer), but which leads to the killing of Polonius, This killing in turn provokes Claudius to act against Hamlet out of political necessity. Hamlet assuages his guilt for the death of Polonius by his verbal onslaught on his mother in the closet scene, an outburst of anger that also perhaps marks his half-conscious awareness of being himself trapped ('Thus [This Q2] bad begins, and worse remains behind'). Claudius, too, who in F has the last major soliloquy, reveals in it his consciousness of being unable to escape the consequences of his murder of old Hamlet: 'Oh limed soul, that struggling to be free / Art more engag'd'. Both Hamlet and Claudius thus become prisoners of their actions, which partly explains the power of the passage added in Act II in F in which Hamlet plays on the image of Denmark as a prison.

The broken Christian rites in the play and the appearance of the Ghost relate to beliefs in a life after death, but there runs through the action too an alternative sense, brought out especially in the graveyard scene in Act V, of death as total oblivion, as in the image of the body rotting in nine years at the most. This anxiety about death makes more poignant the effect of Hamlet's pursuit of revenge, which leads him into a maze of violence in which he becomes the direct or indirect cause of far more deaths than Claudius brought about, including those of Polonius, Ophelia, Rosencrantz and Guildenstern, Laertes, and finally Claudius himself. Ironically, Hamlet is flanked by two other representatives of the heroic code to which he allies himself through his father, namely Laertes and Fortinbras. Laertes reveals through his kneejerk reaction to his father's death, and in his readiness to use poison and commit sacrilege, the horrible aspects of revenge. Fortinbras, as his name suggests, is a conventional throwback to a politics of might as right. Hamlet sees in Laertes the image of his own cause, and gives Fortinbras his dying vote to rule in Denmark, as if in his return from the killing-fields of Poland, Fortinbras appears as the figure of old Hamlet *redivivus*, in whom Hamlet can identify the heroic past he idealized. The play thus moves to a compelling sense of closure, as Claudius appropriately dies by poison and the sword, while Hamlet, in death, is symbolically identified with that heroic ideal, as his body is carried off with martial honours. The ironies and issues opened up in the play reverberate far beyond it, as its afterlife and the endless commentaries on it show, but the design is completed in a powerfully satisfying way.

CHAPTER 7

A shaping for King Lear

DIVISION

No ghosts haunt the play, no voices from the past, such as those that exert an immense influence in *Hamlet*; that play is obsessed with memory, but there is no memory in *King Lear*, except of vague injustices and neglect of the poor. Lear has no history in spite of his great age. We know nothing of how he came to the throne, of the events of his reign, even how long he has reigned, so that it seems he has been in power for ever. We know nothing of his queen, of her life or death, in striking contrast to the old play of *King Leir*, which begins with the obsequies of Leir's 'deceased and dearest Queen', and with lamentation that his daughters will lack 'their mother's good advice'. We know nothing of how Lear came to marry late, as he must have done, and spawn three daughters, one of marriageable age at the beginning of the play, and so, by analogy with Juliet and Viola, in her teens. There is nothing to tell us how it came about that he was over sixty when Cordelia and perhaps his other daughters were born. It is as if Lear has ruled England for so long that all memory of his predecessors has been wiped out. Gloucester may say 'We have seen the best of our time', but we have no sense of what that 'best' was; the past is a blank, and the present is all that matters.

To put this another way, one might say that *King Lear* is released from history, and can always therefore be seen as essentially a contemporary play. This is a necessary point to be made if the design of the play as it now appears is to be appreciated. For long, critics treated the play as a portrayal of an old man's pilgrimage through suffering to rebirth and redemption, and pushed it back into a mythical context, aligning it, as noted earlier, with the story of figures like Job or Prometheus. On the stage until recently the play was set in a prehistoric, or at any rate ancient, period, often with

visual echoes of Stonehenge, so that it was disconnected from the
present for the audience. The sources, of course, indicate that Lear
reigned about a hundred years before the founding of Rome, and
more than 800 before Christ, and Shakespeare made use of the
antiquity of the legend, recorded by Spenser in *The Faerie Queene*,
and in the old play of *King Leir* (entered in the Stationers' Register
1594, printed 1605), to the extent that Lear invokes Classical deities
like Hecate and Apollo, and unidentified 'gods' are appealed to
throughout the play. Shakespeare allows all possibilities; the play is
at once ancient and modern, and because it is not located in a
specific place (except for the vague references to somewhere near
Dover late in the action) or specific time, we are not troubled by a
sense of contradictions or anachronisms.

It therefore has made good sense for new historicists and others to
interrogate the play as a document of the history of Shakespeare's
own time. Their interests, however, tend to be in the local and
particular rather than in the play as a whole (see below, pp. 221–2),
so that although they notice contemporary significances, they are
not concerned with the shaping of the dramatic action. The play was
politicized in the 1960s in relation to the Cold War and the tyranny
of Stalin, but was narrowly conceived as confirming a bleak and
cynical view of the world. Again, such an approach made good
sense, as the overwhelming impact of Peter Brook's production and
film testifies, even if the play was skewed by reshaping and cutting to
support a thesis. What both the new historicists and the political
interpreters have realized is that *King Lear* is not about an ancient
past; rather the vague suggestions of antiquity in the play, and its
mythic resonances, work to enrich and deepen a design that
throughout emphasizes the present moment and looks to the future
that depends upon each act. Thus the play is political in the largest
sense, and its possible local reference to the age of James I is of less
importance than its pervasive concern with wider issues that bear
powerfully on the political consciousness of the present time, ours
and everyone's.

The changes made in F reinforce this sense of the immediacy of the
play, and in my view show that we have not two plays called *King
Lear*, but one in which full weight is given both to Lear as an old man
enduring suffering, and to Lear as a tyrant corrupted by his absolute
power. The first stage of the action coincides with Act I as F divides
the play. This may be mere coincidence, since the act divisions, not

present in Q, may have nothing to do with Shakespeare. It is by no means clear either that Shakespeare thought primarily in terms of scenes as structural units, as some would claim. An attempt to analyse *King Lear* in these terms led Emrys Jones to see the play as falling into two parts, the division coming at the end of Act III, but the form struck him as elusive: 'We seem to move from episode to episode without much sense of what the final destination is to be.'[1] The design appears to me to be somewhat obscured by the familiar act and scene divisions, but is not a mere drifting from episode to episode. Act I ends with a device that signals a structural hinge in the action. For the first time in the play a character, the Fool, directly involves the audience in breaking the dramatic illusion to share a joke about the women out there:

> She that's a maid now, and laughs at my departure,
> Shall not be a maid long, unless things be cut shorter.

These lines can be explained literally in terms of laughter turning to dismay, but a reminder that the play is tragic is hardly necessary here. Explanations of this kind tend to miss the point; the couplet marks the end of a stage in the action, momentarily interrupting it, to switch attention away from Lear, who is offstage for the next three scenes (320 lines).

Lear dominates the first stage of the action, and the additions made in F to his opening announcement are important as clarifying his motives, and significantly qualify our impression of him here:

> Know, that we have divided
> In three our kingdom: and 'tis our fast intent
> To shake all cares and business from our age,
> Conferring them on younger strengths, [while we
> Unburthen'd crawl toward death. Our son of Cornwall,
> And you, our no less loving son of Albany,
> We have this hour a constant will to publish
> Our daughters' several dowers, that future strife
> May be prevented now. (F)] The princes, France & Burgundy,
> Great rivals in our youngest daughter's love
> Long in our court, have made their amorous sojourn,
> And here are to be answer'd. Tell me my daughters,
> [(Since now we will divest us both of rule,
> Interest of territory, cares of state) (F)]
> Which of you shall we say doth love us most?

The added lines not only identify Cornwall and Albany, but

ironically show Lear hoping to prevent the 'future strife' he virtually
guarantees will come by his action. In these lines, more importantly,
he sees himself as shedding all responsibilities, 'rule / Interest of
territory, cares of state', so that he can 'Unburthen'd crawl toward
death'. Death is all he has left to prepare for (see above, p. 109). In
the Folio death is his announced theme; but it soon becomes clear
that he has no sense of the implications of what he is saying. He gives
away his land, the source of his power, and hands over authority to
Cornwall and Albany, yet in the very act of doing so contradicts
himself in retaining the name and observances due ('addition') to a
king, as well as a train of a hundred knights to be maintained by
each in turn. This is not to crawl unburdened toward death, but
rather to hold on to the privileges and lifestyle of a monarch without
the responsibility which makes those privileges and lifestyle tolerable
to others.

Lear can be seen right away both as an authoritarian patriarch
with attendants springing to obey his every whim, and as a pathetic
old man doing everything wrong. He has staged a ceremonial
occasion, in which his daughters appear to compete for the best
share of his lands, a ceremony in which each is to play an assigned
part; only it seems that Goneril and Regan have speeches ready, as
though they had some inkling of the performance to come, and their
formal, empty, overblown assertions of love are right for a playlet in
which no one is expected to speak the truth – except that Lear is so
used to people pleasing him that he can no longer distinguish
between flattery and truth. The speeches of the sisters have been
better understood in the theatre than by critics; so in the Royal
Shakespeare Theatre production of 1982, they came downstage
'straightforwardly to address the audience as if producing a party
piece prepared for public performance'.[2] They do what is required;
but Cordelia, unprepared it seems, refuses to play the ceremonial
game, thus exposing as absurd Lear's demand for a public expression
of love, which is a private and intimate matter between two people.
She also exposes the gap between what Lear thinks he is doing,
generously donating his land and power to loving and grateful
children, and what he is actually doing, giving away everything to
daughters he doesn't know except as ceremonial figures, trappings of
his former power.

Hence the shock of Cordelia's 'Nothing my Lord'. We should be
astonished that this young girl can stand up so boldly against a

powerful tyrant who is her father, but old enough to be her grandfather. As he is a tyrannical old despot making a nonsense of the idea of love, he deserves her effective rebuke; as he is a pathetic old man and her father, he needs her kindness and love. She claims to speak truth, but ceremonial occasions have little to do with truth; in fact she speaks less than truth in saying she loves her father according to her 'bond, no[r Q] more, nor less'. The word 'bond' has legal overtones, and in measuring her love she denies its very nature, for, as Antony knows, 'there's beggary in the love that can be reckoned'. The Folio accentuates the boldness of Cordelia's confrontation of her father by adding the repetitive '*Lear*. Nothing? / *Cor.* Nothing', but removes the scornful second line in her words:

> Sure, I shall never marry like my sisters,
> [To love my father all. Q]

But still Cordelia's response remains, as Lear says, 'untender'. She is right and wrong, both true and false at the same time, and more than a little like her father in their clash over the word 'nothing'.

Lear's outburst now that his preconceived scheme goes wrong is so extreme as to suggest both that no one has dared to contradict him before and that he has so identified with his authority that a denial of it deranges him into the 'hideous rashness' of casting off Cordelia. Kent perceives his behaviour as 'mad' ('man' Q), and so it is, in the sense that Lear, overcome by passion, wilfully blinds himself to the true nature of what he is doing. The Quarto stage direction for Lear's entry calls for him to follow 'one bearing a coronet', but this is omitted from the Folio, suggesting that instead of taking a coronet from an attendant to give it to Cornwall and Albany, he now removes one he is wearing, when he says 'This coronet part between [betwixt Q] you', so making more vivid the surrender of his power. F adds to Kent's attempt to make Lear 'See better' a line for Cornwall and Albany (or just possibly Cordelia; but the speech-heading '*Alb.Cor.*' suggests the usual pairing of the two sons-in-law), 'Dear Sir forbear', as the King draws his sword or takes a weapon from Kent or some attendant, and threatens to kill Kent. The added line, with perhaps a gesture of restraint by Cornwall and Albany (as in Edmund Kean's and some later productions[3]), heightens the violence of Lear and the peremptory nature of his behaviour.

The first words he speaks under Goneril's roof, 'Let me not stay a jot for dinner' (1.4.8), show that he has not surrendered his long

habit of authority, of expecting his capricious wishes to be fulfilled on
the instant. His hiring of the disguised Kent suggests that Lear has
no sense of restraint as to the number of followers he can retain. The
Kent who, in defending Cordelia, stood up to Lear, now and for the
rest of the action serves him like a faithful dog, in his unthinking
loyalty anticipating his master's wishes, as when he trips up Oswald,
and so helps to give rein to rather than to control the excesses of Lear
and his train of a hundred knights. Once more, as the Fool says,
Kent is 'taking one's part that's out of favour', here in supporting
Lear, but he is no longer so clearly in the right. The Fool's role is
sharpened in F by the omission of the sweet and bitter fool passage
(see above, pp. 100–1), and by the change of a speech-heading so
that he attacks Kent as well as Lear:

KENT [LEAR Q]   This is nothing Fool.
FOOL   Then 'tis like the breath of an unfee'd lawyer, you gave me nothing
   for't, can you make no use of nothing nuncle?
LEAR   Why no boy, nothing can be made out of nothing.
FOOL   Prithee tell him, so much the rent of his land comes to, he will not
   believe a fool.

The Fool's attack continues with 'Nuncle, give me an egg, and I'll
give thee two crowns', as throughout the scene he harps on Lear's
folly in giving away his crown, his lands and possessions, the source
of his power. Making the phrase 'Lear's shadow' into an acerbic
response by the Fool in F, instead of an answer Lear in Q gives to his
own question, 'Who is it that can tell me who I am?', also focusses
the Fool's critique of Lear, and incidentally of Kent, whose loyalty
may be admirable in itself, and whose violence to Oswald may draw
a warm gut response, but who is at the same time sycophantically
pandering to Lear's obstinacy. Here Kent's behaviour works to
prevent Lear from understanding his situation, rather than enabling
him, as Kent desired in the opening scene, to 'see better'.

   In F, too, the parts of Goneril and Albany are altered in this scene.
Goneril's brief exchange with Oswald in 1.3 is shortened in F by the
omission of five lines in which she scornfully abuses her father (see
above, p. 106). The omission of these contemptuous lines, and also of
her announced intention to seek opportunities for a quarrel, 'I would
breed from hence occasions, and I shall' (Q only), puts the emphasis
here in her dialogue with Oswald entirely on the misbehaviour of
Lear and his retinue as wronging her and growing 'riotous'. In the

following scene Albany has a few lines added in F expressing his
puzzlement at what is happening, and including his appeal to the
old King, 'Pray Sir be patient' (line 261), as Lear begins to curse
Goneril. Her lines harp on the riots of Lear's 'insolent retinue', and
she begins to assert the power he has given her by asking him to
reduce the number of his followers, a request that provokes his
terrifying and total rejection of her as a 'Degenerate bastard', a
rejection parallel to that of Cordelia. After he rushes off intending to
stay with Regan, F adds lines for Goneril which further elaborate the
dangers inherent in having Lear's train of knights, armed ('At
point'), in her court:

> This man hath had good counsel, a hundred knights?
> 'Tis politic and safe to let him keep
> At point a hundred knights: yes, that on every dream
> Each buzz, each fancy, each complaint, dislike,
> He may enguard his dotage with their powers,
> And hold our lives in mercy.   (1.4.322–7; F only)

In Q Goneril sends Oswald off with a letter to Regan, leaving us to
guess the contents, but in F she explains that she has advised Regan
against sustaining Lear 'and his hundred knights'. The changes in F
make Goneril's behaviour here more reasonable and less disdainful,
so balancing more evenly her behaviour against that of her father.
She has good reasons for curbing the excesses of Lear's knights, as is
shown by Kent's violence to Oswald, and for challenging her father,
who, having given away his power, would continue to act as though
he retained it, expecting everyone, as before, to please him and obey
his whims. If she seems hard, she is reflecting his hardness; like
father, like daughter, an analogy strengthened in F.

The first act of the play ends with Lear's one scene of intimacy
with the Fool, after Kent goes off to deliver his letter to Gloucester.
The scene does not advance the action, and was often cut or
transposed to Act II in eighteenth- and nineteenth-century productions of the play, but in certain respects it is a turning point. In it
Lear for the first time recalls Cordelia in recognizing that he 'did her
wrong', and his final cry, 'O let me not be mad ... I would not be
mad', marks his (and the audience's) recognition that madness
indeed lies ahead. Although he is mostly close to the Fool in this
scene, and even solves one of his riddles, the 'reason why the seven
stars are no mo[re Q] than seven', Lear is beginning to drift away
into the obsession with his daughters that drives him out of his mind.

Lear has thought of himself as having a generous and kind nature ('I will forget my nature, so kind a father'), but what we have seen in his division of the kingdom, dismissal of Cordelia and terrifying curse on Goneril is a generosity corrupted into an extension of power, and a kindness that cannot tolerate insubordination. The way forward to an even harsher confrontation with Regan, and thence to madness and decline, is by now fully signposted. From this point on the Fool's role changes, especially in F, as he becomes more of a choric figure, for the most part ignored by Lear, and so less a 'pestilent gall' (1.4.114) to him than a voice of common sense for the audience in a world where everything goes awry.

EXPULSION

The next stage of the action in some ways echoes the first, with variations, and leads to the expulsion of Lear into the storm, but it also opens up new perspectives through what only this play among Shakespeare's major tragedies has, a subplot that widens the scope of the play while paralleling and forming a commentary on the main action. The absence of Lear from the stage during the first three scenes of Act II is important as establishing a sense of life going on outside his court and immediate circle. Edmund, it is true, had been highlighted in the opening lines of the play, making him the visible topic of conversation between Gloucester and Kent, and then again in the second scene with his eloquent soliloquy on bastardy. No exit is marked for him in Q or in F in the opening scene, though editors usually send him off with Gloucester when he exits on Lear's command to attend France and Burgundy at line 34; but he could either remain on stage as a brooding presence at court, or return with Gloucester at line 187, and go off when Lear and most of the court leave in state at line 266. If Edmund witnesses the casting out of Cordelia, it would underline his own device to bring about the casting out of Edgar. To argue that he has been 'out', or abroad 'nine years', as Gloucester says, and therefore is not known at court does not make sense, since he is apparently at court when the play begins, and Cornwall needs no introduction to him when they meet in II.1.

Edmund's appeal to the law of nature as opposed to the gods is the only major soliloquy in the play, and the only one that conveys a sense of interior life (apart from the brief one with which he closes this same scene), in the sense that in it he interrogates himself, and, with his vitality, independence and intelligence, invites the complicity of the audience in rejecting as unfair and untrue the common stigma attached to bastards. He also interrogates the ruling ideology of Shakespeare's age, which thought it 'an impiety monstrous, to confound God and Nature . . . For it is God, that only disposeth of all things according to his own will . . . It is Nature that can dispose of nothing, but according to the will of the matter wherein it worketh.'[4] Thus this scene gives him a special emphasis, as he turns instantly into a dutiful son on the entrance of his father.

If Edmund is established in our consciousness in Act I as a formidable challenge to the orthodox assumptions about nature and natural relations shared by his father and Edgar, it is in Act II that his challenge strikes home, with the success of his plot to drive out Edgar and replace him in Gloucester's esteem as his 'Loyal and natural boy'. This phrase is capped by Cornwall's, 'I hear that you have shown your father / A child-like office.' The play on what it is to be natural, loyal and childlike echoes the opening scene, and reverberates elsewhere in the play, as Gloucester seeks to disinherit Edgar in a parallel with Cordelia that is reinforced by Regan's anachronistic reference to Edgar as Lear's godson.

Edmund is seen in the entourage of Cornwall and Regan as the one who intervenes to stop Kent from beating Oswald, but he does not speak in the rest of II.2, and does not accompany Cornwall and Regan when they confront Lear in II.4. His rise established, Shakespeare switches attention to Edgar, and as Edmund was highlighted at the opening and again in I.2, so Edgar, a shadowy figure until this point, takes the spotlight, so to speak, in what is conventionally treated as II.3. This is virtually the same in Q and in F, where he addresses the audience as he begins to turn himself into Poor Tom. It is set off as a separate scene by many editors,[5] but not so marked in Q or F, where the action is continuous, so that Kent, asleep in the stocks, is also present on stage. The two are thus visually linked in degradation and as outcasts, anticipating their association in Act III with Lear, when he is shut out to wander in the storm. It is only now, when Edgar speaks directly to the audience in a kind of soliloquy and takes on a new role, that he becomes a significant presence in the play.

Cornwall and Regan, jostling for dominance, are also forcefully established in these scenes as resolute figures, controlling their part of the kingdom with an authority as peremptory as Lear's, even as Regan asserts herself in relation to her dominant husband. They have already effectively displaced Lear, even if the anxiety reflected in Regan's determination to have the last word suggests tensions that could explode. Edmund incidentally hints in II.1 that there is already hostility between rival factions for Albany and Cornwall, when he asks Edgar, 'have you nothing said / Upon his party 'gainst [against Q] the Duke of Albany?', so that a sense of potential fracture and dissension is felt, as the consequences of Lear's folly in dividing the kingdom begin to emerge. Where in Act I Lear is the dominating voice and his the dominating perspective – even if Edmund has his moment as an unruly and subversive presence, and Goneril faces down her father – in the next phase of the action, the effect of giving Cornwall and Regan, Edgar and Kent their independent voices is to open up a range of perspectives, and in some measure to decentre Lear.

While Lear is off stage, further associations of violence are developed in connection with his entourage. Kent's attempt to force Oswald to fight him, and his string of inventive insults, a sustained aria of name-calling, may again satisfy an audience's gut feeling that Oswald deserves to be put down in this way, and that taking a smack at him is the next best thing to rebuking Goneril, but his violence does his master a disservice, confirms evidence of the riotous behaviour of his followers, and exacerbates the conflict between Lear and his daughters. To speak what we feel may be honest, but it can be politically stupid or naive. This scene has some parallels with I.I, with Kent now behaving like Cordelia in uttering unpalatable truths, for which he is put in the stocks by the tough Cornwall (F; Q gives Regan the last word here, 'put in his legs'). F omits the lines in which Gloucester in Q remonstrates with Cornwall (II.2.141–5), saying that to put someone in the stocks is punishment for the 'basest and contemned'st wretches' (Q has 'contaned' corrected to 'temnest') who steal and commit petty crimes, so urging the scandal of punishing the King's messenger in this way. By omitting this passage, F allows us to think that Kent's punishment is not inappropriate for his offence, as indeed is suggested by the orders for discipline in the household of the Earl of Huntingdon issued in 1604: there urging a quarrel or behaving in an unseemly way to one's betters was to be punished by the stocks.[6]

Shakespeare here makes Kent and Edgar speak in turn, each

unaware of the other, as isolated and outcast, and at the same time associates them visually by their simultaneous presence on the stage, just before Lear returns in II.4 to his confrontation with Goneril and Regan. There are marked echoes of Act I, as Lear is once again faced with a flouting of his authority that leaves him incredulous. He cannot accept that Cornwall and Regan have put Kent in the stocks, any more than he could accept Cordelia's 'Nothing'; and it brings on an attack of the mother, the 'Hysterica passio' that rises from the womb, and makes Lear behave alternately like the stereotype of a woman overcome by passion (see below, p. 215; this scene contains his only reference in the play to the mother of Lear's children) and as imperious monarch, a double image caught neatly in F in the conjunction of ordering and begging in his message to Regan, 'The dear father / Would with his daughter speak, commands, tends, service' (Q has 'come and', corrected to 'commands'). When, in speaking to Regan, Lear begins to abuse Goneril again, Regan is given an additional few lines in F in which she once again stresses the 'riots' of Lear's knights:

LEAR   Say? how is that?
REG.   I cannot think my sister in the least
   Would fail her obligation. If sir perchance
   She have restrained the riots of your followers,
   'Tis on such ground, and to such wholesome end,
   As clears her from all blame.   (II.4.140–5; F only)

So in two small touches, in making Cornwall solely responsible for putting Kent in the stocks, and in stressing again the misbehaviour of Lear's knights as what seems a perfectly sound reason for reducing his train, F alters the balance between Lear and Regan and makes it much more even.

   It is Regan who now appeals (as Albany did earlier in F at I.4.261) to her father to be patient; but Lear, who has given away his rule, and so, as Regan not unreasonably says, 'should be rul'd', converts the issue of rule or power into one of age and ingratitude, appealing, ironically in relation to his casting out of Cordelia, to the 'bond of childhood'. It is easy to be so moved by the growing alienation of the old King as to overlook the logic of their case for reducing the number of his followers, and see Goneril and Regan as merely evil, especially when the argument with his daughters leads inexorably to Regan's 'What need[s Q] one?' Yet his terrifying and total rejection of Goneril and his ferocious curses upon her again in this scene help to make compromise impossible, even though he half-recognizes that the corruption of his daughters is also his own corruption, derived from him:

> But yet thou art my flesh, my blood, my daughter,
> Or rather a disease that's in [lies within Q] my flesh,
> Which I must needs call mine. Thou art a boil,
> A plague-sore, or [an Q] embossed carbuncle
> In my corrupted blood.   (II.4.221–5)

If they are corrupted, he is the source of that corruption, and by giving up power yet insisting on his prerogatives, he has himself exposed the disease that infects them all. The issue of his followers becomes crucial in Regan's questions:

>   what, fifty followers?
> Is it not well? What should you need of more?
> Yea, or so many? Sith that both charge and danger,
> Speak[s Q] 'gainst so great a number? How in one house,
> Should many people, under two commands,
> Hold amity? 'Tis hard, almost impossible.   (II.4.237–42)

The problem for her is a political one, and her objections are perfectly rational and focus the contradiction in Lear's attempt to hang on to what he has given away, his authority. Essentially the same point is made by Coriolanus in the larger context of Rome when the Tribunes of the people are established:

>   By Jove himself,
> It makes the consuls base; and my soul aches
> To know, when two authorities are up,
> Neither supreme, how soon confusion
> May enter 'twixt the gap of both, and take
> The one by th'other.   (*Coriolanus*, III.1.107–12)

Lear, however, cannot see the issue in terms of rule, but only in terms of wickedness ('Those wicked creatures yet do look [seem Q] well favour'd / When others are more wicked'), or in terms of love, once again measuring love, when Goneril's offer seems better than that of Regan ('thou art twice her love').

Goneril and Regan put themselves in the wrong by proposing to get rid of all Lear's followers, provoking his magnificent rejoinder to 'What need one?', 'O reason not the need', which climaxes the whole sequence. Indeed, he has no need of a large retinue, but their stripping away of all isolates him pathetically on stage, and forces

upon him the recognition at last that he is no longer in power, but a
'poor old man [fellow Q]', in need of patience more than anything.
To the last Regan is concerned about the 'desperate train' of knights
attending Lear, and what they may provoke him to do. It is
somewhat odd, then, that when Lear enters at the beginning of this
scene he is accompanied by one 'Gentleman' (F; Knight, Q). A
director may choose, as Peter Brook did in 1962 and in his film
version in 1971, to make Lear's train a formidable gang of unruly
ruffians, whose gross behaviour creates mayhem in Goneril's court;
but F suggests that Shakespeare was concerned to heighten the
image of the daughters and the powerful Cornwall, who has the last
word in the scene, as they combine against an increasingly isolated
and vulnerable Lear. This would explain why only one of his
followers has a speaking part in the scene (does Regan point to him
on her question, 'What need one?'). He still has 'five or six and thirty
of his knights' accompanying him to Dover, according to Oswald at
III.7.16, so the absence of them in II.4. would seem to be calculated by
the author. The effect of this may be to reduce the impact of Regan's
anxiety about Lear's riotous followers, by emphasizing visually that
they have by this time begun to abandon him, as the Fool hinted
earlier in the scene:

> That sir which [that Q] serves [and seeks F] for gain
>   And follows but for form;
> Will pack, when it begins to rain,
>   And leave thee in the storm.

The Fool arrives with Lear in II.4, but his is now a different, more
choric role than earlier. Almost all the Fool's comments in the scene
are addressed to Kent, but F adds the lines directed at Lear in which
the Fool generalizes once again on Lear's folly in giving away his
possessions:

> Fathers that wear rags,
>   Do make their children blind,
> But fathers that bear bags,
>   Shall see their children kind.
> Fortune that arrant whore,
> Ne'er turns the key to th'poor.   (II.4.48–53; F only)

But even this speech serves as a choric reminder to the audience,
emphasizing that Lear has nothing to bargain with. Lear does not
seem to notice the Fool's speech, which in F allows the old King to

express silently by gesture the symptoms of the 'mother', a choking in the throat,[7] that begin to affect him. It is only as he goes off that he at last turns to his old companion the Fool, and exits with him, crying 'O fool, I shall go mad', into the storm that is already heard according to the stage direction 'Storm and Tempest' in F at line 282.

It may be that in Shakespeare's revised conception of the play a stage of the action was completed not in II.4, with the exit into the storm after the emotional climax of Lear's great speech, 'O reason not the need' – which so poignantly dramatizes his loss of authority, with all its complex contrasts between, for instance, power and impotence, manliness and effeminacy, need and desire, patience and hysteria – but in III.2, a scene which, like the last scene of Act I, brings Kent, Lear and the Fool together, and ends with another direct address to the audience by the Fool (in F only). Where, in I.5, Lear is still communicating with his companions, in III.2 he is absorbed in anger and self-pity, and only notices the Fool as he goes off to the hovel. In place of his attempt to stave off madness, ('let me not be mad'), he now recognizes that he cannot escape it ('My wits begin to turn'). F adds the Fool's prophecy at the end of the scene (see above, pp. 101–2), when he has the stage to himself for his rhyming speech beginning:

> When priests are more in word than matter;
> When brewers mar their malt with water;
> When nobles are their tailors' tutors,
> No heretics burn'd, but wenches' suitors;
> When every case in law, is right . . .

The audience would recognize the satirical implications for their own world of the confusion predicted here, and this speech highlights the Fool as a choric figure who breaks out of the frame, so to speak, in his final joke, 'This prophecy Merlin shall make, for I live before his time.' Here he drops his role for the moment to speak in direct relationship to the audience, as he had done at the end of I.5 (see above, p. 183), and makes a direct connection between the events of the play and the world outside the theatre.

Until very recently this speech was usually cut in productions of the play,[8] as distracting attention from the pathos of Lear's exit, as he goes off saying 'Come bring us to this hovel.' In his concentration on the storm for most of the scene, he ignores the Fool, before turning to him in a gesture that takes him out of his self-absorption into contact with others, 'Come on, my boy . . . I have one part in [of Q] my heart / That's sorry [That sorrows Q] yet for thee.' In F, however, 'Come bring us to this hovel' must be addressed to Kent, who leads Lear off, leaving the Fool to speak his prophecy. The increasing attention given to political and social issues in the play has led directors in some recent productions to emphasize this speech,[9] so that it becomes a potent satiric vision of the world as it is, set against a utopian possibility, ironically depicted as 'confusion'. The lines at once directly link the play with the world of the audience, one in which brewers are known to adulterate their ale, in which nobles spend extravagantly on clothes, and in which cutpurses abound and usurers, bawds and whores often thrive; and at the same time they symbolize the chaos that Lear has brought about. The speech has a generalizing force, like the songs in a Brecht play, stressing the larger impact of Lear's division of the kingdom, and satirically linking disorder and corruption in the play with the corruptions the audience would be aware of in their own society. The Fool thus doubles in these scenes in F as general commentator, and as the 'boy' noticed sympathetically by Lear from time to time as the old King gradually sheds his preoccupation with himself and recovers a concern for others.

CONFUSION

The sequence of scenes that culminates in the Fool's prophecy dramatizes the humiliation of Kent, the isolation of Edgar and the expulsion of Lear. The next sequence begins with the return in III.3 of Edmund, off stage since II.2, and shows the realm of Albion coming to great confusion. Even as the powerless Lear shifts from rage ('I will punish home') and self-pity to an awareness of the sufferings of others, so the inevitable consequences of his blindness when in power now begin to affect the whole country, and Edmund is a key figure in this development. As Lear begins to attend to others, so the Fool's role withers away. Edgar and Lear himself take over as choric commentators, Edgar using his madness as Poor Tom, and Lear himself becoming a kind of fool. The brilliant episode of the mock-trial in Q, III.6, interrupts this development by restoring the Fool to prominence, and returning to a Lear still harping on his daughters, and it was dropped from F, as was Edgar's rhyming soliloquy at the end of

the scene soliciting sympathy for Lear. In Q Lear ignores the Fool in
III.4, but in F two lines are added in which the King addresses him:

> In boy, go first. You houseless poverty,
> Nay, get thee in; I'll pray, and then I'll sleep.
>
> (III.4.26–7; F only)

These lines immediately precede Lear's 'prayer' (does F imply that
he kneels?), 'Poor naked wretches ...', so that Lear's sudden
attention to the Fool in F leads him to think of other 'wretches'. And
in F Lear's 'prayer' is followed by a second addition, the cry of Edgar
announcing himself as Poor Tom, 'Fathom and half, fathom and
half; poor Tom', as if he is taking soundings in floodwater. Thus in F
Lear's great cry of pity for the poor, 'Take physic, pomp, / Expose
thyself to feel what wretches feel', is sandwiched between his
attending to the Fool, and the discovery in the hovel of Poor Tom, a
naked wretch indeed. The stage image is powerful here, but, of
course, it is only when he is marginalized and lacks the power to do
anything about them that Lear begins to feel for the poor. In Q Lear
speaks only to Kent here, and it is the Fool who names Poor Tom.
These small additions add to the dramatic force of a scene in which
the appearance of Poor Tom triggers in Lear the madness that leads
him from this point on in Q and F to devote all his attention to his
'philosopher' and ignore the Fool, whose brief speeches in the
remaining lines of III.4 serve as general comments on the group
('This cold night will turn us all to fools, and madmen'), while Kent
and Gloucester try their best to communicate with the King.

Lear's identification of himself with Poor Tom leads him to start
tearing off his clothes: 'Thou art the thing itself; unaccommodated
man, is no more but such a poor, bare, forked animal as thou art.
Off, off you lendings: [Come, unbutton here. (F)]' It is a gesture that
seems to symbolize the stripping away of his power, his retinue, his
role and authority, all that he has brought about by his initial error
in dividing the kingdom, but also shows him casting off all the
trappings he no longer needs, and accepting his community with
others. Tearing off his clothes would in fact reduce Lear himself to a
'poor, bare, forked animal', for clothes mark the difference between
human beings and animals. The small addition, if it is one (Q has
'come on', but in its uncorrected state, 'come on bee true', which
looks like a corruption of 'unbutton'), in F of the phrase 'Come,
unbutton here' qualifies 'Off, off you lendings', suggesting that Lear

does not get very far in taking his clothes off, and is stayed by the Fool as the latter says, 'Prithee, nuncle, be contented', and by Kent. The common practice of adding a stage direction for Lear, 'Tears off his clothes',[10] is misleading. From the period of the Restoration until well into the nineteenth century, Lear (played for much of this period in Nahum Tate's version), was traditionally costumed in a regal robe of scarlet bordered with ermine, and a drawing of Macready playing the role in 1838 shows him pulling this off to reveal an undershirt,[11] but with Kent and the Fool preventing him from stripping. Such a costume has nothing to do with the ostensible period of the play, but enforces the symbolism of Lear shedding his royalty. He does not cast off his clothes in order to discover his humanity, as is sometimes claimed, for the finding of himself involves the restoration of proper clothing, and when he is comforted by Cordelia, the first thing done for him is to 'put fresh garments on him' (IV.7.21).

This image of the half-crazed Lear unbuttoning in the company of the almost naked Poor Tom, the Fool and Kent is in F the climax of the storm scenes, and III.6, much abbreviated in this text, becomes a kind of coda, a coda in which Lear, now quite mad in impatience at his daughters, at last falls asleep, and is carried off by Kent to be set on his way to Dover. F adds two brief speeches for the Fool, giving him more prominence (see p. 103 above) as he caps Lear's last words, 'We'll go to supper i'th'morning. [So, so, so Q]', with 'And I'll go to bed at noon'; in this way the Fool is provided with a memorable last line that jokingly underlines the disorder in Lear's mind and in the world around him. The Fool disappears altogether after this scene, and Lear himself is not seen again after this crisis until IV.6. All that remains for him is to be reconciled to Cordelia and to die.

The rejection of Lear by Goneril and Regan, and his wanderings in the storm, have for long been the centre of attention, but the return of Edmund in III.3, and of Edgar as Poor Tom in IV.4, brings a shift of perspective, as the power-struggles of the next generation become central, and Lear is sidelined as a pathetic, mad old man, politically insignificant. Edmund betrays his father to Cornwall, reporting him as 'an intelligent party to the advantages of France' (Q and F). Although many references to France found in Q are omitted from F, several, including this one, Cordelia's reference to 'great France' at IV.4.25, and Cornwall's announcement that the 'army of France is landed' at III.7.2, are retained in F, so that we always have the sense that Cordelia is leading French forces, and that far more than a civil quarrel between Cornwall and Albany is at stake. In supporting the French (Cordelia) Gloucester really is a traitor to his own country. This is emphasized in F by a number of changes made in III.7, the scene of Gloucester's blinding. The last nine lines in Q, in which two 'Servants' of Cornwall plan to assist the now blind old man, direct attention to his 'bleeding face', and channel audience response by their comments on the 'wickedness' of Cornwall and Regan, are omitted from F. In this text, not only is there no coercion of our sympathy for Gloucester, but two other alterations emphasize his treachery. In his opening call to his servants to 'seek out the villain Gloucester' (Q), the word 'villain' is changed in F to 'traitor'; and later F adds the word 'treacherous' in Regan's response to Gloucester's 'Where's my son Edmund?', as she cries, 'Out treacherous villain', words that apply ironically to Edmund, but are hurled at his father. In F, thus, the words 'traitor', 'traitorous' or 'treacherous' occur eight times in a scene of ninety-six lines, so stressing that in changing sides, switching his allegiance from Cornwall and Regan back to Lear, Gloucester is indeed a traitor to them; but this reiteration also makes us aware that in the conditions Lear has brought about by his division of the kingdom, it is impossible not to be a traitor to one side or another; all are traitors. The overall effect of the scene is significantly modified in F.

In this scene the violence threatened since the rumour heard in II.1 of 'likely wars' between Cornwall and Albany now breaks out, though not quite as anticipated. Hitherto the violence in the play has been associated with Lear and his companions, with Lear who drew his sword on Kent and struck Oswald, with Lear's riotous knights, and with Kent, who tripped up, and later beat Oswald; but now the memory of these incidents is overwhelmed by the horror of the physical blinding on stage of Gloucester, and, violence provoking more violence, the killing of Cornwall by his servant, and of the servant by Regan. The first blood is shed in the play, and the visual impact on the audience is notoriously shocking. It drastically alters our perspective on Cornwall and Regan, staining them with a kind of blood-guilt in the sheer cruelty of their torture of Gloucester. It is not merely gratuitous violence, therefore, as it brings into the open what remains latent in their earlier treatment of Lear, and does so in relation to another old man and father-figure who could be a stand-in for him. At the same time, the shock of this scene breaks the spell cast by Lear himself through the storm scenes, and opens out the action by its insistence on the invasion of England by a French force ('the army of France is landed'), its emphasis on the sending of Lear to Dover (mentioned five times), and its stress on the 'treachery' of Gloucester and corresponding 'loyalty' of Edmund, who is 'too good to pity' his father (III.7.90). Here indeed the confusion Lear has brought about in the realm of Albion is powerfully dramatized.

The return of Edgar coincides with Lear's shift from self-pity to a concern with 'Poor naked wretches', and he comes in pat upon his cue. To the audience he is, of course, Edgar in disguise playing madman, whose tears may spoil his 'counterfeiting' (III.6.61). Edgar displaces the Fool as nearest to Lear, and takes Lear's attention away from himself as he becomes the King's 'philosopher'. Edgar presents himself as a former 'servingman', perhaps a lover or court hanger-on, who has relished all the vices available to the fashionable gallant in Jacobean England. Now, reduced to penury, he is punished by the imaginary fiends that haunt him. He catalogues the corruptions of the courtier who is 'false of heart, light of ear, bloody of hand; hog in sloth, fox in stealth, wolf in greediness, dog in madness, lion in prey', and from this perspective the prince of darkness is indeed a 'gentleman'. So Edgar too reminds us of the larger context of the play, even as he provokes Lear's attempt to strip off his clothing. Edgar's importance as symbolic 'unaccommodated man' lies in stirring Lear here, and in IV.1 Gloucester, to a new awareness of what they neglected when in power, or simply failed to see; but for the audience, Edgar is not only a moral consciousness, a rebuke to the 'superfluous and lust-dieted man' (IV.1.67), but also a witness from a younger generation to the sufferings of the old. In maintaining his disguise he always remains in control of himself, aloof from, and when necessary able to manipulate, the feelings of Lear and Gloucester, and so is able to become an agent of their recovery. Only by avoiding emotional commitment does Edgar remain clear-sighted and become a force for renewal and restitution; this is the main reason why Shakespeare does not permit him to reveal himself to his father until the very end.[12] The visual emblem of Poor Tom, the mad, leading the blind (''Tis the time's plague, when madmen lead the blind', IV.1.46), recalls Lear with the Fool in the storm, a connection made for us by the addition of a few lines in F in Edgar's opening speech:

> Welcome then,
> Thou unsubstantial air that I embrace:
> The wretch that thou hast blown unto the worst
> Owes nothing to thy blasts.

Edgar's plaintive line a little later, 'Who is't can say, "I am at the worst"?' (line 25) thus in F again reminds us of Lear and anticipates worse to come, and yet this scene also visually reunites the father with the son he cast out. F also omits Edgar's verbal flourish in which he names the five 'fiends' troubling him, so removing lines which distract from the pathos of the scene, and from Edgar's difficulty in maintaining his mask as Poor Tom.

Edmund returns to initiate the violence of the later part of the play by betraying his father, while Edgar returns as witness to the degradation of Gloucester and agent of his recovery. They set in motion contrasting movements, on the one hand towards conflict and disintegration and on the other towards reunion and order. The substantial changes made in Act iv in F may be seen as intensifying the interaction between these movements. Before the death of Cornwall the division between him and Albany had extended into a quarrel between Goneril and Regan for the favours of Edmund, and Albany finds himself in iv.2 in the impossible position of siding with Gloucester and Lear while caught up in a war in which they are the enemy. This scene is much abbreviated in F, losing thirty-four of its ninety-seven lines, including a reference by Goneril to a French force spreading its 'banners' in England. One omission removes the dialogue in which Albany a second time depicts Goneril as a 'fiend' (he has already called her 'devil' and 'fiend' in lines found in both Q and F), and threatens to attack her (lines 63–8). The other large abridgment in the scene removes the dialogue in which Albany turns on Goneril and moralizes on what she and her sister, 'Tigers, not daughters', have done, in his speech beginning, 'Wisdom and goodness, to the vile seem vile' (iv.2.38–49). Here, as in iii.7, speeches that would coerce the viewer's response are omitted from F, and the emphasis is on preparations for war, on Goneril's display of love for Edmund, on the split between her and Albany, and on the news of the blinding of Gloucester. F adds just one line, Goneril's ironic remark as Edmund leaves, and before Albany enters, 'Oh, the difference of man, and man', pointing for the audience beyond the contrast between her husband and Edmund to the differences and dissensions between other men in the play.

The threat of war escalates rapidly through Act IV, especially in the slimmed down Folio text, and to meet the forces of the army that has landed (from France, IV.2.4), the 'powers' of Albany are in the field by IV.5. The quarrel between Goneril and Regan for the favours of Edmund also gathers pace. It is in this context that Cordelia returns in IV.4. She has been so long off stage that Shakespeare has been able to modify her character so that she now seems at first no longer the girl tough and bold enough to challenge her autocratic father-king and rebuke her older sisters, but rather in Q an almost holy figure, no longer measuring love according to her bond, but the very emblem of caring pity. F omits the elaborate establishment of a quasi-religious aura about this new Cordelia in the Gentleman's description of her 'holy' tears in IV.3. The brief image of her presented in the scene which follows in Q, and which is all we have in F, is enough to restore her as a figure of love and pity, notably in the echo of Christ's words (Luke 2.49) in her 'O dear father, / It is thy business that I go about'. The scene also starts with the news that Lear has been found, and so points to the reunion of another cast-off child with her father. At the same time, in F the opening stage direction calls for Cordelia to enter 'with Drum and Colours' (not in Q), and 'soldiers' ('others', Q), so making it clear that she is at the head of an army; and since here again Cordelia mentions the French connection,

> Therefore great France
> My mourning, and importun'd [important Q] tears hath pitied,
> (IV.4.25–6)

the 'colours' presumably sufficiently indicated to the audience a French army opposed to the 'British powers' a Messenger reports as 'marching hitherward' (line 21). Her presence leading an army does relate to her boldness in the opening scene, as now Cordelia has made it her business, she says, to restore 'our ag'd father's right [rite F]'. Her use of the royal plural is notable, as is her concern for the 'right' of Lear; does she mean to restore her father to the power he has given away, to a royalty he has relinquished? It would seem that there is after all, and in spite of her denial, some 'blown ambition' (line 27) in what she is doing; she is not merely rescuing Lear, but aiming to give him back the power he so abused. It seems that she is caught up in the horrible confusions caused by her father's initial act, for here she defends herself as acting out of pity and love, which merge with and at the same time paradoxically are alien to the

image of the war she is seeking. Here the opposing impulses towards
conflict and restoration of accord are poignantly dramatized.

When Cordelia translates her love for her father into a determination to restore him to power, she exercises power over him. When
Edgar, who resurfaces as himself in iv.6, no longer playing Poor
Tom, claims to be curing his father's despair, he is exercising power
over Gloucester. The usual roles of father and child are reversed.
The mime of Gloucester's 'death' staged by Edgar has an actor
pretending to be blind fall over a 'cliff' he and we know isn't there,
for the purpose, Edgar says, of curing Gloucester's 'despair'; but
though his recovery from his 'fall' leads him to acquire a measure of
patience and renounce thoughts of suicide, the effect does not last,
for Gloucester soon wishes for death at the hands of Oswald (line
230), and falls into 'ill thoughts again' (v.2.8) when we next see him.
The mime of Gloucester throwing himself, as he supposes, over a cliff
is the same in F as in Q, and seems to be there for its effect on the
audience as much as for its uncertain effect on Gloucester. Critics,
actors and directors do not agree on whether the episode is meant to
be grotesque, tragic, absurd, or farcical, and argue about 'how much
of an illusion his [Shakespeare's] audience might have been under
about the presence of a cliff'.[13] As far as illusion is concerned, the
audience is aware visually all the time that there is no cliff, and the
point of the incident would be lost if they were under such an
illusion. The sequence relates to a conventional device of having a
character 'die' and return to life (like Bottom as Pyramus, Falstaff or
Imogen) which is basically comic, both because we know the actor is
not really dead, and because we and the characters are delighted to
see them come to life again. But in *King Lear* Shakespeare transforms
the convention: whatever other qualities may be detected in this
scene, there is an element of gratuitous cruelty about it, as Gloucester is drawn into a charade which raises his hopes for the one thing
he wants, death, only to deprive him of what he calls 'that benefit'
(line 61); if it helps him temporarily to 'bear / Affliction', it leaves
him in the end still waiting for the death he has been offered and
then denied ('a man may rot even here', v.2.8). Peter Brook made
his Gloucester faint as he fell, and come to convinced that he had
died, and the more successful the actor is in conveying a sense of his
illusion of suicide, the more cruel the effect seems to be, as he revives
to cry 'Away, and let me die.'

This episode also brings the gods momentarily into the action, but

they exist only as created and stage-managed by Edgar, so that the
spectacle of Gloucester kneeling in prayer, 'O, you mighty gods! /
This world I do renounce . . .', is at once pathetic and empty – there
is no other world, except as Edgar produces it in his words, deceiving
his father for the time being into believing his 'life's a miracle', and
telling him what to think:

> Think that the clearest gods, who make them [made their Q] honours
> Of men's impossibilities, have preserved thee.

Gloucester may credit this for a little while, but we get no nearer to
the gods in the play than as Edgar here creates them. It is an
extraordinary contrast to *Hamlet*, where a Christian dispensation, a
belief in God, in Providence and in another world are taken for
granted in the action, if frequently questioned, and set against a sense
of death as final, as mere oblivion. The action of *King Lear*, on the
other hand, takes place in a present without a past, and in a secular
world where the gods are verbal constructs, made present as Edgar
produces them imaginatively for the dubious benefit of his father.[14] In
relation to this, the single association of Cordelia with Christ in IV.4
merely helps to confirm her emblematic rehabilitation as a figure of
pity, and does not have further reverberations in the play.

   Political confusion in the realm of Albion, complicated by
Edmund's machinations, Regan's lust for him, and Cordelia's
invasion with a French army, is paralleled by the confusion in the
minds of Gloucester and Lear in their encounter in IV.6. Lear has
been off stage for about 370 lines (in F; much longer in Q), and is
changed, in his madness now significantly enacting a mockery of his
former power, a parody of the 'great image of authority', conducting
a 'trial' of Gloucester for adultery, and of his own daughters, that
becomes at once a searing outburst of misogyny, and, in F, an
indictment of the use of power and wealth to pervert the course of
justice. Lear's vision here extends the Fool's prophecy into the
cynicism of total corruption, notably in the lines added in F (and
printed there as prose):

> Through tatter'd clothes great [rags, small Q] vices do appear:
> Robes and furr'd gowns hide[s Q] all. [Place sins with gold,
> And the strong lance of justice, hurtless breaks:
> Arm it in rags, a pigmy's straw does pierce it.
> None does offend, none, I say none, I'll able 'em;
> Take that of me my friend, who have the power
> To seal th'accuser's lips. (F)]   (IV.6.164–70)

These lines become the culmination of Lear's new perception of the
nature of authority, 'A dog's obeyed [so bade Q] in office', and they
add a further dimension: if gold can 'place' or put in office 'sins',[15]
then offence loses its meaning, so that 'None does offend, none, I say,
none.' The lines also ironically expose the nature of the power the
now impotent Lear once had to authorize anyone ('I'll able 'em') to
corrupt the course of justice.

The scene begins with a mock-death, goes on to the encounter of
two old men conscious of ruin and mortality, with Lear imagining
killing his sons-in-law ('Then kill, kill, kill, kill, kill, kill'), and
running off to 'die bravely', and ends with the violent death on stage
of Oswald. If Gloucester's passage through a kind of death and
coming to life again is intended to parallel Lear's oblivion in the loss
of his wits and return to sanity, it also belongs with the other forms of
violence in the scene, and the harping on death. Edgar grows in
power and stature, mentally in manipulating his father, physically in
defeating and killing Oswald. At the same time this scene registers a
sense of reconciliation between Gloucester and Edgar (who nevertheless, in spite of his claim to having learned to be 'pregnant to good
pity', does not here reveal who he is to his father), and between Lear
and Gloucester. The power of the scene lies in its extension of the
sense of confusion, in its extraordinary combination of violence and
pathos, cruelty and pity, hostility and reconciliation, and in its visual
and verbal reminders that Lear and Gloucester have death on their
minds, as dying well is all that they can hope for.

The meeting of Gloucester and Lear is sandwiched between the
'death' and revival of Gloucester under Edgar's supervision, and the
bringing back to consciousness of Lear under Cordelia's supervision.
When Lear is brought on 'in a chair carried by Servants' (F; not in
Q), and clothed in 'fresh garments' to be reunited once more with
Cordelia, a dramatic point of Gloucester's mimed suicide becomes
clearer, for both men go through a symbolic death and an unwanted
return to life. Lear's reconciliation with Cordelia, his kneeling to her
when she asks his blessing, and his acceptance at last that he is 'a
very foolish fond old man, / Fourscore and upward' (F adds, 'Not an
hour more, nor less'), are very affecting. But the scene is double-
edged, like that between Gloucester and Edgar at the beginning of
IV.6, for again there is an element, unintended on Cordelia's part, of
cruelty about it. We have seen Lear come to new perceptions in

madness, exposing the corruptions of authority and making a mockery of kingship, perceptions that make it impossible for him to take on such authority again, and it is a further confusion that in her well-meaning love this 'kind and dear princess', as Kent calls her, is determined not only to restore her father to a life he would be glad to relinquish, but also to restore him to the power and majesty he can no longer command, and has given up. His first words are 'You do me wrong to take me out o'th'grave', so that her address to him, 'How does my Royal Lord? How fares your Majesty?', is doubly ironic in that she treats him as a monarch rather than as her father, and would give him back what he no longer wants (his life), and no longer has or can have (his power and status). In F the number of characters is reduced, as the Doctor who ministers to Lear (Q) vanishes, to be amalgamated with the 'Gentleman' who put fresh clothes on him, and eight lines are omitted from the dialogue of Cordelia and the Gentleman. F also leaves out the final sequence of twelve lines in Q, a conversation between Kent and the Gentleman about the latest news and rumours, and the expectation of battle, so that in F the scene ends with Lear's exit line, 'Pray [you F] now forget, and forgive, I am old and foolish.' This line gains extra weight in F, and its open syntax generalizes its meaning, allowing the possibility that Lear says not simply 'forgive me for my injustice to you', but 'forget and forgive all wrongs done in the past'. It is thus especially poignant that Cordelia cannot, as his words suggest he would do, forget or forgive her sisters, and in seeking to restore him to his 'right', his rule, by heading an army in battle against the British forces led by Albany and Edmund, she ends by inflicting on him yet more suffering.

WAR

The last part of the play has to do with war, and the war is between England and France. In F Lear's departure is followed by the entry 'with Drum and Colours' (F; not in Q) of Edmund, Regan and their army, to join with the army of Albany and Goneril, who also lead their soldiers 'with Drum and Colours' (F), the banners emphasizing for the audience that these are British forces. The scene is shortened in F by the omission of twelve lines. The jealousy of Regan is well established by now, so that the economy of leaving out part of her questioning of Edmund about his relations with Goneril can be afforded. F also omits Albany's lines in which in Q he makes it known that he fights against France, not 'the king', and two lines in which Edmund speaks respectfully to Albany. Thus the motives of Albany in fighting are left less clear, and the relationship between him and Edmund uncertain, perhaps in preparation for the breach between them in the next scene. After Edgar slips in to give Albany his letter denouncing Edmund, and to issue his challenge, Edmund returns to have the last word, his final soliloquy in which, in Q and F, he ponders on the fix he is in, having sworn love to both Regan and Goneril, and sees in his usual ruthless and clear-sighted fashion that his only course is let the two sisters sort it out, and to ensure the deaths of Albany, Lear and Cordelia. Here the vivid visual presentation of forces gathering for war, and reminders of discord between brothers (Edmund and Edgar), sisters (Goneril and Regan), and partners in battle (Edmund and Albany), brings also a threat to the lives of Lear and Cordelia, and so provides a shattering response to Lear's wish to 'forget, and forgive'. The scene shows how sentimental, indeed impossible, that desire is in the context of the sequence of events triggered by his division of the kingdom and by Gloucester's errors.

The visual image at the beginning of v.2 sharpens this contradiction, for Cordelia and Lear march across the stage with their army, accompanied likewise by 'Drum and Colours' (F). Are the colours those of Lear, as perhaps displayed in the opening scene, or those of France? The logic of the play would suggest the latter as more appropriate here. Although, as noted earlier (see pp. 106–7), F removes some references to France and changes the entry as it appears in Q ('Enter the powers of France over the stage, Cordelia with her father in her hand'), enough indications remain in the text that Cordelia is at the head of a French invading force moving against 'British powers' (iv.4.21). In any case, Lear's 'Pray you now forget, and forgive' is followed by his next appearance leading an army assembled to fight his own countrymen and marshalled by his own children. Why does Cordelia not simply take him back with her to France?[16] The play does not raise this question, but it does show her determination to seek conflict, to restore Lear to power, and, apparently, to revenge herself on her sisters. Almost at once in this brief scene, after Edgar and Gloucester have exchanged only four lines, the sound of an 'Alarm and Retreat' (Q and F), 'within' added in F, marks the defeat of Lear and Cordelia, and their capture by the enemy. Some directors have introduced a full-scale battle at this point, with the silent Gloucester on stage tormented by the noise, or they have elaborated noises off stage spotlighting the isolation of Gloucester in the middle of battle,[17] and it is important that the sense of a large-scale fight is registered as two nations clash. At the same time, the text in Q and F emphasizes above all the rapidity with which the fortunes of Lear change, and how quickly affliction strikes again. Edgar's pious platitudes are almost absurdly inadequate to the situation:

> Men must endure
> Their going hence, even as their coming hither,
> Ripeness is all come on.   (v.2.9–11)

Both Gloucester and Lear have gone beyond 'ripeness', if this word has to do with being reconciled to dying; they have both wished for and been denied death only to have their suffering prolonged, and both have become irrelevant to the struggles for power of a new generation.

In any case, entries of marching armies and the battle set the tone for most of Act v, which is full of stage action, and foregrounds a series of events and discoveries that have been seen as more appropriate to romance than to tragedy, but which deliberately engage the audience's immediate attention, and allow the matter of Lear and Gloucester to fade into the background. The victory of Edmund becomes a defeat as Albany arrests him for high treason and emerges unexpectedly as a claimant to power ('I hold you but a subject of this war'). The quarrel of Goneril and Regan for love of Edmund is brought into the open by Goneril in a sequence that is shortened in F by the omission of six lines that merely expand what has already been said; and at the same time F sharpens the interchange of dialogue by adding Goneril's comment 'An interlude', so making the characters conscious of the element of black farce in the bitter conflict of the sisters:

ALB.   For your claim fair sister[s F],
  I bar it in the interest of my wife,
  'Tis she is sub-contracted to this lord,
  And I her husband contradict your [the Q] bans.
  If you will marry, make your loves [love Q] to me,
  My lady is bespoke.
[GON.   An interlude. F]   (v.3.89–94)

Goneril's remark points up Albany's rewriting of the plot Goneril
has in mind into a new play-script, and heightens the new toughness
and independence shown by Albany in the later scenes of the play.
The intensity of feeling generated here as Albany arrests his own
wife, 'this gilded serpent' who is sub-contracted to Emund, and the
absorption of the characters in their own affairs, leads into Albany's
challenge to Edmund if a champion does not appear for him. The
clash of the brothers is the centrepiece of the scene, and one reason
Shakespeare has the battle between the British and French forces
take place off stage in v.2 is that he wanted to highlight the fight
between these two, in which the forces of evil are overcome
symbolically by the forces of good.

The rapid unfolding of new events continues with Edgar shedding
his disguise and reporting the death of Gloucester (and in Q the
return of the banished Kent in eighteen lines omitted from F); and
this is followed by the startling entry of one 'with a bloody knife' to
report the mutual destruction of Goneril and Regan by stabbing and
poison. There is yet more busy stage action as Kent arrives, the
bodies of Goneril and Regan are brought on, and Edmund is carried
off. In the headlong rush of events it might seem that confusion has
turned to chaos, but the ceremonial trial by combat of Edmund and
Edgar symbolizes a restoration of order according to established
rules, and coincides with the deaths of Goneril and Regan. The
wheel for all three is come 'full circle', as Edmund says, leaving the
future of the country assured in the hands of Albany and Edgar.

The reconciliation of Edgar and Albany, marked visually by their
physical contact (Albany says 'I must embrace thee'), is thus a very
important moment, and it seems that Edgar may have it right when
he says to Edmund,

> The gods are just, and of our pleasant vices [virtues Q]
> Make instruments to plague [scourge Q] us.   (v.3.171–2)

But if there is justice in this play, it comes about through the various
ways in which the vices that give pleasure, the exercise of domination, the lust for power, or sexual lust, and ambition, recoil upon the
characters, not in any intervention of the inscrutable heavens. This is
the justice that operates in the cases of Goneril, Regan, Edmund,
and Gloucester. Edgar's account of his father is equivocal, of how he

> Led him, begg'd for him, sav'd him from despair.
> Never (O fault) reveal'd myself unto him,
> Until some half-hour past, when I was arm'd ...   (v.3.192–4)

Here he speaks of how he kept Gloucester alive, admits his 'fault' (F; in Q the word is 'father') in not revealing himself, yet when he does do so he in fact brings on his father's death, the death he had worked hard to stave off. So much for 'ripeness is all'; we might ask by what right Edgar takes it upon himself to keep his father alive, and determine whether he is in a state of despair, when to have revealed himself as the long lost and now desired son was the obvious way for Edgar to restore his father to a condition in which his heart could 'burst smilingly' (line 200), as it now has done.

It is often a problem in staging Shakespeare's plays to know when and how bodies of the 'dead' are removed from the stage, and it is rare for bodies to be brought on. So it is an unusual and powerful theatrical moment when the dead bodies of the two sisters and the dying Edmund are foregrounded in Albany's and in our attention. It takes the arrival of Kent, at first unremarked by those on stage, to jolt Albany and us back to a consciousness of Lear. His cry, 'Great thing of us forgot', is double-edged. It may cause an audience to laugh uneasily, I suspect because they too have half-forgotten the matter of Lear and Cordelia, being so caught up in the vivid and absorbing action, including two murders and a fight to the death, that has accompanied the 230 lines since these characters were on stage. The audience responds to the double perspective here on Lear, who is at once the great thing in the play in terms of pathos, and of no importance any longer politically, which is to say in terms of the action now being played out.

In the hectic sequences of war, challenge and combat, and murder of the final scene the brief highlighting of Lear clutching Cordelia ('Have I caught thee? / He that parts us, shall bring a brand from heaven') is intensely moving, not least in that the effect of Cordelia's attempt to give him back his authority (she still addresses him as 'King') is here to reduce him to a pathetic self-centred possessiveness, as he sentimentalizes over their situation and turns the horror of it to prettiness, as if they two could create their own golden world and 'wear out / In a walled prison, packs and sects of great ones' when we know Edmund's intention is to have them killed. They have each other for the moment, it is true, and Lear's temporary happiness in the consolation of being with her – 'We two alone will sing like birds in a cage' – is very moving; but he sees her selfishly, as existing solely for him, and his vision of them enduring in prison as mere by-standers, relishing court gossip and outlasting the 'great ones' who rise and fall, 'ebb and flow by the moon', marks the self-delusion of an old man who wishes too late for what he has thrown away. Cordelia makes no reference to her husband in the last scenes, and Lear's holding on to her here as though they two alone can exist, independent of others, might remind us of the demand he made at the beginning of the play for all her love, and her rebuke she made to him then, that her husband should 'carry / Half my love with him, half my care, and duty' (1.1.101–2). This episode registers at once Lear's renewed love for Cordelia as a devotion that blinds him to everything else and makes suffering tolerable, and at the same time expresses a false and self-deceiving vision that is shattered when Edmund at once sends a Captain after them to execute them. F omits the lines that in Q give this Captain some individuality ('I cannot draw a cart, nor eat dried oats, / If it be man's work, I'll do it'), perhaps to avoid any distraction from the ruthless order Edmund gives for their deaths 'instantly'.

When Lear enters 'with Cordelia in his arms' (Q and F), the stage direction does not say she is dead, but the symbolism of the scene requires that she must be,[18] for Shakespeare has taken care to have the bodies of Goneril and Regan displayed on stage, so that for Lear too the wheel has come full circle, as the presence on stage of all three of his children dead strikingly shows what he has brought upon himself by dividing the kingdom and casting out Cordelia. Lear, preoccupied with himself and Cordelia, wants to believe she is alive ('This feather stirs, she lives'), but chorus-like, Kent, Albany and Edgar see his entrance carrying her as an image of horror, as if it were the 'promis'd end', the end of the world, for they and we know she is dead, and can see the bodies of Goneril and Regan, as Kent reminds us by trying to tell Lear 'Your eldest daughters have fordone [foredoome Q] themselves, / And desperately are dead.' Lear, it seems, is spared an awareness of their deaths; when Kent speaks, Lear does not appear to listen:

> ALB. He knows not what he says, and vain is it [it is Q]
> That we present us to him.   (V.3.294–5)

Lear is absorbed in himself and his burden, so much that he does not really communicate with Albany or Edgar or Kent, except in the brief momentary recognition of Kent, until just before he dies, when he turns, probably to Edgar, to ask, 'Pray you undo this button.' Edgar, attending to him, cries, 'He faints', and Lear comes to only to

wish for death, saying, 'Break heart, I prithee break.' In F Kent
speaks this last line, and Lear's last words are an addition,

> Do you see this? Look on her? Look her lips,
> Look there, look there.

What he sees or thinks he sees has been much debated; to some it
seems a final cruel delusion if he imagines Cordelia to be alive, to
others a blessed release for him in a moment of imagined reunion.
Lear has lost his power and all he had, he has destroyed his world,
and outlived all his children, and the final scene stretches out his
suffering beyond the point at which to have died would have been
fitting ('You do me wrong to take me out o'th'grave'), as Gloucester
died at the moment of recognition of his lost child. And yet at the
end the only thing to wish for him is a gentle death, and in F this is
what he gets. His ending is, indeed, both cruel and gentle, and full of
irony in relation to his aim in dividing the kingdom so that he could
'Unburthen'd crawl toward death' (I.I.140, F only). For at the last
he enters burdened, carrying in Cordelia, and if Albany had his way,
would be further weighed down by the return of his power:

> for us, we will resign
> During the life of this old majesty
> To him our absolute power, you [i.e. Kent and Edgar] to your rights
> With boot, and such addition as your honours [honour Q]
> Have more than merited. All friends shall taste
> The wages of their virtue, and all foes
> The cup of their deservings.   (v.3.299–305)

Albany's words have been seen as simply inadequate, and as refuted
by the death of Lear,[19] since virtue does not have its reward in the
case of Cordelia. Albany, however, reminds us here of a central
concern of the play, rule and power; after all that Lear has done to
abuse his power, it would be sentimental in the extreme to give it
back to him, but Albany is making a fitting gesture to an aged man,
'this [great F] decay', for whom death is very near. Albany is
concerned about the future of the realm, and in the 'general woe' of
the moment, offers after the death of Lear to hand over power to
Edgar and Kent. F gives the last speech to Edgar ('Duke', i.e.,
Albany, Q), so that it becomes a reminder that Albany is saying what
he feels, not what he ought to say; but at least we can imagine that

things will not be the same now Lear has gone, and under Albany and Edgar the 'gor'd state' will be renewed and better ruled.

What I take to be the revised *King Lear* of F is thus significantly different from Q, though not as radically different as the authors of *The Division of the Kingdoms* would have us think. In the later part of the play, from III.6 onwards, F omits 216 lines found in Q, adding only seventeen, so that the action is speeded up. Many of the omissions, such as Edgar's rhyming moralizing at the end of III.6, the Servants' comments on Cornwall, Regan and Gloucester at the end of III.7, the moralizing speech of Albany in IV.2, the account of Cordelia in IV.3, and Edgar's report of an encounter between Gloucester and Kent in V.3, are all passages that exert a coercive pressure by telling us what to think or how to feel. Their removal leaves the play more open, makes the motives of Albany more obscure,[20] and reduces substantially the sense that Edgar, Kent and Albany may at times be spokesmen for the author, guiding the sympathies of the audience. The changes, as is now well known, include the omission of a number of references to France and a French invading force, but F still shows Cordelia commanding a French army against British forces, and the visual image of her with Lear leading troops into battle in V.2 suggests not only that she may be in the wrong to make war against her own country, but also that she is wilful in seeking a fight against the combined forces of Edmund and Albany. Again, the F text, by removing the coercive account of Cordelia as a saintly emblem of pity and reducing her rôle significantly in the play, opens her part to interrogation, and makes it much more ambiguous.

If, as some claim, the emergence of the bourgeois subject, 'the unified subject of liberal humanism', can be located in the later seventeenth century,[21] the subject as an individual valued for his or her uniqueness is adumbrated in the drama at least from the late sixteenth century onwards, as well as increasingly in works of poetry and fiction. As the bourgeois subject gains greater freedom of expression, and asserts his or her own individuality and difference from others, so at the same time the growth of mass societies, the inscrutability of market forces and the increasing remoteness of the sources of power all tend to diminish the ordinary person to a cipher. Shakespeare may be said to have unmasked this contradiction, and

notably in *King Lear*. For this play shows us the reduction of Lear
from a position of economic and political domination to a 'cipher', as
he is stripped of power and of all his retinue. The action of the play
shows us the progressive marginalization of Lear in relation to the
economic and power struggles he activates by his division of the
kingdom. It is indeed a major irony that as he becomes less a role
and more a person, with a growing awareness of himself as subject
('Who is it that can tell me who I am?'; 'I am a very foolish fond old
man'), so we are made to appreciate him as a 'uniquely valuable
individual', even as politically he is reduced to nothing. So it is only
superficially true to claim, as Annabel Patterson does, that the play
retreats 'into the domestic and familial' at the end, abandoning its
socio-economic 'message' embodied in 'Take physic, pomp';[22] for at
a deeper level *King Lear* exposes the contradiction between, on the
one hand, the importance our society places upon individual expression and fulfilment, upon the freedom and autonomy of each person,
and on the other, the diminution of the individual to a nobody,
another entry in the computer lists of the government, banks, police
and advertisers, marking the social, economic and political insignificance of each person in a mass society. In this sense *King Lear*
remains to the end a powerfully political play, and the pathos of the
final image of Lear is largely generated by our awareness of this
contradiction, as it is embodied in what has happened to him.
Perhaps there is yet another political dimension to the play, reflected
in its resurgence as Shakespeare's 'greatest' play since the Second
World War and especially since 1960 or so, at least as it relates to
Britain, where it has been staged more often in recent years than ever
before. For these years mark the final decline of Britain as an
imperialist and economic power, with the dissolution of the empire,
much of it given away in a withdrawal from or division of the
colonies once dominated from London. Yet it seems that many
British people, and certainly the notorious tabloid press that wields
such influence there, cling to the 'name, and all th'addition' of
imperial pride in a fantasy that Britain is still a major world power;
so the country enters on wars it cannot afford, and maintains all the
trappings of glory while unemployment increases and welfare systems disintegrate. Perhaps it is not altogether fanciful to associate
Lear, clinging to the power he has given away and losing everything,

with Britain, clinging to an imperial role it no longer has any claim to, having given its empire away, while declining all too rapidly into one of the poorest countries of Europe.

In contrast to *Hamlet*, *King Lear* has, as noted earlier, no voices from the past, in spite of being set nominally in an ancient, pre-Christian period. Only Kent's long service to Lear hints at a past, but every action in the play springs from its immediate context, and is without known precedent, so that Shakespeare can interweave images and echoes that suggest primitive and contemporary worlds, ancient and modern, pagan and Christian. Also in contrast to *Hamlet*, *King Lear* has no visitors from a world beyond the grave, and no sense of religious sanctions, or of a Providence that might be concerned in human affairs. Characters invoke the gods when it suits them, but there is no sign that the gods listen, or are even there. Lear projects them into the storm in Act III, and Edgar invents a miracle to deceive his father into better thoughts when there seems no reason why Gloucester should not choose death by suicide as a release from suffering. *King Lear* is an old man's play, while *Hamlet* is a young man's play; both have to do with death, but whereas in *Hamlet* the young treat death casually as if it could not happen to them, and so court it in the codes they adopt – as in the devotion Hamlet and Fortinbras have to an heroic code, and the adherence of Laertes to a code of revenge – the old men in *King Lear* linger on in life against their will. Gloucester and Lear are the only tragic figures in Shakespeare's plays who die natural deaths. Yet there is a sense in which the prospect of death shapes this play much more strongly than it does *Hamlet*: it is introduced at the beginning in Lear's abdication from cares of state, and strengthened in the Folio text, in which he speaks of crawling toward death.

King Lear also differs from *Hamlet* in the power attributed to women in the play. Hamlet can be seen as rejecting his mother and Ophelia, and suppressing the feminine part of himself, in the effort to convert himself into a revenger and adopt the masculine ethos represented by his father. There may be some truth in the claim made by a well-known feminist essay on *King Lear*, arguing that the play endorses the ideology of a patriarchal society and displays a 'representation of patriarchal misogyny' in a demonstration that 'the institution of male power in the family and the State is . . . the only form of social organisation strong enough to hold chaos at bay'.[23] But such an argument seems to miss the point, even if in general, Shakespeare, like other authors of his age, assumed as natural a patriarchal order derived ultimately from God. For *King Lear* is dominated by its women. When Goneril and Regan have power, indeed, they are as strong and ruthless as Lear himself had been, and show they have the courage and toughness to hold sway in a masculine world. Lear's preference is for a male society, as he surrounds himself with an armed guard, his hundred knights, and he is shattered by discovering that his two elder daughters, whom he seems not to have known except as adornments to the court, are just like him in their masculine imperiousness. In contrast to Hamlet who suppresses the feminine part of himself, Lear, rendered impotent by his own actions, can only give way to the 'mother' in response to Goneril and Regan. When Goneril demands he send away fifty of his followers within a fortnight, he bursts into tears:

> Life and death, I am asham'd
> That thou hast power to shake my manhood thus,
> That these hot tears, which break from me perforce,
> Should make thee worth them.   (1.4.296–9)

His response to Regan similarly is to try to fight back tears:

> touch me with noble anger,
> And let not women's weapons, water-drops,
> Stain my man's cheeks.   (II.4.276–8)

Tears, women's weapons, are all he has, until he is rescued by Cordelia, who also, like a man, insists on leading an army against the British, and fighting to put her father back into power. The controlling image at the end of the play is that of the three dead daughters, destroyed, it might be said, by their intervention in a man's world, but at the same time having shown they could compete in it, and change the course of future events.

   I think we may see a sequence of stages in the action, beginning with Act I, which is devoted mainly to establishing Lear's division of the kingdom, and the subsequent self-division in him, at once arbitrary tyrant and kind father, impossibly demanding even in generosity, and reduced to asking 'Who is it that can tell me who I am?' As Lear began by expelling Kent and Cordelia, so the second stage leads to the stocking of Kent and the internal exile of Edgar and Lear himself; the play opens out as Edmund, Cornwall, Goneril and Regan effectively take charge, and we begin to see the effects of Lear's actions on the realm of Albion. In the next stage the realm is brought into confusion, with developing threats of civil dissension and foreign invasion, and with violence bringing bloodshed in the blinding of Gloucester and the killing of Cornwall and Oswald. This violence culminates in the chaos of war, which is foregrounded in the final stage of the action, when Lear and Gloucester, sidelined by the upheavals they triggered, can only look for death with dignity in the context of the dissolution of what had been Lear's kingdom.

This is to summarize rather crudely the shaping I have been proposing, one that supports a political emphasis in reading the play. In *King Lear* there are no precedents for what the characters do, and actions are taken without thought of their consequences. Lear's idea of rule extends to little beyond having others do what pleases him, and his daughters use power to do what pleases them. He continues to retain the trappings of power with his train of a hundred knights, and to behave imperiously, and Goneril and Regan have good political reasons, emphasized in the Folio text, for restraining and diminishing his retinue. Lear condemns their behaviour, which politically makes sense, as wicked, invoking a moral valuation he has not applied to his own actions, and turns his horrible curses on them, so rejecting all three of his daughters in turn. The effect, as it leads to Lear being shut out in the storm, is to spotlight the blindness and the arrogance of those in power, and to bring home to us the pathetic reduction of Lear from a despotic patriarchal monarch into a poor old man exposed to feel what wretches feel. It is this change that has given some plausibility to a perception of Lear's progress, or even, as some would say, pilgrimage, as a movement towards self-discovery or even redemption, though this is hardly what the full scope of the action portrays.

The Fool as surrogate child or 'boy', and Kent as loyal, unquestioning follower, channel sympathy for Lear during this change in him, a sympathy which is reinforced by the blinding and casting out of Gloucester. In the early part of the play, violence is associated with Lear, with his train of knights, with Kent, who trips and beats Oswald, with Gloucester in the act of adultery, possibly rape, by which Edmund was begot, and in a way with Edgar, who is said by Edmund to have wounded him, and who is thought by Regan to be a companion of Lear's 'riotous knights' (II.1.93). All of these, Lear, Kent, Gloucester and Edgar, are subjected to the natural violence of the storm in Act III, which brings out their humanity through companionship in misery. From the end of Act III, when Gloucester is blinded, the source of violence is transferred, so to speak, to Goneril, Regan, Cornwall and Edmund. The horror of the act of blinding is physically overwhelming, and marks Regan and Cornwall with blood-guilt; Cornwall, then Oswald, seeking to kill Gloucester, and then Edmund, all die by the violence they provoke, as do Goneril and Regan.

The later part of the action moves simultaneously towards conflict and reconciliation. Edgar leads his father to safety, yet fails to reveal himself, and is at once cruel and kind in practising on him by letting him experience a mock-death and return to life again. So too, Cordelia lovingly helps to restore her father to his senses, yet insists on leading him into battle to recover for him a power he no longer wants or can wield. Both Gloucester and Lear undergo a symbolic death and restoration, and both are denied the release they desire from suffering; both might say, as Lear does, 'You do me wrong to take me out o'th'grave', since the play offers no hint of a life beyond death, and to prolong their life in this world is only to test their endurance further. The end is thus full of paradoxes, as Gloucester is left almost to the last in ignorance that Edgar lives, and Lear is not allowed to forget or forgive, but is marched by Cordelia into a battle which brings her death, destroying the one thing that now matters to him. Lear is ironically offered his kingdom again when he no longer cares about it, and when he is visually linked to the dead bodies of all three of his children, whose destruction is the outcome of his initial division of the kingdom. Lear's death, like that of Gloucester, is thus a defeat in victory, both cruel and kind, a necessary release and a stretching out of him still further on the cruel rack of the world he has made. And it is a world *he* has made – he begins the play as a despot locked inside his role, unable to see the consequences of his actions, because he has lost ordinary human contact with others. In the last act we are not shown the battle in which Lear and Cordelia are defeated, in spite of the build-up towards it and the display of soldiers and colours; the fight we do see, shown at length, is that between Edgar and Edmund, which symbolizes in the victory of Edgar the restoration of a better order, one 'pregnant to good pity' – a restoration confirmed in the final speeches of the play, when Edgar and Albany are left to pick up the pieces and sustain the 'gor'd state', and it does not much matter which of them has the closing lines. At the same time there is a powerful sense of closure, of the end of an era, of reaching a point of rest; it is a moment for taking stock, and for looking to a future that will be different because of what has happened in the play – that is to say, because of now past events:

> The oldest hath [have Q] borne most; we that are young
> Shall never see so much, nor live so long.

The lines sound almost trite, but in F they refer explicitly to Lear, and they mark the huge gap between the beginning of the play, where there is no past to influence his actions, and a new condition, in which awareness of past suffering, it is hinted, will make for a better world.[24]

As the two old men become the focus of suffering in the play, so in their reunion when mad or blind in iv.6 they act out a parody of the power relations once so important to them, Lear 'every inch a king', Gloucester anxious to kiss Lear's hand in submission, and it is only by this reduction of them to political insignificance that recovery can come. The great curve of the action takes them from security and immense power out into the storm, and into what seems an endless renewal of suffering: 'Who is't can say we are at the worst?' Yet it also restores to them the love of their lost children, and brings them to an acceptance of the mortality and humanity they have to learn they share with others. Their deaths are at once painful and a blessing, the fulfilment of a long process that makes them aware of the wrongs they have done, and that enables them as a consequence to find release through suffering at the end. The Folio text strengthens this design by making the later action more direct and less cluttered by moralizing, so sharpening the sense of cruelty in kindness, of suffering in reconciliation, of victory in defeat and defeat in victory, of love as selfish and as selfless, and of the inadequacy of moralizing and of ordinary notions of justice to account for what the play has shown us. The reason for the addition in F at the end of Lear's final speech becomes clearer:

> Do you see this? Look on her? Look her lips,
> Look there, look there!

These words, together with the transfer in F of 'Break heart, I prithee break' to Kent, round out the design of the play and the paradoxes of the ending by allowing Lear the momentary joy of imagining Cordelia may be alive, a joy which is heart-breaking because it recalls an earlier moment when he hoped she would speak and her lips said nothing, and because it is delusory, so that, with Kent, we know there is nothing left to wish for Lear except the oblivion of death.

CHAPTER 8

Epilogue

Let me recapitulate briefly to put the last two chapters in context. The success of post-structuralism in abolishing the traditional parameters of literature and literary criticism has been stimulating and in some ways liberating. It has brought about an important shift in the criticism of Shakespeare, generating methods of opening the plays out rather than seeking to pin them down. It has challenged three major traditional critical principles: firstly, that the business of criticism was to seek for determinate meanings; secondly that any work must possess fixed, inherent principles of structure or design; and lastly that a final authoritative text could be traced for each play. So far, so good; but in rejecting these principles, post-structuralism has given critics power over the text and a sanction to display their own critical virtuosity, however tangential to the author and his work. For its demolition of the boundaries between literature and other forms of discourse, and consequent equalizing of all texts including critical ones, has led to a kind of critical cowardice, since no one wants to be seen claiming special status for art or artistry at a time when literature and criticism merge with sociology and history, so that debates about such topics as poverty, ideology, class conflict, the construction of gender, commercialization, patriarchy, and commodification are likely to be high on the agenda at academic conferences devoted to 'literary' topics.

I welcome the challenge to the critical tradition, but not the abandonment of any real concern with works of literature as art. What I have aimed to do in the last two chapters on *Hamlet* and *King Lear* is to reclaim them as aesthetic experiences, in the recognition that our perception of design is bound up with our perception of meaning, and both relate to our own world and time as well as to the plays Shakespeare wrote. I have therefore concentrated on three levels of awareness, to the neglect of other aspects of the plays.

The first has to do with the revision of the plays, probably undertaken by Shakespeare himself; in both plays the changes made in the later versions, those printed in the First Folio, show a process of development towards a clearer design and a more richly nuanced range of meanings. The second relates to politics, not Shakespeare's own, which we cannot know for certain, or the politics of his age, some knowledge of which is obviously relevant to a full understanding of the texts, but the political issues raised in the plays as these issues now manifest themselves to a reader or viewer at the end of the twentieth century. The analyses of critical responses to the plays in the early chapters shows that critics have generally been affected, whether they acknowledge it or not, by the political atmosphere of their own day even when they ostensibly avoided political issues. Both *Hamlet* and *King Lear* are profoundly concerned with politics, and since in writing on them I cannot avoid bringing my own political consciousness to bear, I do so freely. The third level of awareness concerns the artistry of the plays. I argued earlier that we have at once a subjective and an objective relation to a text, and that just as each of us 'completes' its meanings, so our sense of a play as a work of art is generated through our interaction with it. The design we perceive, like the meanings of a text, will vary for readers or viewers at different times, even while certain features, such as the story line, remain more or less constant, if subject to differing emphases. Meaning and design are both there in the text and not there, so it is not impossible to speak of Shakespeare's artistry, if it is done in the recognition that our perception of artistry relates to the beholder as well as to the text itself.

In other words, I have been concerned with the plays as wholes, using the process of revision and the politics in the plays to reinforce a sense of their totality and overall design. In deploying the three kinds of awareness I have described, my accounts of *Hamlet* and *King Lear* run counter to common critical concerns at a time when, as Alan Liu has shown, 'We live in an age of "detailism" characterized by the "pervasive valorization of the minute, the partial, and the marginal"'.[1] He is describing what he calls 'high cultural criticism', or various forms of post-structuralism, including new historicism, new pragmatism and new marxism, and is able to cite numerous examples from a wide range of theorists to support the argument that[2]

Detail is the very instrument of the antifoundational and antiepistemologi-
cal imperative in high cultural criticism: its contention is that there is no
reason (other than fidelity to quaint notions of philosophy) why contexts of
discretely perceived particulars should resolve into culture as a single,
grounded, and knowable order.

Liu is writing about current cultural criticism and its roots in
Romanticism, but what he says applies more generally to the various
post-structuralist modes of literary criticism, and specifically Shakespeare criticism, referred to earlier in this book.

Let me illustrate by citing one influential example. In his book
Shakespearean Negotiations, Stephen Greenblatt begins by rejecting the
notion of a 'total artist and a totalizing society',[3] and he pulls back
from any 'notion of artistic completeness' in order to glimpse what is
'at the margins of a text'; so he says his vision will be 'fragmentary' –
'the circulation of social energy by and through the stage ... was
partial, fragmentary, conflictual' – and his concern is with 'particular social practices' in Shakespeare's age.[4] He offers this method as a
counter to the usual straw man set up to be scornfully demolished by
post-structuralist critics, the idea of the work of art as possessing 'a
permanently novel, untranslatable formal perfection',[5] thus cutting
away the possibility of an aesthetic criticism in favour of criticism
concerned with specific cultural practices. We live in an age that has
good reason to be dismayed at the idea of totalizing societies, and
perhaps a distrust of all totalities is a consequence. It seems to me,
however, that the value and pleasure we gain from watching or
reading a play as a work of art that unfolds in time on the page as we
read, or in space and time in the theatre, is finally determined by our
sense of the design of the whole. An emphasis on the particular, the
fragmentary, the anecdotal, the borders of literature, tends to
marginalize the text while enabling the critic to transcend the detail
and become a source for totalization. So 'The project for localization
sets itself resolutely against the general and the universal, but has its
own ways of creating generalities, leaping over difference to construct an alternative order of "essences" out of the materials of
history.'[6] Starting from the position that there are no wholes, only
aggregates of particulars, has the curious effect of leading back to
some kind of universalizing. I suspect that in the end this is
inescapable, and a function of the structuring of argument with its
own narrative impetus towards conclusiveness. In the last chapter of
his book, Greenblatt considers the art in and of *The Tempest*, both

Prospero's and Shakespeare's, and describes art (he is thinking of Prospero's betrothal masque) as 'pure plenitude': 'The magic of art resides in the freedom of the imagination and hence in liberation from the constraints of the body.'[7] Here 'plenitude' returns us to the notion of completeness or fullness, which is contrived by the magic of art, as the freedom of the imagination is employed to bring particulars into a formal pattern or design.

The analysis of critical responses to *Hamlet* and *King Lear* in the early chapters of the present book shows the extent to which criticism relates to the period when the critic writes as much to the works discussed. So the various forms of post-structuralist criticism are manifestations of anxieties about our own age even as they proclaim their novelty in treating art as merely one of the 'products, practices, discourses of a given culture'.[8] The method of seeing Shakespeare's plays in this way, as embedded in the culture of Elizabethan and Jacobean London and as the product of a negotiation between the dramatist and 'the institutions and practices of society', has been stimulating, and has opened up new perspectives on Shakespeare. But at the same time, in its concentration on particulars and its lack of interest in the plays as artistic wholes, this method has revealed its own limitations. The preoccupation with particulars, traces, exchanges at the margins of the culture of Elizabethan and Jacobean England becomes a means for exerting critical power over the text and the reader. Greenblatt himself confesses that he believes 'sustained, scrupulous attention to formal and linguistic design will remain at the center of literary teaching and study',[9] and perhaps it is time to return such a concern to criticism as well. The analysis of past criticism teaches us that forms of post-structuralism such as new historicism are temporary phases in criticism, and will be replaced by other schemata and no doubt more isms. I have tried to suggest in the present book (which even as it is published becomes part of that history) a direction in which the criticism of Shakespeare might go, towards recuperating a sense of the whole play and of artistic design not in an immutable 'formal perfection', but as generated, like meaning, out of a collaboration between viewers or readers and Shakespeare's texts in a process that is always subject to change; and this requires attending to the cultural transactions and political mood of the age in which the reader or viewer lives as much as to the particular conditions and practices that affected Shakespeare in the writing of his plays.

As to the question from which this book started, whether *Hamlet* or *King Lear* in the greatest of Shakespeare's plays, establishing a pecking order for Shakespeare's works may be fun as a sort of academic game, but it is a game for which the rules change all the time. I think we can now see that when critics claim the status of 'greatest' for one play or the other, they are likely to mean something different from what they seem to be saying. The critic is in effect asserting that the play concerned is the one he or she finds most significant for the time, and most relevant to himself or herself at a particular historical moment; and by attributing exceptional status to the play concerned, the critic is also validating the importance of the interpretation offered. So the question is not in itself important, except that it figures as a way of continually revalidating the canon. I suspect that for the immediate future *King Lear* will continue to be regarded as the central achievement of Shakespeare, if only because it speaks more largely than the other tragedies to the anxieties and problems of the modern world.

Notes

1 INTRODUCTION: *HAMLET* VERSUS *KING LEAR*

1 Seyom Brown, *The Faces of Power* (New York: Columbia University Press, 1968), p. 196.
2 A preliminary account, '*King Lear* and the Displacement of *Hamlet*', was published in *Huntington Library Quarterly*, 50 (1987), 263–78; see also G. R. Hibbard, '*King Lear*: A Retrospect 1939–1979', *Shakespeare Survey*, 33 (1980), 1–12.
3 Spencer R. Weart, *Nuclear Fear: A History of Images* (Cambridge, Mass.: Harvard University Press, 1988), p. 183.
4 *Ibid.*, p. 205.
5 *Ibid.*, p. 279.
6 *Ibid.*, p. 258.
7 Louis Montrose, 'Professing the Renaissance: The Poetics and Politics of Culture', in *The New Historicism*, ed. H. Aram Veeser (New York and London: Routledge, 1989), p. 23.
8 Ruby Cohn, *Modern Shakespeare Offshoots* (Princeton: Princeton University Press, 1976).
9 Roland Barthes, 'From Work to Text', in *Textual Strategies: Perspectives in Post-Structuralist Criticism*, ed. Josue V. Harari (Ithaca: Cornell University Press, 1979), p. 80.
10 See Grace Ioppolo, *Revising Shakespeare* (Cambridge, Mass.: Harvard University Press, 1991), Chapter 1, pp. 19–43.
11 Michael J. Warren, 'Quarto and Folio *King Lear* and the Interpretation of Albany and Edgar', in *Shakespeare, Pattern of Excelling Nature*, ed. David Bevington and Jay Halio (Newark: University of Delaware Press, 1978), pp. 95–107, citing p. 105.
12 See, for instance, Kenneth Muir, *Shakespeare: Contrasts and Controversies* (Brighton: Harvester Press, 1983), pp. 51–66, and Marion Trousdale, 'A Trip through the Divided Kingdoms', *Shakespeare Quarterly*, 37 (1986), 218–23.
13 'Textual Properties', *Shakespeare Quarterly*, 37 (1986), 213–7, citing p. 215.

14 Gary Taylor, *Reinventing Shakespeare: A Cultural History from the Restoration to the Present* (New York: Weidenfeld and Nicolson, 1989), p. 360.
15 'Shakespeare Imagines a Theater', in *Shakespeare, Man of the Theater*, ed. Kenneth Muir, Jay Halio and D. J. Palmer (Newark: University of Delaware Press, 1983), pp. 34–46, citing p. 43.
16 Taylor, *Reinventing Shakespeare*, p. 384.
17 *Ibid.*, p. 411.

2 HAMLET AND HAMLETISM

1 *Lectures 1808–1819: On Literature*, ed. R. A. Foakes. Collected Works of Samuel Taylor Coleridge, 5; Bollingen Series LXXV (2 vols., Princeton: Princeton University Press, 1987), I, 82. Hereafter abbreviated to *LL* (*CC*).
2 *LL* (*CC*) I, 495. The angled brackets denote an insertion in the MS.
3 *LL* (*CC*) I, 367–8.
4 Cited in *Readings on the Character of Hamlet 1661–1947*, compiled by Claude C. H. Williamson (London: Allen and Unwin, 1950; reprinted New York: Gordian Press, 1972), p. 77.
5 Williamson, *Readings*, p. 79.
6 *Ibid.*, p. 313.
7 *Ibid.*, pp. 107, 111.
8 Herbert Beerbohm Tree, *From an Actor's Promptbook* (1895), cited in *ibid.*, p. 190.
9 Ten Brink, *Shakespeare as Tragic Writer* (1874), cited in *ibid.*, p. 128.
10 *Shakespeare's Heroines*, cited in *ibid.*, pp. 75–6.
11 H. N. Hudson, *Lectures on Shakespeare* (1848), cited in *ibid.*, p. 84.
12 A. C. Swinburne, *A Study of Shakespeare* (1880), cited in *ibid.*, p. 152.
13 *William Shakespeare*, cited in *ibid.*, p. 104.
14 *Shakespeare and his Time*, cited in *ibid.*, p. 185.
15 Review in the *London Chronicle*, 32 (17–19 December 1772), cited in *Shakespeare: The Critical Heritage*, ed. Brian Vickers, V (London: Routledge, 1979), p. 46. Garrick cut out 898 lines of the 1002 in Act V to rescue this 'noble play' from 'all the rubbish of the 5th act' (Vickers, *Critical Heritage*, V, 11).
16 *Johnson on Shakespeare*, ed. Arthur Sherbo, *The Yale Edition of the Works of Samuel Johnson*, VIII (New Haven and London: Yale University Press, 1968), p. 1011.
17 *A Philosophical Illustration of Some of Shakespeare's Characters*, in Vickers, *Critical Heritage*, VI, 124.
18 Cited in Cohn, *Modern Shakespeare Offshoots*, pp. 118–19.
19 Essay in *The Mirror*, 22 April, 1780; cited in Williamson, *Readings*, pp. 25, 26.
20 *LL* (*CC*), I, 390.

21 *Table-Talk*, 24 June 1827.
22 *The Tragedies of Shakespeare* (1812), cited in Williamson, *Readings*, p. 41.
23 *Characters of Shakespeare's Plays* (1817), in *The Complete Works of William Hazlitt*, ed. P. P. Howe (21 vols., London: Dent, 1930–4), IV, 232.
24 *Hamlet*, cited in Williamson, *Readings*, p. 189.
25 *Shakespearean Tragedy*, cited in *ibid*., p. 294.
26 *The Plays of Shakespeare*, cited in *ibid*., pp. 270, 273.
27 *Ibid*., p. 271.
28 Morley, *Shakespeare and his Time* (1893), cited in *ibid*., p. 184.
29 Frank Walters, *Studies of Shakespeare's Plays* (1902), cited in *ibid*., p. 251.
30 Georg Brandes, *William Shakespeare* (1911), cited in *ibid*., p. 316.
31 *Ten More Plays of Shakespeare*, cited in *ibid*., p. 330.
32 Cited in *ibid*., p. 331.
33 *Collected Works of Ralph Waldo Emerson*, ed. Robert E. Spiller, I (Cambridge, Mass.: Belknap Press of Harvard University Press, 1971), p. 66.
34 Preface to *Poems* (1853), in *The Poems of Matthew Arnold*, ed. Kenneth Allott (London: Longmans, 1965), p. 591.
35 *Tennyson's Maud: A Definitive Edition*, ed. Susan Shatto (London: Athlone Press, 1986), p. 162.
36 A translation of Freiligrath's poem is printed in *Hamlet. A New Variorum Edition of Shakespeare*, ed. H. H. Furness (2 vols., Philadelphia: J. P. Lippincott & Co., 1877; reprinted New York: Dover Publications, 1963), II, 376–8; this volume (hereafter referred to as *Hamlet*, ed. Furness) also includes an excerpt from H. T. Roetscher's commentary on Shakespeare's dramatic characters (1844), p. 294, from which I also quote.
37 Eleanor Rowe, *Hamlet: A Window on Russia* (New York: New York University Press, 1976), pp. 53–64. For Mickiewicz, see Grigori Kozintsev, *Shakespeare: Time and Conscience*, trans. Joyce Vining (London: Dennis Dobson, 1967), p. 116.
38 Rowe, *Hamlet*, p. 48.
39 *Ibid*., p. 59.
40 Cited in *Hamlet*, ed. Furness, II, 300–1.
41 *Hamlet*, ed. Furness, 1877; the dedication was removed from later reprints, and does not appear, for instance, in that of 1905.
42 Cited in Williamson, *Readings*, p. 104.
43 Rowe, *Hamlet*, p. 58.
44 *Shakespeare's Mind and Art*, cited in *Hamlet*, ed. Furness, II, 190.
45 Williamson, *Readings*, p. 185.
46 *Ibid*., p. 189.
47 *Pierre*, ed. Harrison Hayford, Hershel Parker and G. Thomas Tanselle (Evanston and Chicago: Northwestern University Press, for the Newberry Library, 1971), pp. 135–6.
48 Cited in *A Supplement to the Oxford English Dictionary*, ed. R. W.

Burchfield, II (Oxford: Clarendon Press, 1976), under 'Hamletism', p. 20.

49 *Women in Love*, ed. David Farmer, Lindeth Vasey and John Worthen (Cambridge: Cambridge University Press, 1987), pp. 186–7.

50 T. S. Eliot, *Collected Poems 1909–1962* (London: Faber, 1963), p. 17.

51 *Ibid.*, p. 14.

52 See Cohn, *Modern Shakespeare Offshoots*, p. 138; René Taupin, 'The Myth of Hamlet in France in Mallarmé's Generation', *Modern Language Quarterly*, 14 (1953), 432–47, especially p. 439.

53 Isaiah Berlin, 'Fathers and Children: Turgenev and the Liberal Predicament', *New York Review of Books*, 18 October 1973, cited in Rowe, *Hamlet*, p. 59.

54 Isabel Hapgood, trans., *Novels and Stories of Ivan Turgenieff*, IV (New York: Scribner's Sons, 1904). Turgenev does not mention Hamlet in this story, but Chekhov links Layevsky in his story 'The Duel' both with the 'superfluous man' and with Hamlet. See also Kozintsev, *Shakespeare: Time and Conscience*, pp. 126–7.

55 Hapgood, trans., *Novels and Stories of Ivan Turgenieff*, II (1903), citing p. 190.

56 *Hamlet and Don Quixote*, trans. Robert Nichols (London: Hendersons, 1930), p. 26.

57 Konstantin Mochulsky, *Dostoevsky: His Life and Work*, translated Michael A Minihan (Princeton: Princeton University Press, 1971), p. 248, cited in Rowe, *Hamlet*, p. 86.

58 *Notes from Underground* (1860), trans. David Magarshack, in *Great Short Works of Fyodor Dostoevsky* (New York: Harper and Row, 1968), pp. 267, 276.

59 'The Duel', in *The Oxford Chekhov*, trans. Ronald Hingley (9 vols., London: Oxford University Press, 1965–80), V, 150.

60 *The Oxford Chekhov*, V, 144, 147.

61 *Ivanov* (1887–9), *The Oxford Chekhov*, II, 6, p. 193; IV, 10, p. 225.

62 *Histoire de l'art dramatique en France depuis vingt-cinq ans* (6 vols., Paris: Librairie Magnin, 1859), III, 326; see also Taupin, 'Myth of Hamlet', p. 434.

63 See Lee Johnson, *The Paintings of Eugène Delacroix: A Critical Catalogue 1832–63*, (2 vols., Oxford: Clarendon Press, 1986), I, 86–7 and II, Plate 85, and Theodore Child, 'Hamlet in Paris', *Atlantic Monthly*, 50 (December 1882), 766–76, citing p. 772.

64 Rosette Lamont, 'The Hamlet Myth', *Yale French Studies*, 33 (1964), 80–91, especially p. 82.

65 Peter Brooks, 'The Rest is Silence: Hamlet as Decadent', in *Jules Laforgue: Essays on a Poet's Life and Work*, ed. Warren Ramsey (Carbondale: Southern Illinois University Press, 1969), pp. 93–110, especially p. 97; see also Wallace Fowlie, *Mallarmé* (Chicago: University of

Chicago Press, 1953), p. 244, and Martin Scofield, *The Ghosts of Hamlet*
(Cambridge: Cambridge University Press, 1980), pp. 11–44.

66 Albert Sonnenfeld, 'Hamlet the German and Jules Laforgue', *Yale French Studies*, 33 (1964), 92–100, citing p. 99. See also Helen Phelps Bailey, *Hamlet in France from Voltaire to Laforgue* (Geneva: Librairie Droz, 1964), and Mary Ann Caws, *The Eye in the Text* (Princeton: Princeton University Press, 1981), pp. 143–7.

67 Brook, 'The Rest is Silence', especially p. 104.

68 See *ibid.*, pp. 94, 104; Bailey, *Hamlet in France*, pp. 152–3.

69 Brooks, *ibid.*, p. 109; Taupin, 'Myth of Hamlet', pp. 444–5.

70 Brooks, *ibid.*, pp. 93–4.

71 'Variété', in *Œuvres complètes* (Paris: Editions de N.R.F., 1950), IV, 20–1, as translated by Taupin, 'Myth of Hamlet', p. 446. See also Bailey, *Hamlet in France*, p. 154.

72 *Curiosités esthétiques*, cited in Taupin, *ibid.*, p. 434.

73 Some female Hamlets from Sarah Siddons down to Eve la Gallienne (1937) and Esmé Beringer (1938) are listed in Raymond Mander and Joe Mitchenson, *Hamlet through the Ages* (London: Rockliff, 1952, revised 1955), p. 24. See also Charles H. Shattuck, *Shakespeare on the American Stage*, I, *From the Hallams to Edwin Booth*, (Washington: Folger Shakespeare Library, 1976), pp. 37, 91–5, and II, *From Booth and Barrett to Sothern and Marlowe* (1987), Chapter 3, 'The Feminization of Shakespeare', pp. 93–141. William Winter, *Shakespeare on the Stage* (New York: Moffat, Yard & Co, 1911), lists twenty-one women who acted Hamlet on the American stage.

74 E. C. Steadman in the *Atlantic Monthly*, 1866, as reported in Charles H. Shattuck, *Shakespeare on the American Stage*, II, p. 136. Bernard Grebanier, *Then Came Each Actor* (New York: David McKay, 1975), claims there have been more than fifty female Hamlets, down to Judith Anderson, who played the role in 1971 at the age of seventy-three.

75 Edward P. Vining, *The Mystery of Hamlet* (Philadelphia: J. P. Lippincott & Co, 1881). In an essay to be published in *Shakespeare Survey*, 45, Lawrence Danson deals with the feminization of Hamlet, with special reference to Vining and to Asta Nielsen.

76 Vining, *ibid.*, p. 46; for Morley and Chambers, see above, p. 16.

77 *Ibid.*, p. 54; his heading for Chapter 6 reads, 'Hamlet's Nature Essentially Feminine'.

78 *Ibid.*, p. 59.

79 This film is described in Robert Hamilton Ball, *Shakespeare on Silent Film* (London: Allen and Unwin, 1968), pp. 272–8.

80 Her appearance is described in Ball, *Shakespeare on Silent Film*, pp. 26–7; see also Shattuck, *Shakespeare on the American Stage*, II, pp. 136–8.

81 *Ibid.*, p. 138.

82 Cited in *ibid.*, p. 137.

83 Winter, *Shakespeare on the Stage*, p. 435.

84 David Leverenz, 'The Woman in Hamlet: An Interpersonal View', in *Representing Shakespeare*, ed. Murray M. Schwartz and Coppélia Kahn (Baltimore: Johns Hopkins University Press, 1980), pp. 110–28, citing p. 121. See also Leverenz, *The Language of Puritan Feeling* (New Brunswick: Rutgers University Press, 1980), especially pp. 103–4.

85 Leverenz, 'The Woman in Hamlet', p. 121.

86 'Tonio Kröger', in Thomas Mann, *Stories of Three Decades*, trans. H. T. Lowe-Porter (London: Secker and Warburg, 1936), pp. 103–4.

87 Marilyn French, *Shakespeare's Division of Experience* (New York: Summit Books, 1981), p. 158.

88 W. J. Courthope, *A History of English Poetry* (1903), cited in Williamson, *Readings*, p. 256.

89 W. P. Andrew, *Our Scientific Frontier* (1880), p. 74; cited in V. G. Kiernan, *The Lords of Human Kind* (London: Weidenfeld and Nicolson, 1969), p. 312.

90 Winter, *Shakespeare on the Stage*, p. 431.

91 Charles Dickens, *Great Expectations* (1861); New Oxford Illustrated Dickens (London: Oxford University Press, 1953), p. 240.

92 Bernard Shaw, *The Theatre of the 90's* (1897), cited in Williamson, *Readings*, p. 216.

93 Lawrence W. Levine, *Highbrow/Lowbrow: The Emergence of Cultural Hierarchy in America* (Cambridge, Mass.: Harvard University Press, 1988), p. 23.

94 *Ibid.*, p. 41, citing Dunn's 'My Shakespeare Progress', *Atlantic Monthly*, 98 (1906), 528–33. Martha Baker Dunn (1848–1915) was a minor New England novelist and frequent contributor to this journal.

95 Levine, *Highbrow/Lowbrow*, p. 79.

96 'Uses of Shakespeare off the Stage', *Harper's New Monthly Magazine*, 65 (1882), 431–8, cited in Levine, *ibid.*, p. 73.

97 Levine, *ibid.*, p. 72, citing an advertisement for the New International Shakespeare in 1903.

98 See Michael D. Bristol, *Shakespeare's America, America's Shakespeare* (London and New York: Routledge, 1990), Chapter 3, 'The Function of the Archive', pp. 62–90, and James M. Gibson, 'Horace Howard Furness: Book Collector and Library Builder', in *Shakespeare Study Today*, edited Georgianna Ziegler (New York: AMS Press, 1986), pp. 169–89.

99 Levine, *Highbrow/Lowbrow*, p. 72.

100 Lascelles Abercrombie, *The Idea of Great Poetry* (1925), cited in Williamson, *Readings*, p. 445.

101 Abercrombie, in Williamson, *ibid.*, p. 447.

102 E. A. J. Honigmann, *Shakespeare: Seven Tragedies. The Dramatist's Manipulation of Response* (London: Macmillan, 1976), p. 68.

103 J. W. Draper, *The Hamlet of Shakespeare's Audience* (Durham, North Carolina: Duke University Press, 1938), p. 243.

104 Harry Levin, *The Question of Hamlet* (New York: Oxford University Press, 1959), p. 132.

105 Peter Alexander, *Hamlet Father and Son* (Oxford: Clarendon Press, 1955), p. 166.

106 *Ibid.*, pp. 184, 174.

107 G. K. Hunter, 'The Heroism of Hamlet', in *Hamlet*, ed. J. R. Brown and Bernard Harris (Stratford-upon-Avon Studies, 5; London: Arnold, 1963), pp. 90–109, citing pp. 104, 105. On the decline of the hero, see Joseph Wood Krutch, *The Modern Temper* (New York: Harcourt Brace, 1929), and George Steiner, *The Death of Tragedy* (London: Faber, 1967).

108 Andrew Gurr, *Hamlet and the Distracted Globe* (Edinburgh: Scottish Academic Press, for Sussex University Press, 1978), p. 64.

109 *Ibid.*, p. 76.

110 Bertram Joseph, *Conscience and the King* (London: Chatto and Windus, 1953), p. 151; Reuben A. Brower, *Hero and Saint: Shakespeare and the Graeco-Roman Heroic Tradition* (Oxford: Clarendon Press, 1971), 'Hamlet Hero', pp. 277–316.

111 Meredith Anne Skura, *The Literary Use of the Psychoanalytic Process* (New Haven: Yale University Press, 1981), p. 47.

112 This is Harley Granville-Barker's phrase, in *Prefaces to Shakespeare* (Princeton: Princeton University Press, 1946), p. 258.

113 Roland Mushat Frye, *The Renaissance Hamlet: Issues and Responses in 1600* (Princeton: Princeton University Press, 1984), pp. 263, 251.

114 See Sonnenfeld, 'Hamlet the German and Jules Laforgue', pp. 99–100.

115 James Joyce, *Ulysses* (1922; London: Bodley Head, 1937), p. 176; see also Brooks, 'The Rest is Silence', p. 99.

116 *La Nausée*, trans. Lloyd Alexander (New York: New Directions, 1959, reset 1969), p. 170.

117 Cited in Rowe, *Hamlet*, p. 148.

118 *Dr Zhivago* (1957), trans. Max Hayward and Manya Harari (London: Collins and Harvill Press, 1958), p. 523; see also Rowe, *Hamlet*, pp. 159–61.

119 *Herzog* (Harmondsworth: Penguin Books, 1965), p. 102.

120 *Ibid.*, p. 113.

121 *La Nausée*, pp. 99–100.

122 *Herzog*, p. 99.

123 Trans. John Strachey (New York: Norton and Co, 1961), pp. 69, 81 and n.

124 *Essays in Applied Psycho-Analysis* (1923), cited in Williamson, *Readings*, p. 433. Sigmund Freud's first note relating Hamlet to Oedipus appeared in *The Interpretation of Dreams* (1900); see *The Complete Psychological Works*, trans. James Strachey in collaboration with Anna Freud, assisted by Alex Strachey and Alan Tyson (London: Hogarth Press, 1953), I, 264–6.

125 *The Wheel of Fire* (1930, revised 1949; New York: Meridian Books, 1957), pp. 32, 41.

126 *Ibid.*, p. 45. In 1947 Knight added a reconsideration of the play, maintaining the same general view but admitting that he had exaggerated in his earlier chapter.

127 *Obiter Scripta* (1936), cited in Williamson, *Readings*, p. 636.

128 *Explorations* (1946), cited in *ibid.*, p. 753.

129 *Ibid.*, p. 754.

130 'Hamlet's Hallucination', *Modern Language Review*, 12 (1917), 393–421, citing pp. 401, 406. See also Terence Hawkes, 'Telmah', in *That Shakespeherian Rag: Essays on a Critical Process* (London and New York: Methuen, 1986), pp. 92–119.

131 *What Happens in Hamlet* (Cambridge: Cambridge University Press, 1935; 3rd edition, 1951), pp. 237, 45, 15–16.

132 *Ibid.*, pp. 183–4, 261.

133 *Ibid.*, p. 268.

134 Maynard Mack, 'The World of Hamlet', *Yale Review*, new series, 41 (1951–2), 502–23, citing p. 507.

135 *Ibid.*, pp. 518, 519, 515.

136 *Ibid.*, pp. 515, 503.

137 A. P. Rossiter, *Angel with Horns* (London: Longmans, 1961), p. 181.

138 See Francis Barker, *The Tremulous Private Body: Essays on Subjection* (London: Methuen, 1984).

139 Robert Speaight, *Nature in Shakespearian Tragedy* (London: Hollis and Carter, 1955), p. 43.

140 *Hamlet*, edited Harold Jenkins (New Arden edition, London: Methuen, 1982), pp. 139–40.

141 Martin Dodsworth, *Hamlet Closely Observed* (London: Athlone Press, 1985), p. 297.

142 Ruth Nevo, *Tragic Form in Shakespeare* (Princeton: Princeton University Press, 1972), p. 162.

143 Linda Bamber, *Comic Women, Tragic Men* (Stanford: Stanford University Press, 1982), p. 7.2

144 Barker, *The Tremulous Private Body*, p. 37. The pervasive influence of *Hamlet* on *Lord Jim* is analysed by Eloise Hay in 'Lord Jim et le Hamletisme', *L'Époque Conradienne: première partie des Actes du Colloque de Marseille*, 13–17 septembre 1990, pp. 9–27; a revised version will appear in a volume to be published by Stanford University Press in honour of Thomas C. Moser.

145 Hazlitt, *Complete Works*, ed. P. P. Howe (21 vols., London: Dent, 1930–4), IV, 233.

146 E. K. Chambers, Introduction to his edition of *Hamlet* (1894), cited in Williamson, *Readings*, p. 186.

147 D. H. Lawrence, *Twilight in Italy* (1916; London: Heinemann, 1956), p. 56. Lawrence was describing Enrico Persevalli's performance in the

role as 'the modern Italian'. Lawrence says 'I had always felt an aversion from Hamlet: a creeping, unclean thing he seems, on the stage ...' (p. 68).

148 W. B. Yeats, 'The Statues' (1938), in *Collected Poems* (2nd edition, London: Macmillan, 1950), pp. 375–6.

149 Lawrence, *Twilight in Italy*, p. 69.

150 Rowe, *Hamlet*, p. 133, quoting a Russian history of theatre that refers especially to the period 1933–41. Her chapter on 'Soviet Reality and Hamlet' gives a fuller account of the treatment of the play by critics and in the theatre, which is more complex than a brief reference might suggest.

151 Kozintsev, *Shakespeare: Time and Conscience*, p. 174.

152 Max Plowman, *The Right to Live* (1942), cited in Williamson, *Readings*, p. 717.

153 Charles Marowitz, *The Marowitz Shakespeare* (New York: Drama Book Specialists, 1978), p. 13.

154 Jan Kott, *Shakespeare our Contemporary*, trans. Boleslaw Taborski (London: Methuen; New York: Doubleday, 1964), citing the Preface by Peter Brook, p. ix. This appears only in the English edition; it was replaced in the American edition by a much tamer foreword written by Martin Esslin, which contains the extraordinary statement (in view of Kott's treatment of the plays), 'it is one of the roots of Shakespeare's universality that his work seems free of any definite ideological position' (p. xvii).

155 *Financial Times*, 20 August 1965, B. A. Young reviewing.

156 *A Supplement to the Oxford English Dictionary* citing an article in *Encounter* (1959).

157 Peter Hall's address to his company as reported in the *Observer*, 15 August 1965. See also Stanley Wells, *Royal Shakespeare: Four Major Productions at Stratford-upon-Avon* (Furman Studies, Manchester: Manchester University Press, 1977), pp. 23–42, especially pp. 24–5.

158 Sheridan Morley's review in *Punch*, 16 July 1980, p. 111.

159 James L. Calderwood, *To Be and Not To Be: Negation and Metadrama in Hamlet* (New York: Columbia University Press, 1983), p. 189.

160 *Ibid.*, p. 194.

161 Catherine Belsey, *The Subject of Tragedy: Identity and Difference in Renaissance Drama* (London and New York: Methuen, 1985), p. 33.

162 Nigel Alexander, *Poison, Play and Duel* (London: Routledge, 1971), p. 3.

163 These are the New Arden, ed. Harold Jenkins (1982); the Oxford, ed. G. R. Hibbard (Oxford and New York: Oxford University Press, 1987); and New Cambridge, ed. Philip Edwards (Cambridge: Cambridge University Press, 1985).

164 Tom Stoppard, *Rosencrantz and Guildenstern are Dead* (London: Methuen, 1967), p. 82.

165 *Ibid.*, p. 60.
166 *Ibid.*, p. 89.
167 *Ibid.*, p. 90.
168 *Ibid.*, pp. 80, 78.
169 Belsey, *The Subject of Tragedy*, p. 35.
170 Tom Stoppard, *Dogg's Hamlet, Cahoot's Macbeth* (London: Faber, 1980); Charles Marowitz reduced *Hamlet* to a twenty-eight-minute collage (London: Penguin Books, 1968); and Joseph Papp, *William Shakespeare's 'Naked' Hamlet* (Toronto: Macmillan, 1969).
171 Papp, *ibid.*, pp. 30–1.
172 Kott, *Shakespeare our Contemporary*, p. 76.
173 Sir Philip Sidney, *A Defence of Poetry*, in *Miscellaneous Prose of Sir Philip Sidney*, ed. Katherine Duncan-Jones and Jan van Dorsten (Oxford: Clarendon Press, 1973), p. 83.
174 Seamus Heaney, *North* (London: Faber, 1975), p. 23.

3 THE RECEPTION OF *KING LEAR*

1 Samuel Johnson, notes on *King Lear*, from his edition of 1765, in Vickers, *Critical Heritage*, v, 139.
2 Shakespeare, *King Lear*, ed. J. S. Bratton, Plays in Performance, Bristol: Bristol Classical Press, 1987), p. 16. The edition includes on pp. 220–38 key passages from Tate's version of the play.
3 A. W. Schlegel, *A Course of Lectures on Dramatic Art and Literature* (1809–11; trans. John Black, revised A. J. W. Morrison, London: Bohn, 1846), p. 413.
4 Charles Lamb, 'On the Tragedies of Shakespeare' (1811), in *The Works of Charles and Mary Lamb*, ed. E. V. Lucas (7 vols., London: Methuen, 1903), I, 107.
5 *Ibid.*, I, 107.
6 William Hazlitt, 'Characters of Shakespeare's Plays' (1817), in *Works*, ed. P. P. Howe, IV, 259–60.
7 *Ibid.*, IV, 271, 257.
8 S. T. Coleridge, *LL* (*CC*), II, 328, 325. See also pp. 74–6 below.
9 Hazlitt, *Works*, IV, 214.
10 *Ibid.*, IV, 215.
11 *Ibid.*, IV, 259; cf. 'the greatest strength of genius is shewn in describing the strongest passions' (IV, 271).
12 *Ibid.*, IV, 257.
13 *The Letters of John Keats*, ed. Hyder Rollins (2 vols., Cambridge, Mass.: Harvard University Press, 1958), I, 214–15.
14 P. B. Shelley, 'A Defence of Poetry' (1821; published 1840), in *Shelley's Critical Prose*, ed. Bruce R. McElderry Jr. (Lincoln: University of Nebraska Press, 1967), p. 15.

15 Hazlitt, *Works*, iv, 258.

16 Coleridge, *LL (CC)*, ii, 329.

17 Hazlitt, *Works*, iv, 269.

18 Anna Jameson, *Characteristics of Women, Moral, Political and Historical* (1833), reissued as *Shakespeare's Heroines* (London: George Bell, 1897), pp. 213, 204.

19 Hermann Ulrici, *Shakespeare's Dramatic Art* (1839), trans. Rev A. J. W. Morrison (1846), cited in L. L. Harris and M. W. Scott, eds., *Shakespearean Criticism* (Detroit: Gate Research Company, 1985), ii, 115.

20 G. C. Odell, *Shakespeare from Betterton to Irving* (2 vols., New York: Charles Scribner's Sons, 1920; reprinted Dover Books, 1966), ii, 210, referring to Macready's 1838 production; he first used Shakespeare's text, cutting out the role of the Fool, in 1834, according to J. S. Bratton, 'The Lear of Private Life: Interpretations of *King Lear* in the Nineteenth Century', in *Shakespeare and the Victorian Stage*, ed. Richard Foulkes (Cambridge University Press, 1986), pp. 124–37, especially pp. 128–9.

21 Bratton, *King Lear*, pp. 43–4.

22 G. G. Gervinus, *Shakespeare Commentaries* (1849–50), revised edition, trans. F. E. Bunnett (1877), cited in Harris and Scott, *Shakespearean Criticism*, ii, 120.

23 Gervinus, *Shakespeare Commentaries*, ii, 120.

24 A. C. Swinburne, *A Study of Shakespeare* (1880; 3rd edition, revised, London: Heinemann, 1918), p. 171.

25 Edward Dowden, *Shakespeare: A Critical Study of his Mind and Art* (1875; 3rd edition, revised 1881, London: Routledge, reprinted 1967), p. 257.

26 *Ibid.*, p. 259.

27 *Ibid.*, p. 274.

28 Denton Snider, *The Shakespearian Drama, a Commentary: The Tragedies* (New York: Ticknor, 1887), cited in Harris and Scott, *Shakespearean Criticism*, ii, 134.

29 *Ibid.*, ii, 135.

30 *Ibid.*, ii, 136.

31 A. C. Bradley, *Shakespearean Tragedy* (London: Macmillan, 1904; 2nd edition, 1905), pp. 248, 261.

32 *Ibid.*, p. 244.

33 *Ibid.*, p. 279.

34 *Ibid.*, p. 291.

35 E. K. Chambers, *Shakespeare: A Survey* (1906; London: Sidgwick and Jackson, 1925), pp. 245–6, 248.

36 G. Wilson Knight, *The Wheel of Fire*, p. 191.

37 D. G. James, *The Dream of Learning* (Oxford: Clarendon Press, 1951, reprinted 1965), pp. 80, 92–3.

38 Wilson Knight, *Wheel of Fire*, p. 222.
39 Harley Granville-Barker, *King Lear* (1927, revised 1935), in *Prefaces to Shakespeare*, p. 266.
40 R. B. Heilman, *This Great Stage* (Baton Rouge: Louisiana State University Press, 1948), pp. 266, 287, 283, 221.
41 R. W. Chambers, *King Lear* (W. P. Ker Memorial Lecture, 1939; Glasgow: Jackson, Son & Co., 1940), pp. 25, 32.
42 O. J. Campbell, 'The Salvation of Lear', *ELH*, 15 (1948), 94.
43 Irving Ribner, 'The Gods are Just: A Reading of *King Lear*' (1958), *Patterns in Shakespearean Tragedy* (London: Methuen, 1960), p. 136.
44 Robert Ornstein, *The Moral Vision of Jacobean Tragedy* (Madison: University of Wisconsin Press, 1960), pp. 272–3.
45 Kenneth Muir, ed., *King Lear* (London: Methuen, 1952), p. lix.
46 *Ibid.*, p. lv; on p. lix Muir says his analysis is partly based on that of Bradley, who 'suggested that the play might be called "The Redemption of King Lear"'.
47 Geoffrey Bickersteth, 'The Golden World of *King Lear*', in *Proceedings of the British Academy*, 32 (1946), 25.
48 Theodore Spencer, *Shakespeare and the Nature of Man* (New York: Macmillan, 1942), p. 136.
49 *Ibid.*, pp. 15–16, 141–3.
50 *Ibid.*, pp. 142, 146.
51 Edwin Muir, 'The Politics of *King Lear*' (W. P. Ker Memorial Lecture, 1946; Glasgow: Glasgow University Publications, LXXII, 1947), p. 49.
52 *Ibid.*, pp. 18, 16.
53 *Ibid.*, pp. 19, 23–4.
54 See Bristol, *Shakespeare's America, America's Shakespeare*, pp. 151–7; the quotation is from p. 157.
55 John F. Danby, *Shakespeare's Doctrine of Nature* (London: Faber, 1949, reprinted 1951, 1958, 1961), p. 41.
56 *Ibid.*, p. 46.
57 *Ibid.*, p. 50.
58 *Ibid.*, p. 138.
59 *Ibid.*, p. 133.
60 *Ibid.*, pp. 176, 169.
61 *Ibid.*, p. 189.
62 Bradley, *Shakespearean Tragedy*, pp. 284–5.
63 *Ibid.*, p. 330.
64 *Ibid.*, pp. 285, 303.
65 *Ibid.*, p. 302.
66 Danby, *Shakespeare's Doctrine of Nature*, p. 195.
67 *Ibid.*, p. 138.
68 Hibbard, '*King Lear*: A Retrospect 1939–1979', p. 5.
69 Edwin Muir, 'The Politics of *King Lear*', pp. 7–8, 15, 23–4.
70 Danby, *Shakespeare's Doctrine of Nature*, p. 169.

71 *Ibid.*, p. 194.
72 See Joseph Summers, *Dreams of Love and Power* (Oxford: Clarendon Press, 1984), p. 113.
73 Russell Fraser, *Shakespeare's Poetics in Relation to King Lear* (London: Routledge, 1962), p. 133.
74 Paul Jorgensen, *Lear's Self-Discovery* (Berkeley and Los Angeles: University of California Press, 1967), p. 135; see also the quotation from Kenneth Muir's edition, p. 50 above and note 45.
75 Stephen Greenblatt, '*King Lear* and Harsnett's "Devil Fiction"', in Greenblatt, ed., *The Power of Forms in the English Renaissance* (Norman, Oklahoma: University of Oklahoma Press, 1982), pp. 241, 242.
76 L. C. Knights, *An Approach to Hamlet* (London: Chatto and Windus, 1960), pp. 119, 117.
77 Arthur Sewell, *Character and Society in Shakespeare* (Oxford: Clarendon Press, 1951), pp. 110, 118.
78 *Ibid.*, p. 108.
79 *Ibid.*, p. 118.
80 Richard Sewall, *The Vision of Tragedy* (New Haven: Yale University Press, 1959), p. 79.
81 John Holloway, *The Story of the Night: Studies in Shakespeare's Major Tragedies* (London: Routledge, 1961), pp. 79, 98.
82 Maynard Mack, *King Lear in our Time* (Berkeley and Los Angeles: University of California Press, 1965), p. 117.
83 *Ibid.*, p. 117.
84 *Ibid.*, p. 111.
85 *Ibid.*, p. 97.
86 *Ibid.*, p. 90.
87 *Ibid.*, pp. 116–17.
88 *Ibid.*, p. 116.
89 Helen Gardner, *King Lear* (John Coffin Memorial Lecture, 1966; London: Athlone Press, 1967), p. 28. Others who have seen a kind of pietà at the end include R. G. Hunter and James Siemon (see below, notes 144, 151).
90 Mack, *King Lear in our Time*, p. 32. See also Bristol, *Shakespeare's America, America's Shakespeare*, pp. 184–7; he sees Mack as mapping 'a strategic retreat from ontological and theological certainty through the domain of political and social relations to the sphere of private ethical sensibility'.
91 Mack, *ibid.*, p. 47.
92 *Ibid.*, p. 66.
93 *Ibid.*, p. 70.
94 *Ibid.*, p. 76.
95 *Ibid.*, p. 77.
96 *Ibid.*, pp. 78–9.
97 *Ibid.*, pp. 59.

98 *Ibid.*, p. 116.

99 Barbara Everett, 'The New *King Lear*', *Critical Quarterly*, 2 (1960), 325–39, especially pp. 330, 339.

100 J. Stampfer, 'The Catharsis of *King Lear*', *Shakespeare Survey*, 13 (1960), 1–10, citing pp. 5, 10.

101 Mack, *King Lear in our Time*, p. 25.

102 For example, Michael Long and R. G. Hunter (see below, notes 142 and 158).

103 Mack, *King Lear in our Time*, p. 38.

104 Herbert Blau, *The Impossible Theater: A Manifesto* (New York: Macmillan, 1964), p. 279.

105 *Ibid.*, pp. 279, 281.

106 *Ibid.*, p. 282.

107 *King Lear*, ed. J. S. Bratton, p. 161.

108 Marowitz, 'Lear Log', *Encore*, 10 (1963), 20–33, citing pp. 28–9; reprinted with a postscript in *Tulane Drama Review*, 8, no. 2 (1963), 103–21 (citing p. 114).

109 Everett, 'The Figure in Professor Knights' Carpet', *Critical Quarterly*, 2 (1960), 171–6, citing p. 175.

110 Jan Kott, *Shakespeare our Contemporary*, p. 152.

111 N. S. Brooke, *King Lear* (London: Edward Arnold, 1963), p. 57.

112 Holloway, *The Story of the Night*, p. 94.

113 Kott, *Shakespeare our Contemporary*, p. 162.

114 William R. Elton, *King Lear and the Gods* (San Marino: Huntington Library, 1966), p. 334.

115 Stanley Cavell, 'The Avoidance of Love', in *Disowning Knowledge in Six Plays by Shakespeare* (Cambridge: Cambridge University Press, 1987), pp. 39–123, citing pp. x, 70, 111, 114.

116 V. A. Kolve, 'The Modernity of *Lear*', in *Pacific Coast Studies in Shakespeare*, ed. Waldo F. McNeir and Thelma N. Greenfield (Eugene: University of Oregon Press, 1966), p. 188.

117 Marowitz, *Tulane Drama Review*, p. 103.

118 The *Observer*, 5 April 1964, p. 23.

119 Marowitz, *Tulane Drama Review*, p. 106.

120 Peter Brook, 'Politics of Sclerosis: Stalin and Lear'. Interviewed by A. J. Liehm, trans. by Richard Seaver, *Theatre Quarterly*, 3, no. 10 (1973), 13–17, citing p. 15.

121 Kolve, 'The Modernity of *Lear*', p. 188.

122 Kozintsev, *Shakespeare: Time and Conscience*, p. 62.

123 *Ibid.*, p. 93.

124 *Ibid.*, p. 94.

125 *Ibid.*, p. 102.

126 Kozintsev, '*Hamlet* and *King Lear*: Stage and Film', in *Shakespeare 1971: Proceedings of the World Shakespeare Congress*, Vancouver, August 1971, edited Clifford Leech and J. M. R. Margeson (Toronto: University of Toronto Press, 1972), p. 195.

127 *Ibid.*, p. 198.
128 *Ibid.*, p. 198.
129 Frank Kermode, *The Sense of an Ending* (New York: Oxford University Press, 1967), p. 82.
130 Kozintsev, *Shakespeare: Time and Conscience*, p. 89.
131 *Lear* (London: Methuen, 1972; edited with commentary and notes by Patricia Hern, 1983), p. 88.
132 *Ibid.*, p. 84.
133 *Ibid.*, p. xxvi.
134 *Ibid.*, p. 85.
135 *Ibid.*, p. 84.
136 W. B. Yeats, *Letters*, ed. Allan Wade (London: Rupert Hart-Davis, 1954), p. 876, remarks in his lofty way, 'Joy is the salvation of the soul. You say we must love, yes but love is not pity. It does not desire to change its object. It is a form of the eternal contemplation of what is.'
137 See 'Edward Bond: The Long Road to *Lear*', *Theatre Quarterly*, 2 (1972), 3–31, especially p. 9.
138 See Laurilyn J. Harris, 'Peter Brook's *King Lear*: Aesthetic Achievement or Far Side of the Moon?', *Theatre Research International*, 11 (1986), 223–39.
139 Helen Gardner, 'Shakespeare in the Directors' Theatre', in *In Defence of the Imagination* (Cambridge, Mass.: Harvard University Press, 1982), p. 72.
140 Michael Goldman, *Shakespeare and the Energies of Drama* (Princeton: Princeton University Press, 1972), p. 106.
141 Richard Fly, *Shakespeare's Mediated World* (Amherst: University of Massachusetts Press, 1976), p. 98.
142 Robert G. Hunter, *Shakespeare and the Mystery of God's Judgments* (Athens: University of Georgia Press, 1976), p. 194.
143 Nevo, *Tragic Form in Shakespeare*, pp. 294, 304.
144 Fly, *Shakespeare's Mediated World*, p. 96.
145 Howard Felperin, *Shakespearean Representation* (Princeton: Princeton University Press, 1977), p. 96.
146 *Ibid.*, p. 105.
147 The seminal work was E. A. J. Honigmann's *The Stability of Shakespeare's Text* (London: Arnold, 1965), but revision became an issue effectively in the 1980s; see below, pp. 83–4.
148 Stephen Orgel, 'Shakespeare Imagines a Theater', in *Shakespeare Man of the Theater*, p. 43.
149 James R. Siemon, *Shakespearean Iconoclasm* (Berkeley and Los Angeles: University of California Press, 1985), p. 251.
150 Stephen Booth, *King Lear, Macbeth, Indefinition and Tragedy* (New Haven: Yale University Press, 1983), pp. 1–11.
151 *Ibid.*, pp. 27–8.
152 *Ibid.*, p. 43.

153 *Ibid.*, p. 56.
154 Harry Berger Jr., 'Text against Performance: The Gloucester Family Romance', in *Shakespeare's Rough Magic*, ed. Peter Erickson and Coppélia Kahn (Newark: University of Delaware Press, 1985), p. 225.
155 Berger here cites S. L. Goldberg, *An Essay on King Lear* (Cambridge: Cambridge University Press, 1974), p. 121.
156 Berger, 'Text against Performance', p. 227.
157 Bernard McElroy, *Shakespeare's Mature Tragedies* (Princeton: Princeton University Press, 1973), pp. 161–2.
158 Michael Long, *The Unnatural Scene: A Study in Shakespearean Tragedy* (London: Methuen, 1976), pp. 214, 216.
159 Emrys Jones, *Scenic Form in Shakespeare* (Oxford: Clarendon Press, 1971), p. 159.
160 Joseph Wittreich, *'Image of that Horror': History, Prophecy and Apocalypse in King Lear* (San Marino: Huntington Library, 1984), pp. 33, 122.
161 J. W. Lever, *The Tragedy of State* (London: Methuen, 1971), p. 4.
162 Rosalie Colie, 'Reason and Need: *King Lear* and the "Crisis" of the Aristocracy', in *Some Facets of King Lear: Essays in Prismatic Criticism*, edited Rosalie Colie and F. T. Flahiff (Toronto: University of Toronto Press, 1974), p. 212.
163 *Ibid.*, p. 216.
164 Alvin Kernan, '*King Lear* and the Shakespearean Pageant of History', in *On King Lear*, ed. Lawrence Danson (Princeton: Princeton University Press, 1981), p. 23.
165 James H. Kavanagh, 'Shakespeare in Ideology', in *Alternative Shakespeares*, ed. John Drakakis (London and New York: Methuen, 1985), pp. 144–65, citing p. 159.
166 *Ibid.*, p. 160.
167 John Turner, 'King Lear', in *Shakespeare: The Play of History*, ed. Graham Holderness, Nick Potter and John Turner (Iowa City: University of Iowa Press, 1988), p. 101.
168 *Ibid.*, p. 105.
169 *Ibid.*, p. 111.
170 Greenblatt, 'Shakespeare and the Exorcists', in *Shakespearean Negotiations* (Berkeley and Los Angeles: University of California Press, 1988), pp. 94–128, citing p. 119; this is a revised version of the essay referred to above, n. 75.
171 *Ibid.*, p. 125.
172 John Drakakis, 'Theatre, Ideology and Institution: Shakespeare and the Roadsweepers', in *The Shakespeare Myth*, ed. Graham Holderness (Manchester: Manchester University Press, 1988), p. 36.
173 Leonard Tennenhouse, *Power on Display: The Politics of Shakespeare's Genres* (London and New York: Methuen, 1986), p. 134.

174 *Ibid.*, pp. 141–2.
175 Annabel Patterson, *Shakespeare and the Popular Voice* (Oxford and Cambridge, Mass.: Blackwell, 1989), p. 115.
176 *Ibid.*, p. 111.
177 *Ibid.*, p. 116.
178 Kathleen McLuskie, 'The Patriarchal Bard: Feminist Criticism and Shakespeare: *King Lear* and *Measure for Measure*', in *Political Shakespeare*, ed. Jonathan Dollimore and Alan Sinfield (Manchester: Manchester University Press; Ithaca: Cornell University Press, 1985), p. 100.
179 *Ibid.*, p. 106.
180 For current debunking of Shakespeare, see Graham Holderness, ed., *The Shakespeare Myth* (Brighton: Harvester Press, 1988), and Gary Taylor, *Reinventing Shakespeare*. For Taylor, Shakespeare's standing as a dramatist is a testimony more to 'the virility of British imperialism' than to his worth as a writer, and he is demoted to a mere hack writer; but it is a facile, if deliberately iconoclastic, Taylor who finds Shakespeare to be facile, 'the poet contracting to a mere technician of language, a verbocrat in the literary meritocracy' (pp. 379, 398).
181 Robin Headlam Wells, *Shakespeare, Politics and the State* (London: Macmillan, 1986), p. 160.
182 Coleridge, *LL (CC)*, II, 346.
183 *Ibid.*, 322.
184 Lamb, *Works*, I, 107.
185 *King Lear*, ed. J. S. Bratton, p. 35.
186 *Ibid.*, p. 58.
187 Hazlitt, *Works*, IV, 259.
188 Madeleine Doran, *The Text of King Lear* (Stanford: Stanford University Press, 1931; reissued New York: AMS Press, 1967); E. A. J. Honigmann, *The Stability of Shakespeare's Text* (1965).
189 See Leonard Tennenhouse, *Power on Display*, pp. 134–6; Annabel Patterson, *Shakespeare and the Popular Voice*, p. 106.
190 Richard Levin, 'Leaking Relativism', *Essays in Criticism*, 38 (1988), 267–77.
191 David Margolies, 'Teaching a Handsaw to Fly: Shakespeare as a Hegemonic Instrument', in Holderness, ed., *The Shakespeare Myth*, pp. 42–53, citing p. 43.
192 Jonathan Dollimore, *Radical Tragedy* (Brighton: Harvester Press, 1984; 2nd edition, 1989), p. 197.
193 *Ibid.*, pp. 198, 201.
194 *Ibid.*, p. 198.
195 Coleridge, *Essays on his Times*, ed. David Erdman, 3 vols. The Collected Works of Samuel Taylor Coleridge, Bollingen Series, LXXV (Princeton: Princeton University Press; London: Routledge, 1978), I, 717. Hereafter *EOT (CC)*.
196 *EOT (CC)*, I, 314.

197 *Ibid.*, 319.
198 Coleridge, *Collected Notebooks*, ed. Kathleen Coburn, III (London: Routledge, 1973), 3845.
199 *Ibid.*
200 *LL (CC)*,II, 326.
201 *Ibid.*, 327.
202 *Ibid.*, 328.
203 *Ibid.*, 325.
204 *Ibid.*, 329, and see above, p. 69.
205 Martin Orkin, *Shakespeare against Apartheid* (Craighill, South Africa: Ad. Donker, 1987), p. 160.
206 Holderness, ed., *Shakespeare: The Play of History*, p. 117.

4 PLAYS AND TEXTS

1 See the review by Mark Almond of Tocilescu's production at the Lyttelton Theatre in London, *Times Literary Supplement*, 5–11 October 1990, p. 1069.
2 *Political Shakespeare: New Essays in Cultural Materialism*, ed. Jonathan Dollimore and Alan Sinfield (Manchester: Manchester University Press, 1985), editorial preface, p. viii; and see Terence Hawkes, 'Lear's Maps: A General Survey', *Deutsche Shakespeare Gesellschaft West Jahrbuch* (1989), pp. 138–9.
3 Hawkes, 'Lear's Maps', p. 139.
4 John Drakakis, 'Theatre, Ideology, and Institution: Shakespeare and the Roadsweepers', pp. 24–41, citing p. 36; see also Stephen Greenblatt, *Shakespearean Negotiations*, especially pp. 30–5.
5 *Ibid.*, p. 7.
6 *Ibid.*, p. 65. For the quotation from Coleridge, see *LL (CC)*, I, 35. See also Juliet Sychrava, *Schiller to Derrida: Idealism in Aesthetics* (Cambridge: Cambridge University Press, 1989), pp. 45–57 for a discussion of Coleridge's aesthetics, and of the contradiction between organicism as a subjective process and as a function of the poem or play as object.
7 Michael D. Bristol, *Shakespeare's America, America's Shakespeare*, p. 18.
8 *Ibid.*, p. 115.
9 Greenblatt, *Shakespearean Negotiations*, pp. 2, 20.
10 See Bristol, *Shakespeare's America, America's Shakespeare*, especially pp. 1 and 19, and Levine, *Highbrow/Lowbrow*, pp. 13–81.
11 Hawkes, 'Lear's Maps', p.135.
12 See Greenblatt, *Shakespearean Negotiations*, p. 7; Hawkes, 'Lear's Maps', p. 135.
13 See Alan Liu, 'The Power of Formalism: The New Historicism', *ELH*, 56 (1989), pp. 721–71, and in this general context, Alasdair MacIntyre, *After Virtue: A Study in Moral Theory* (London: Duckworth; Notre

Dame, Indiana: Notre Dame University Press, 1981), especially Chapters 11 to 15.

14 Bristol, *Shakespeare's America, America's Shakespeare*, p. 115.
15 Stephen Orgel, 'The Authentic Shakespeare', *Representations*, 21 (1988), 1–26, citing p. 7.
16 Marion Trousdale, 'A Trip through the Divided Kingdoms', p. 223.
17 *The Division of the Kingdoms: Shakespeare's Two Versions of King Lear*, ed. Gary Taylor and Michael Warren (Oxford: Clarendon Press, 1983), pp. 20 (Stanley Wells) and 138 (Thomas Clayton).
18 Stephen Urkowitz, *Shakespeare's Revision of King Lear* (Princeton: Princeton University Press, 1980), p. 147.
19 D. F. McKenzie, *Bibliography and the Sociology of Texts* (The Panizzi Lectures; London: British Library, 1986), p. 28. Sociology, McKenzie argues, 'directs us to consider the human motives and interactions which texts involve at every stage of their production, transmission, and consumption. It alerts us to the roles of institutions, and their complex structures, in affecting the forms of social discourse, past and present' (pp. 6–7). For the debate about revision, see Grace Ioppolo, *Revising Shakespeare*, especially Chapter 6.
20 Bristol, *Shakespeare's America, America's Shakespeare*, p. 117.
21 *Ibid.*, p. 118.
22 Terence Hawkes, *That Shakespeherian Rag*, p. 76.
23 See Bristol, *Shakespeare's America, America's Shakespeare*, p. 95.
24 *Ibid.*, p. 109.
25 Hawkes, *That Shakespeherian Rag*, pp. 88–9. E. A. J. Honigmann had earlier shown that Shakespeare and other dramatists used 'O' to signal a variety of noises, such as sighs, groans and roars, in 'Re-Enter the Stage-Direction: Shakespeare and Some Contemporaries', *Shakespeare Survey*, 29 (1976), 117–25, citing p. 123.
26 *Hamlet*, ed. Philip Edwards (New Cambridge Shakespeare, Cambridge: Cambridge University Press, 1985), p. 241; ed. G. R. Hibbard (The Oxford Shakespeare, Oxford: Oxford University Press, 1987), p. 352.
27 Hawkes, *That Shakespeherian Rag*, p. 86.
28 Orgel, 'The Authentic Shakespeare', p. 7.
29 Bristol, *Shakespeare's America, America's Shakespeare*, p. 119.
30 *Hamlet*, ed. Edwards, p. 67.
31 The phrase is from Bristol, *Shakespeare's America, America's Shakespeare*, p. 109, where he says play-texts were not treated as 'finished literary productions' except by the 'atypical' Ben Jonson.
32 See *Hamlet*, ed. Hibbard, p. 88.
33 *Hamlet*, ed. Edwards, pp. 66–7, citing Charles Shattuck, *The Hamlet of Edwin Booth* (Urbana: University of Illinois Press, 1969).
34 Goldberg, 'Textual Properties', p. 216.

35 *Hamlet*, ed. Hibbard, p. 126.
36 Stanley Wells, 'The Once and Future *King Lear*', in *The Division of the Kingdoms*, pp. 18, 1.
37 Hawkes, *That Shakespeherian Rag*, p. 77.
38 Hawkes, 'Lear's Maps', p. 135; Bristol, *Shakespeare's America, America's Shakespeare*, p. 30.
39 *Hamlet*, ed. Edwards, p. 32.
40 Hawkes, *That Shakespeherian Rag*, p. 76; Bristol, *Shakespeare's America, America's Shakespeare*, p. 23.
41 So Hibbard devotes sixty-four pages of his introduction in his edition to a discussion of textual problems (pp. 67–130).
42 A suggestion supported by Janet Clare, '*Art made Tongue-Tied by Authority*': *Elizabethan and Jacobean Dramatic Censorship* (The Revels Plays Companion Library; Manchester: Manchester University Press, 1990), p. 108.
43 *Hamlet*, ed. Edwards, p. 4; E. A. J. Honigmann, 'The Date of *Hamlet*', *Shakespeare Survey*, 9 (1956), 27–9; *Hamlet*, ed. Hibbard, pp. 5, 112.
44 See Harold Jenkins, 'Playhouse Interpolations in the Folio Text of *Hamlet*', *Studies in Bibliography*, 13 (1961), 31–47.
45 *Hamlet*, ed. Hibbard, p. 126.
46 *Hamlet*, ed. Harold Jenkins (The New Arden Shakespeare; London and New York: Methuen, 1982), p. 154; see also *Hamlet*, ed. Hibbard, p. 48.
47 *Hamlet*, ed. Jenkins, p. 488.
48 *Hamlet*, ed. Hibbard, p. 112.
49 William Shakespeare, *The Complete Works Original-Spelling Edition*, ed. Stanley Wells, Gary Taylor, John Jowett and William Montgomery (Oxford: Oxford University Press, 1986), p. 735.
50 *Hamlet*, ed. Wells and Taylor, p. 1121.
51 *King Lear*, ed. Kenneth Muir (The New Arden Shakespeare; London: Methuen, 1952), p. xvi.
52 *Hamlet*, ed. Hibbard, p. 112.
53 See Peter Blayney, *The Texts of King Lear and their Origins: Volume One, Nicholas Okes and the First Quarto* (Cambridge: Cambridge University Press, 1982), pp. 28–30. Blayney accuses Okes, printer of the Quarto, of 'Cheap-minded expedience' (p. 30).
54 Stanley Wells, 'The Once and Future *King Lear*', p. 17.
55 Gary Taylor, 'Monopolies, Show Trials, Disaster, and Invasion: King Lear and Censorship', in *The Division of the Kingdoms*, pp. 75–119; Annabel Patterson, *Censorship and Interpretation* (Madison: University of Wisconsin Press, 1984), pp. 58–73; Clare, *Art made Tongue-Tied by Authority*, pp. 131–6.
56 Patterson, *Shakespeare and the Popular Voice*, p. 106.
57 *Ibid.*
58 See Wells, 'The Once and Future *King Lear*', pp. 8–20.
59 John Bayley, *Shakespeare and Tragedy* (London: Routledge, 1981), p. 61.

The varying and contradictory accounts of the Fool can be tracked in Larry Champion (compiler), *King Lear: An Annotated Bibliography* (2 vols., New York and London: Garland, 1980), starting with the compiler's own sketch of them, I, xxiv.

60 Citing Nicholas Shrimpton's description in his review in *Shakespeare Survey*, 36 (1983), p. 152.

61 Grigori Kozintsev, *King Lear: The Space of Tragedy* (1973; translated by Mary Mackintosh, Berkeley: University of California Press, 1977), pp. 71–2.

62 Jack Jorgens, *Shakespeare on Film* (Bloomington: Indiana University Press, 1977), p. 243.

63 John Kerrigan, 'Revision, Adaptation and the Fool in *King Lear*', in *The Division of the Kingdoms*, pp. 195–245, citing p. 219.

64 *Ibid.*, p. 219.

65 *Ibid.*, p. 221.

66 *Ibid.*, p. 223.

67 P. W. K. Stone, *The Textual History of King Lear* (London: Scolar Press, 1980), pp. 121ff., and Kerrigan, 'Revision, Adaptation and the Fool', pp. 221–3, both argue for topical allusions here, but differ in their dating and interpretation.

68 Kerrigan, *ibid.*, p. 218–19.

69 See Huntington Brown, 'Lear's Fool: A Boy, not a Man', *Essays in Criticism*, 13 (1963), 164–71; and Neil McEwan, 'The Lost Childhood of Lear's Fool', *Essays in Criticism*, 26 (1976), 209–17.

70 See Stephen Booth, *King Lear, Macbeth, Indefinition and Tragedy*, pp. 129, 153–5.

71 Maynard Mack, 'The Jacobean Shakespeare: Some Observations on the Construction of the Tragedies', in *Jacobean Theatre*, ed. John Russell Brown and Bernard Harris (London: Arnold, 1960), pp. 10–42, citing p. 24.

72 See John Danby, 'The Fool', *Durham University Journal*, 38 (1945), 17–24.

73 Kerrigan's differentiation of the Fool in Q and in F; 'Revision, Adaptation and the Fool', p. 230.

74 Gary Taylor, 'The War in *King Lear*', *Shakespeare Survey*, 33 (1980), 27–34. E. A. J. Honigmann has criticized Taylor's argument that there are two accounts of the war in Q and F *Lear* as much too categorical, and has also noted the use of 'colours' in F as possible French emblems; see his review of *The Complete King Lear, 1608–1623*, ed. Michael Warren, in *The New York Review of Books*, 25 October 1990, 58–60.

75 Ioppolo, *Revising Shakespeare*, p. 173.

76 *Ibid.*, pp. 179–80; she was influenced by Gary Taylor's arguments that the Folio changes a French invasion into a civil war (*The Division of the Kingdoms*, p. 426), arguments not borne out either by the text, which in F, in spite of omissions, still emphasizes that Cordelia leads a French

army, or by the stage directions calling for the 'colours' of what must be a French army; see above, p. 107.

77 In his *Shakespeare and Revision*, the Hilda Hulme Lecture published by the University of London (1988), Stanley Wells says that the two texts of *King Lear* 'represent the play at different stages of its evolution', but still claims that the two versions 'create, in effect, two separate plays' (pp. 14–15).

5 *HAMLET, KING LEAR* AND ART

1 James Joyce, *Ulysses* (1922), ed. Hans Walter Gabler (3 vols., New York and London: Garland Publishing Co., 1984); this edition 'traces and records the work's evolution towards publication' (I, viii) on left-hand pages, but does present a reading text on facing pages.

2 David Wiles, *Shakespeare's Clown: Actor and Text in the Elizabethan Playhouse* (Cambridge: Cambridge University Press, 1987), p. 165.

3 Elizabeth W. Bruss, *Beautiful Theories: The Spectacle of Discourse in Contemporary Criticism* (Baltimore and London: Johns Hopkins University Press, 1982), pp. 64, 73. For her, theory itself takes the place of literature, and, with the 'abolition of literature' (p. 69), absorbs the aesthetic role formerly assigned to it; hence her title.

4 *The Theory of Criticism from Plato to the Present*, ed. Raman Selden (London and New York: Longman, 1988), p. 187; Selden is paraphrasing the views of Hans Robert Jauss, *Towards an Aesthetic of Reception* (1970; trans. Timothy Bahti, 1982).

5 Josue V. Harari, 'Critical Factions/Critical Fictions', in *Textual Strategies: Perspectives in Post-Structuralist Criticism* (Ithaca:. Cornell University Press), pp. 17–72, citing p. 40.

6 Goldberg, 'Textual Properties', p. 216; see also Stephen Orgel, 'The Authentic Shakespeare', especially pp. 7–8.

7 See Michel Foucault, 'What is an Author?', trans. Josue Harari, in *Textual Strategies*, pp. 141–60.

8 As in Holderness, ed., *The Shakespeare Myth*, and Gary Taylor, *Reinventing Shakespeare*. See also Levine, 'William Shakespeare in America', in *Highbrow/Lowbrow*, pp. 17–81.

9 Hawkes, *That Shakespeherian Rag*, p. 76; and see Levine, *Highbrow/Lowbrow*, pp. 72–3.

10 Levine, *ibid.*, pp. 70–81.

11 Bristol, *Shakespeare's America, America's Shakespeare*, p. 112.

12 *Ibid.*, p. 106.

13 See below, p. 170.

14 Bristol, *ibid.*, p. 117; and see Goldberg, 'Textual Properties', p. 213.

15 Levine, *Highbrow/Lowbrow*, p. 39, citing H. N. Hudson, *Lectures on Shakespeare* (1848), I, 79.

16 Ian Hunter, *Culture and Government: The Emergence of Literary Education*

(Basingstoke and London: Macmillan, 1988), p. 152; see also Tony Bennett, *Outside Literature* (London: Routledge, 1990), p. 181.

17 Hunter, *ibid.*, p. 153.
18 *Ibid.*, p. 152.
19 See John M. Mackenzie, *Propaganda and Empire: The Manipulation of British Public Opinion, 1880–1960* (Manchester: Manchester University Press, 1984), Chapter 7.
20 Cited in Stephen J. Brown, 'The Uses of Shakespeare in America: A Study in Class Domination', in *Shakespeare, Pattern of Excelling Nature*, pp. 230–1.
21 Hunter, *Culture and Government*, p. 214.
22 Stanley Fish, *Is There a Text in This Class? The Authority of Interpretive Communities* (Cambridge, Mass.: Harvard University Press, 1980), pp. 16–17.
23 *Ibid.*, p. 368.
24 Stanley Fish, *Doing What Comes Naturally: Change, Rhetoric, and the Practice of Theory in Literary and Legal Studies* (Durham, North Carolina and London: Duke University Press, 1989), p. 141.
25 Fish, *Is There a Text in This Class?*, p. 355.
26 Brown, 'The Uses of Shakespeare in America', p. 230.
27 *Hamlet*, ed. Jenkins, p. 154.
28 The title of Chapter 1 in his *Shakespearean Negotiations* (1988).
29 Tony Bennett, *Outside Literature*, p. 129, citing Pavlev Medvedev and Mikhail Bakhtin, *The Formal Method in Literary Scholarship* (Baltimore: Johns Hopkins University Press, 1978), p. 29.
30 Herbert Marcuse, *The Aesthetic Dimension: Toward a Critique of Marxist Aesthetics* (Boston: Beacon Press, 1978), pp. 8, 23.
31 *Ibid.*, p. 13.
32 Terry Eagleton, *Literary Theory: An Introduction* (Minneapolis: University of Minnesota Press, 1983), p. 11.
33 *Ibid.*, pp. 216–17.
34 Terry Eagleton, *The Function of Criticism: From The Spectator to Post-Structuralism* (London: Verso Editions, 1984), p. 123; Bennett, commenting on Eagleton's theories in *Outside Literature*, p. 227.
35 Eagleton, *Literary Theory*, p. 208.
36 Eagleton, *Function of Criticism*, pp. 123–4.
37 Bennett, *Outside Literature*, p. 173.
38 *Ibid.*, pp. 174, 173.
39 Eagleton, *Literary Theory*, p. 202.
40 Fish, *Is There a Text in This Class?*, pp. 16, 355; Eagleton, *Literary Theory*, pp. 86–7; Eagleton, *Function of Criticism*, p. 124.
41 Fredric Jameson, *Marxism and Form: Twentieth-Century Dialectical Theories of Literature* (Princeton: Princeton University Press, 1971), pp. 329, 352.
42 Eagleton, *Literary Theory*, p. 202.

43 Jameson, *Marxism and Form*, p. 313.
44 Taylor, *Reinventing Shakespeare*, p. 384. In *The Ideology of the Aesthetic* (Oxford: Blackwell, 1990), p. 374, Terry Eagleton opposes élitist art to popular art, 'one aesthetically aloof from everyday life as against one which embraces the motifs of common experience'. This is a typically narrow and falsifying definition of élitist art, which, in Shakespeare's plays, as in the plays of Harold Pinter or Samuel Beckett, is much concerned with 'the motifs of common experience'.
45 Eagleton, *Literary Theory*, p. 213.
46 Stephen Greenblatt, *Shakespearean Negotiations*, p. 4; *cf.* Eagleton, *Literary Theory*, p. 21, on art treated as a 'solitary fetish'.
47 Eagleton, *ibid.*, p. 11; Bristol, *Shakespeare's America, America's Shakespeare*, p. 117 (my italics).
48 See A. D. Nuttall, *A New Mimesis: Shakespeare and the Representation of Reality* (London and New York: Methuen, 1983), Chapter 2, 'The Dissolution of Mimesis'.
49 Thomas Heywood, *An Apology for Actors* (1612), Sig.F1v; see also Madeleine Doran, *Endeavors of Art* (Madison: University of Wisconsin Press, 1954, reprinted 1964), pp. 71–2. This and the following paragraphs are reworked from my essay, '"Forms to his Conceit": Shakespeare and the Uses of Stage-Illusion', *Proceedings of the British Academy*, 66 (1982), 103–19.
50 For an account of the debates about the staging and interpretation of this scene, see M. R. Woodhead, 'Deep Plots and Indiscretions in "The Murder of Gonzago"', *Shakespeare Survey*, 32 (1979), 151–61.
51 *Timon of Athens*, 1.1.35; *The Winter's Tale*, v.3.19; Shakespeare was also fascinated by what was called 'perspective' in art, or the anamorphic possibilities of works 'which rightly gazed upon, / Show nothing but confusion – eyed awry, / Distinguish form' *Richard II*, 11.2.18–20; see Ernest Gilman, *The Curious Perspective: Literary and Pictorial Wit in the Seventeenth Century* (New Haven: Yale University Press, 1978), pp. 88–165.
52 A point made by Madeleine Doran, *Endeavors of Art*, p. 72.
53 E. H. Gombrich, *Art and Illusion* (London: Phaidon Books, 1960, new edition 1962), pp. 176–7, and p. 182, where he cites this stanza.
54 Cited in E. K. Chambers, *The Elizabethan Stage* (4 vols., Oxford: Clarendon Press, 1923), II, 308–9; Burbage died in 1619.
55 Thomas Heywood, *An Apology for Actors*, Sig. B4r.
56 By T. Palmer in *The Works of Francis Beaumont and John Fletcher*, ed. A Glover (10 vols., Cambridge: Cambridge University Press, 1905–12), I, xlviii.
57 Cited in Chambers, *The Elizabethan Stage*, IV, 321–2.
58 John Rainolds, *Th'Overthrow of Stage-Playes* (1599), p. 108.
59 Kendall L. Walton, *Mimesis as Make-Believe: On the Foundation of the*

Representational Arts (Cambridge, Mass.: Harvard University Press, 1990), p. 53.

60 *Ibid.*, pp. 53, 209.
61 *Ibid.*, pp. 225, 235, 236.
62 *Ibid.*, p. 237.
63 *Ibid.*, p. 272.
64 Nuttall, *A New Mimesis*, p. 75.
65 *Ibid.*, p. 78.
66 *Ibid.*, p. 76.
67 *Ibid.*, p. 100.
68 *Ibid.*, p. 77, and see pp. 83–4.
69 See my essay, 'Making and Breaking Dramatic Illusion', in *Aesthetic Illusion: Theoretical and Historical Approaches,* ed. Frederick Burwick and Walter Pape (Berlin and New York: Walter de Gruyter, 1990), pp. 219–20, and Richard Altick, *The Shows of London* (Cambridge, Mass.: Belknap Press of Harvard University Press, 1978), pp. 117–40, 163–72, 184–97.
70 James Boaden, *Memoirs of the Life of Philip Kemble* (2 vols., London, 1825), II, 91.
71 'A Discourse upon Comedy' (1702), in *The Complete Works of George Farquhar,* ed. Charles Stonehill (2 vols., London: Nonesuch Press, 1930), II, 341.
72 *Ibid.*, II, 338.
73 'Preface to Shakespeare' (1765), in *Johnson on Shakespeare,* in Arthur Sherbo, ed., *The Yale Edition of the Works of Samuel Johnson* (New Haven and London: Yale University Press, 1968), VII, 76–7.
74 *Ibid.*, I, 77.
75 In the *Monthly Review,* October and November 1765; cited in Vickers, *Critical Heritage,* V, 191–2; and see *Johnson on Shakespeare,* I, 62: 'Shakespeare is above all modern writers, the poet of nature; the poet that holds up to his readers a faithful mirrour of manners and life.'
76 Kenrick, cited in Vickers, *ibid.*, V, 191–2.
77 Henry Lord Kames, *Elements of Criticism,* 6th edition, with the Author's last Corrections and Addition, 2 vols. (1785), II, 418.
78 *The Botanic Garden* (2 vols., 1789), II, 87. The quotation comes from the second prose 'Interlude' inserted on probability in art in 'The Loves of the Plants'.
79 *LL (CC),* I, 133–4. This and the next two paragraphs are adapted from 'Making and Breaking Dramatic Illusion', pp. 219–21.
80 *LL (CC),* I, 134, 133.
81 *The Works of Charles and Mary Lamb,* II, 163.
82 *The Messingkauf Dialogues,* trans. John Willett (London: Methuen, 1965, reprinted 1978), p. 51.

83 *The Shakespeare Revolution* (Cambridge: Cambridge University Press, 1977), in a chapter headed, 'Shakespeare, Peter Brook and Non-Illusion', pp. 206–31. Styan thought the absence of scenic illusion, which is what he meant by saying 'Brook's approach was to deny all stage illusion', would leave a 'vacuum to be filled by the imagination of the spectator' (p. 230); just so, giving scope to the spectator's 'inward illusion'.

84 *Collected Letters*, ed. E. L. Griggs (6 vols., Oxford: Oxford University Press, 1956–71), IV, 641.

85 *Biographia Literaria*, II, 6.

86 *Collected Letters*, IV, 642.

87 *LL* (*CC*), I, 543.

88 In *Twelfth Night*: see above, p. 127.

89 See E. A. J. Honigmann, *The Stability of Shakespeare's Text*, (London: Arnold, 1965), pp. 52–3 (on Keats), 92–3, 110–11.

90 The authority of Aristotle lies behind the belief that artistic coherence is a property of the work, inherent in it, and so eternal and immutable, and behind the notion of organic unity; see *Poetics*, trans. G. F. Else (Ann Arbor: University of Michigan Press, 1967, reprinted 1983), pp. 31–2, and Humphry House, *Aristotle's Poetics* (London: Rupert Hart-Davis, 1961), pp. 48–50.

91 *LL* (*CC*), I, 495.

92 Frederick Burwick, *Illusion and the Drama: Critical Theory of the Enlightment and Romantic Era* (University Park: Pennsylvania State University Press, 1991), p. 222; Burwick's chapter on Coleridge, 'Illusion and the Poetic Imagination', pp. 191–229, provides an excellent account of the development of Coleridge's thinking on aesthetic issues.

93 *LL* (*CC*), I, 352.

94 Hunter, *Culture and Government*, p. 58.

95 *Ibid.*, p. 157.

96 Robert Scholes, *Textual Power: Literary Theory and the Teaching of English* (New Haven and London: Yale University Press, 1985), p. 33.

97 Eagleton, *The Function of Criticism*, p. 123.

98 Dollimore and Sinfield, eds., *Political Shakespeare*, p. 4.

99 Nuttall, *A New Mimesis*, p. 75.

100 Bennett, *Outside Literature*, p. 185.

101 William Empson, *Seven Types of Ambiguity* (London: Chatto and Windus, 1930), p. 25; in the 3rd edition (1956), Empson qualified his remarks in a note, p. 20, but added, 'I don't think my treatment of it [i.e., the passage] was wrong as far as it went.'

102 *Hamlet*, ed. Jenkins, pp. 277–80, 484–93.

103 Sychrava, *Schiller to Derrida*, p. 181.

104 *Ibid.*, p. 181. This is not the place to do justice to her complex analysis in which she traces the ancestry of post-structuralist critical theories in Romantic or 'sentimental' concepts of literature in order to estab-

lish a way of re-evaluating the poetry of John Clare. She links aesthetic and cognitive experience, relying for some of her distinctions on the theory developed by Nelson Goodman in *Languages of Art: An Approach to a Theory of Symbols* (Indianapolis: Hackett Publishing Co., 1976).

105 *Ibid.*, p. 193.
106 Frank Kermode, *History and Value* (Oxford: Clarendon Press, 1988), p. 127.
107 Stanley Cavell, *Disowning Knowledge*, p. 83.
108 Jones, *Scenic Form in Shakespeare*, pp. 33, 81. The books mentioned here seem curiously isolated from the mainstream of critical inquiry, and in the main are not concerned with larger aesthetic issues so much as with identifying building blocks in particular scenes or sequences.
109 Mark Rose, *Shakespearean Design* (Cambridge, Mass.: The Belknap Press of Harvard University Press, 1972), pp. 68, 125.
110 Jean E. Howard, *Shakespeare's Art of Orchestration. Stage Technique and Audience Response* (Urbana: University of Illinois Press, 1984), p. 114.
111 *Ibid.*, p. 43.
112 Nevo, *Tragic Form in Shakespeare*, pp. 6, 26.
113 Charles and Elaine Hallett, *Analyzing Shakespeare's Action* (Cambridge: Cambridge University Press, 1991), p. 7.

6 A DESIGN FOR *HAMLET*

1 *Hamlet*, ed. Hibbard, pp. 41–2; Eleanor Prosser, *Hamlet and Revenge* (Stanford: Stanford University Press, 1967), p. 138.
2 *Hamlet*, ed. Hibbard, p. 355.
3 As argued by George Walton Williams in 'Antique Romans and Modern Danes in *Julius Caesar* and *Hamlet*', in *Literature and Nationalism*, ed. Vincent Newey and Ann Thompson (Liverpool: Liverpool University Press, 1991), pp. 41–55.
4 Prosser, *Hamlet and Revenge*, pp. 120, 255: 'The spirit that visits Elsinore is like no other in the drama of the English Renaissance' (p. 255).
5 Jenkins shows that this is what the term 'parle' probably meant, in his edition of *Hamlet*, p. 427.
6 *Hamlet*, ed. Hibbard, p. 185.
7 *Hamlet*, ed. Edwards, pp. 39, 45.
8 MacIntyre, *After Virtue* p. 115.
9 *Ibid.*, p. 117.
10 Jacqueline Rose, 'Sexuality in the Reading of Shakespeare: *Hamlet* and *Measure for Measure*', in *Alternative Shakespeares*, ed. John Drakakis (London: Methuen, 1985), pp. 95–118, citing pp. 95, 101.
11 *Ibid.*, p. 102.
12 Elaine Showalter, 'Representing Ophelia: Women, Madness, and the Responsibilities of Feminist Criticism', in *Shakespeare and the Question of*

Theory, ed. Patricia Parker and Geoffrey Hartman (London and New York: Methuen, 1985), pp. 77–94, citing pp. 83, 91.

13 Showalter (pp. 78–9) comments on this passage: Hamlet seizes on 'nothing' as meaning the female genitalia in his retort, 'That's a fair thought to lie between maids' legs.'

14 Wilson Knight, perhaps taking a hint from A. C. Bradley, who saw Iago as 'The counterpart of Hamlet' (p. 184), found a stronger relationship: 'Hamlet thus takes a devilish joy in cruelty towards the end of the play: he is like Iago' (*Wheel of Fire*, p. 27).

15 *Hamlet*, ed. Jenkins, p. 131.

16 Knights, *An Approach to Hamlet* (London: Chatto, 1960), pp. 41–2.

17 Greenblatt, *Shakespearean Negotiations*, p. 56.

18 *Ibid.*, pp. 52–3.

19 Corinne Sweet writing in the *Observer*, 7 July 1991, and citing Elean Thomas's new book, *The Last Room*.

20 Robert Burton, *The Anatomy of Melancholy*, ed. A. R. Shilleto (3 vols., London: George Bell and Sons, 1890), I, 149–50.

21 A word used by Hibbard (p. 48), by Jenkins (p. 153), and implicit in Edwards's 'directive, a commission that is also a mission' (p. 45); see also above, pp. 26, 36.

22 *Hamlet*, ed. Hibbard, p. 63.

23 This is the emphasis in much mid-twentieth-century criticism, as Edwards noted (*Hamlet*, p. 37); see especially R. N. Alexander, *Poison, Play and Duel* (London: Routledge, 1971); and see above, pp. 40–1.

24 Mack, 'The World of *Hamlet*', p. 518, citing E. M. W. Tillyard.

25 Michel Foucault, *Discipline and Punish*, trans. Alan Sheridan (New York: Pantheon Books, 1977), and see D. A. Miller, *The Novel and the Police* (Berkeley and Los Angeles: University of California Press, 1988), pp. 16–18.

26 *Johnson on Shakespeare*, VIII, 990; and see *Hamlet*, ed. Hibbard, p. 56.

27 Some would take literally Hamlet's statements that heaven has appointed him as scourge and minister and argue that 'divine providence works out the catastrophe with justice' (Fredson Bowers, *Hamlet as Minister and Scourge and Other Studies in Shakespeare and Milton* (Charlottesville: University of Virginia Press, 1989), p. 101; but for a sceptical view by someone who shares Bowers's belief that *Hamlet* is a religious play, see *Hamlet*, ed. Edwards, pp. 56–8. See also R. A. Foakes, 'The Art of Cruelty: Hamlet and Vindice', *Shakespeare Survey*, 26 (1973), p. 25.

28 Paul Werstine, 'The Textual Mystery of *Hamlet*', *Shakespeare Quarterly*, 39 (1988), 1–26, citing p. 6.

29 *Hamlet*, ed. Edwards, p. 50; and see Werstine, 'Textual Mystery', p. 21.

30 Michael Neill, '"Exeunt with a Dead March": Funeral Pageantry on the Shakespearean Stage', in David M. Bergeron, ed., *Pageantry in the*

Shakespearean Theater (Athens: University of Georgia Press, 1985), pp. 153–93; see especially pp. 177–8.

31 Neill, '"Exeunt with a Dead March"', p. 180.

32 I commented on this imagery in '*Hamlet* and the Court of Elsinore', *Shakespeare Survey*, 9 (1956), p. 37.

7 A SHAPING FOR *KING LEAR*

1 Jones, *Scenic Form in Shakespeare*, p. 155.

2 *King Lear*, ed. Bratton, p. 65.

3 *King Lear*, ed. Bratton, p. 73. For a spirited argument in support of the claim that '*Cor.*' here refers to Cordelia, see Beth Goldring's essay, '*Cor.*'s Rescue of Kent', in *The Division of the Kingdoms*, pp. 143–51. It seems to me much more likely that the speech-heading '*Cor.*' here relates to two other changes in F; one is the alteration of '*Glost.*' (Q) to '*Cor.*' to announce the entry of France and Burgundy at 1.1.188, and the other the addition of references to Cornwall and Albany in Lear's speech in F at 1.1.41–2. All three changes go together, and show Shakespeare identifying for the audience two important characters who in Q remain silent and unnoticed in the background.

4 Sir Walter Raleigh, *The History of the World* (1614), Sig. E2v.

5 As in the editions by Muir and Bratton, and in, for example, *The Riverside Shakespeare*, ed. G. Blakemore Evans (Boston: Houghton Mifflin, 1974).

6 *King Lear*, ed. Muir, p. 73, citing G. M. Young, *Times Literary Supplement*, 30 September 1949, p. 633.

7 Stephen Greenblatt relies on Shakespeare's use of Samuel Harsnett's *Declaration of Egregious Popish Impostures* to argue that *hysterica passio* could be regarded as a sign of demonic possession, but Harsnett specifically refers to the 'mother' as a disease; and as one especially though not exclusively associated with women, it suggests primarily the emergence in Lear of the woman, the word recalling the mother of his children whose memory is virtually suppressed in the play, and also the dawning of 'womanish' feelings and breaking down of his masculine hardness.

8 *King Lear*, ed. Bratton, p. 139: 'It was commonly cut, for its obscurity and dramatic difficulty, up to 1970; but after that point the satirical Utopian vision it contains began to be recognised by socially and politically oriented interpreters of the play as of central significance.'

9 It was, for instance, moved to III.6, and used to preface an interval in the recent production by Kenneth Branagh for the English Renaissance Company.

10 So Muir in his edition and the *Riverside* add 'Tearing off his clothes'; Bratton has 'Tears off his clothes'.

11 *King Lear*, ed. Bratton, p. 142.
12 In *Disowning Knowledge*, Stanley Cavell assumes that Edgar wants to avoid being recognized: 'There are no lengths to which we may not go in order to avoid being revealed, even to those we love and are loved by' (pp. 55–6).
13 *King Lear*, ed. Bratton, p. 175.
14 The whole play is, of course, in one sense a verbal construct; but as represented on the stage, Edgar here appears within Shakespeare's construct as the author of his own fiction in the layered illusions of reality in the play.
15 F's 'Place sins' was emended to 'Plate sin' by Theobald, an emendation accepted by most editors, including Muir in the Arden edition.
16 Stanley Cavell thinks Lear's love for Cordelia is not the 'plain love of a daughter for father', and is 'incompatible with the idea of her having any (other) lover', *Disowning Knowledge*, p. 70.
17 *King Lear*, ed. Bratton, p. 197.
18 E. A. J. Honigmann argues that Cordelia could be alive here, and opens her eyes but is unable to speak in this final scene; see *Myriad-Minded Shakespeare* (London: Macmillan, 1989), pp. 90–2.
19 See, for example, N. S. Brooke, *King Lear* (London: Arnold, 1963), pp. 54–5.
20 But it does not change him so completely as Stephen Urkowitz claims in arguing that Albany has 'moral elevation' in Q, and espouses 'no positively defined ethical standards' in F; he produces a reading 'utterly and irreconcilably at odds with the conventional view'; see *Shakespeare's Revision of King Lear* (Princeton: Princeton University Press, 1980), pp. 92–3 and 126.
21 Belsey, *The Subject of Tragedy*, p. 33.
22 Patterson, *Shakespeare and the Popular Voice*, p. 116.
23 McLuskie, 'The Patriarchal Bard', pp. 98–9.
24 Philip C. Maguire argues ingeniously in *Speechless Dialect: Shakespeare's Open Silences* (Berkeley and Los Angeles: University of California Press, 1985) that the play ends with the silence of either Edgar (in Q) or Albany (in F), which can be interpreted in various ways; Edgar's and Albany's 'silence' may show their refusal to take on power after Lear dies. This argument is another way of destabilizing the play, and the silences of Edgar and Albany here are invented by the critic: the absence of a speech becomes a presence, pregnant with meanings.

EPILOGUE

1 Alan Liu, 'Local Transcendence: Cultural Criticism, Postmodernism, and the Romanticism of Detail', *Representations*, 32 (1990), 75–113, citing p. 78; Liu is in turn quoting from Naomi Schor, *Reading in Detail:*

Aesthetics and the Feminine (New York: Methuen, 1987), p. 3; see also Eagleton, *Ideology of the Aesthetic* pp. 380–1.
2 Liu, *ibid.*, p. 81.
3 Greenblatt, *Shakespearean Negotiations*, p. 2.
4 *Ibid.*, pp. 3, 4, 19.
5 *Ibid.*, p. 4.
6 Leah Marcus, *Puzzling Shakespeare: Local Reading and its Discontents* (Berkeley and Los Angeles: University of California Press, 1988), p. 213; Liu cites this passage, 'Local Transcendence', p. 92.
7 Greenblatt, *Shakespearean Negotiations*, p. 159.
8 *Ibid.*, p. 13.
9 *Ibid.*, p. 4.

Index

Printed in the United Kingdom
by Lightning Source UK Ltd.
135801UK00001B/280-282/A